*Jill Julius Matthews is Director
of the Centre for Women's Studies
at the Australian National University, Canberra.
She is author of* Good and Mad Women.

Sex in public

Australian sexual cultures

Edited by Jill Julius Matthews

ALLEN & UNWIN

Copyright © this collection Jill Julius Matthews 1997
The copyright in individual pieces remains with the authors.

All rights reserved. No part of this book may be reproduced or transmitted in any form or by any means, electronic or mechanical, including photocopying, recording or by any information storage and retrieval system, without prior permission in writing from the publisher.

Every effort has been made to contact persons owning copyright in the works of art reproduced in this book. However, in cases where this has not been possible, owners are invited to notify Allen & Unwin as soon as possible.

First published in 1997 by
Allen & Unwin Pty Ltd
9 Atchison Street, St Leonards, NSW 2065 Australia
Phone: (61 2) 9901 4088
Fax: (61 2) 9906 2218
E-mail: frontdesk@allen-unwin.com.au

National Library of Australia
Cataloguing-in-Publication entry:

Sex in public: Australian sexual culture

   Includes bibliographical references and index.
   ISBN 1 86448 049 1.

   1. Lesbianism—Australia. 2. Homosexuality—Australia.
   3. Gays—Australia—Sexual behaviour. 4. Lesbians—
   Australia—Sexual behaviour. I. Matthews, Jill Julius.

306.760994

Set in 11/13 pt Sabon by DOCUPRO, Sydney
Printed by Southwood Press Pty Limited, Sydney

10 9 8 7 6 5 4 3 2 1

Contents

Contributors	vii
Introduction *Jill Julius Matthews*	xi
1 Nothing personal: sex, gender and identity in the media age *Catharine Lumby*	1
2 Screen sex: from television to teledildonics *Barbara Creed*	16
3 The economy of pleasure and the laws of desire *Fiona Patten*	31
4 Grief and the lesbian queer/n: a love story *Rebecca Cox*	50
5 Bisexual mediations: beyond the third term *McKenzie Wark*	63
6 Sexual conduct, sexual culture, sexual community: gay men's bodies and AIDS *Gary W. Dowsett*	78
7 A short history of facial hair *David McDiarmid*	91
8 Degrees of separation: lesbian separatist communities in northern New South Wales, 1974–95 *Judith Ion*	97
9 Dangerous desire: lesbianism as sex or politics *Kimberly O'Sullivan*	114

10	Lesbian erotica and impossible images *C.Moore Hardy*	127
11	Sex and the single T-cell: the taboo of HIV-positive sexuality in Australian art and culture *Ted Gott*	139
12	Stirred heart and soul: the visual representation of lesbian sexuality *Elizabeth Ashburn*	157
13	I was a teenage romance writer *Jenny Pausacker*	170

References 182
Index 193

Contributors

ELIZABETH ASHBURN is an artist, writer and activist. She is a professor at the College of Fine Arts, the University of New South Wales, and is co-president of the Centre for Gay and Lesbian Research at the University of Sydney. She is the author of *Lesbian Art: An Encounter with Power* (Craftsman House 1996).

REBECCA COX is a writer and PhD student at the University of Western Sydney. She has published stories in *Wicked Women* and *Pink Ink* (Wicked Women Press 1991). She has also appeared in the films *Lipstick* and *None of the Above*. She is a natural blonde.

BARBARA CREED is a senior lecturer in Cinema Studies in the Department of Fine Arts at Melbourne University. She has spoken and published widely in the areas of film, feminist theory, psychoanalysis and cultural studies. She is author of *The Monstrous-Feminine: Film, Feminism, Psychoanalysis* (Routledge 1993).

GARY W. DOWSETT is a lecturer in Sociology at Macquarie University, Sydney. He has spent the last twenty years researching and writing about sexuality, HIV/AIDS, masculinity, gay men and education. He is the author of *Practicing Desire: Homosexual Sex in the Era of AIDS* (Stanford University Press 1996), co-author of *Making the Difference: Schools, Families and Social Division* (Allen & Unwin 1982) and *Sustaining Safe Sex: Gay Communities Respond to AIDS* (Falmer Press 1993), and co-editor of *Rethinking Sex: Social Theory and Sexuality Research* (Melbourne University Press 1992).

TED GOTT is Curator of European Art, National Gallery of Australia, Canberra. He curated the exhibition, 'Don't Leave Me This Way: Art in the Age of AIDS', NGA, 1994–95, and maintains an active interest in issues surrounding HIV/AIDS and art. He is currently researching the life and work of David McDiarmid.

C.MOORE HARDY is a Sydney photographer who has been publishing and exhibiting since 1988. She has held solo exhibitions in both Melbourne and Sydney, and she has curated a number of Sydney Gay & Lesbian Mardi Gras Exhibitions. Her work is held at the National Portrait Gallery in Canberra, National Art School Collection in Sydney, the National Library of Australia in Canberra, the Sydney Melanoma Unit Collection, the Woman's Gallery Collection in Melbourne, the NSW State Library and private collections.

JUDITH ION has been variously connected to the Centre for Women's Studies at the Australian National University for some years: as graduate student, research assistant and tutor. She dreams of being a full-time *funded* student (all donations welcome) but in the meantime pays the bills by driving a taxi and doing research. Her PhD topic is 'An ethno-history of lesbian community in Canberra, 1965–84'. She is the co-author of *History of Sexualities in Australia: Bibliography No. 2* (Centre for Women's Studies, ANU 1995) and has written a brief history of the Canberra Rape Crisis Centre to commemorate its twentieth year.

CATHARINE LUMBY lectures in Mass Communications at Macquarie University. She has worked as a print and television journalist and still writes regularly for the *Sydney Morning*

Herald and the *Australian*. Her book *Bad Girls: TV, Sex and Feminism in the 90s* will be published in 1997 by Allen & Unwin.

DAVID MCDIARMID was a leading Sydney artist until his death from AIDS in 1995. Since his first exhibition in 1976, his work has been shown throughout Australia, as well as in Germany, Norway, the Netherlands and the United States. As a community artist he was extensively involved with gay liberation, the Sydney Gay & Lesbian Mardi Gras and HIV support groups. His work is held at the National Gallery of Australia, the Mitchell Library in Sydney, the Powerhouse Museum in Sydney, the National Gallery of Victoria and private collections.

JILL JULIUS MATTHEWS has been involved in both women's liberation and gay liberation since the early 1970s. She is currently Reader in Women's Studies at the Australian National University. She has published widely in the history of femininity and of sexuality, and was the co-convener of the ANU Humanities Research Centre's year on Sexualities and Culture in 1993. She is the author of *Good and Mad Women: The Social Construction of Femininity in Twentieth Century Australia* (Allen & Unwin 1984).

FIONA PATTEN has worked in and around the sex industry since 1990. She is currently the president of the Eros Foundation, a national sex industry organisation established to lobby for sensible law reform in all areas of the sex industry in Australia. She is editor of *Sex Files*, the bi-monthly magazine of the Eros Foundation.

KIMBERLY O'SULLIVAN came out in 1978 and has been causing political and sexual trouble ever since. She is an archivist, an activist and a writer and has written widely for the feminist, gay and lesbian press. She has worked in the sex industry, as an erotic dancer and B&D mistress. She is one of the four authors of *Kink* (Wicked Women Press 1990), and was editor of *Wicked Women* until 1996.

JENNY PAUSACKER has a PhD in children's literature. As an academic, her main interest was in genre fiction; as a freelance writer, she has written 27 romances or thrillers under a variety of pen names, as well as eleven books for children and young adults under her own name. Her young adult novel *Mr Enigmatic* won the NSW Premier's Literary Award for Children's Fiction in 1995 and she is currently working on a novel about the 1970s Women's Liberation Movement.

MCKENZIE WARK is the author of *Virtual Geography: Living with Global Media Events* (Indiana University Press 1995). His essays on sexuality have appeared in the journals *Meanjin* and *Burn* and in the *Fruit* anthology, and the *Weekend Australian*. He lectures in media studies at Macquarie University.

Introduction

JILL JULIUS MATTHEWS

In the late 1960s populations of urban youth in Australia, as elsewhere, generated a millenarian cult under the name of sexual revolution. Its social origins were various, its fervour unmistakable. Permissiveness, libertarianism, moral anarchy, sex-drugs-and-rock & roll, freedom: there was something for everybody. Sex became impassioned talk, alongside guilty secrets, self-righteous umbrage and exuberant practice. Sex also became organised and went on marches, demanding freedom for the bodies of children[1] and women and gays. Feminism and gay liberation were born; revolution was in the air. In only a little while, all would be changed and the world as it had been known would be gone forever.

But what happens when the end of the world doesn't? When the revolution doesn't come? The answer seems to be that the elements that were once united into a total vision of liberation become separated out. The moral and political fervour to change everything, all at once and now, dissipates or becomes channelled into narrower single issues. For some there develops a slight embarrassment in remembering youthful naivete, idealism or folly. For others there remains the belief that the struggle

---

1 The small but vocal Children's Liberation movement of the late 1960s is often forgotten in the stories of the rise of the sexual liberation movements.

for the new world of sexual freedom must continue, or at least its rhetoric. And then, of course, there rises a new generation which hears the stories of the early seventies radicals, and variously mocks the old, admires the heroes, takes up what it sees as the unfinished task or goes its own way without a thought that anything precedes this moment. So the Australian sexual revolution came and went. It did not change the world, but it did leave its mark. Its constitutive elements have unravelled across the next three decades but are still identifiable in the sexual cultures and politics of the 1990s: transgressive libertarianism, anti-consumerist populism, liberal civil rights, utopian moralism.

One important element of this continuing but contradictory heritage remains—a space and a language to speak about sex in a positive and optimistic way. Much of the rhetoric of the sexual revolution itself may now seem old-fashioned and irrelevant, but the possibility it opened up stands, no matter how tenuously, against many decades, if not centuries, of sex negativity. As the American critic Gayle Rubin writes about it, sexuality has historically been viewed as a dangerous phenomenon, to be rigidly constrained into heterosexual marriage for purposes of procreation, with all other manifestations condemned by church, State and the professions (Rubin 1984). The international sexual revolution of the sixties challenged that negativity. Its starting assumption was that consensual sex of all descriptions was a good thing. It challenged the rules about who one could have sex with, where one could have it, what acts one could engage in, and it proclaimed that sex was to be enjoyed, not compelled or endured.

In this, of course, the sexual revolutionaries were naive. The practicalities of personal and social life conspired against their utopian vision of open and joyful sex. As well, many feminists began to point out the unhappy consequences for women of men's greater power in sexual as in all other matters. For a while in the early seventies, feminism was able to hold on to both positions: the end to be achieved by overcoming women's oppression was a human liberation in which true equality and freedom in sexuality as in all else would be enjoyed by all. That vision, too, faded. In particular, the radical feminist emphasis on sexual violence came to be all-encompassing. What were initially vitally important and targeted campaigns against the abuses of masculine power—rape, incest, domestic violence, representations of violent sexuality, coerced prostitution—came in time to be presented as the whole truth of sex.

By the late 1970s, and continuing into the eighties, this negativity and pessimism had become the dominant understanding about sex within feminism. During this same period, considerable numbers of feminists took up jobs in state and federal public services, many of them working in areas specifically concerned with the provision of services to women.[2] State-run campaigns were soon directed against those issues of masculine sexual violence that radical feminism had identified. One could hypothesise that the negativity about sexuality that radical feminism had developed so strongly made femocrat incursion into the State both easier and more powerful. The traditional negativity of that institution could recognise an ally.

Nonetheless, while the negative view clearly remained dominant, and perhaps even increased its hold in public and political life, its historically taken-for-granted status had been challenged. The small public space forged by the sexual revolution, in which the pleasures of sex could legitimately be spoken of, remained open. Feminism was not monolithic and there were other strands, as well as elements of gay liberation, which opposed the negative stance of radical feminism and sustained the discourse of sexual optimism. Major cultural changes, discussed below, have enlarged its space. The balance between an attitude of optimism about sexuality and one of negativity is constantly shifting, and most public discussions about sex inevitably involve elements of each.

Since the late 1980s, variants of the more optimistic or positive discourse of sex have returned to talkshows, television and classrooms. Australia since the early 1990s has seen a

---

[2] This phenomenon has been discussed by Eisenstein (1991), Yeatman (1990), and Watson (1990), among others.

burgeoning of university courses dealing with aspects of the history and politics of sex. From a mere trickle of arcane publishing, academic sex has become at least a good sized creek.[3] Not only has the academic market for writing about sex expanded, so too have other forms of communication: magazines, film, computer-based information, art, performance.

This book provides a selective mapping of this expanding space of sexual optimism. It is an incomplete ethnography, a discussion of a range of cultural phenomena in contemporary Australia that have fashioned themselves out of various understandings of sexuality. Aspects of this selectivity can be immediately identified. In terms of standard classification of sexualities, most of the authors in this collection write from a standpoint that would not be termed heterosexual or straight. They largely share a common Anglo- and European-Australian ancestry and an educated, middle-class background. They also predominantly come from and write about urban Sydney, with a few contributors coming from urban Melbourne and Canberra. The rest of the country is largely unrepresented, though there is considerable reference to the abstract internationalism of cyberspace and to the international gay community. Now, while a sexual ethnography of a modern society would never aspire to 'completeness', this distinct skewing of the range

---

[3] For example, in the month-long 1996 Sydney Gay & Lesbian Mardi Gras Festival alone, at least five books dealing with gay and lesbian sexualities were launched by mainstream publishers, while one of the country's major cultural journals published a special issue on queer sexualities and a new specialist queer journal joined the fray: Elizabeth Ashburn 1996, *Lesbian Art: An Encounter with Power*, Sydney: Craftsman House; Michael Hurley 1996, *Guide to Gay and Lesbian Writing in Australia*, Sydney: Allen & Unwin; Tony Ayres (ed.) 1996 *String of Pearls: Stories about Cross-Dressing*, Sydney: Allen & Unwin; Jenny Pausacker (ed.) 1996, *Hide and Seek*, Melbourne: Reed Books; Mark Macleod (ed.) 1996, *Ready or Not*, Sydney: Random House Australia. *Meanjin* 1996 Vol. 55 No. 1. published a special issue on 'Australian Queer' and just before the Festival rush of publications, *Media International Australia*, November 1995 No. 78, presented a special issue on Queer Media. The specialist journal is *InQueeries* 1996, from Melbourne University.

INTRODUCTION

towards middle-class, white, inner-city, queer lifestyles and preoccupations needs some explanation.

Simply put, that configuration of social characteristics seems, at this stage, to mark the limits of the variety of communities in Australia that define themselves in relation to sexuality rather than to some other characteristic. Individuals in these communities sustain a personal identity that is self-consciously (if usually complicatedly) sexual. They have a collective identification, they identify with others, on the basis of that understanding and those practices of sexuality. At least for some of the time, when such identification matters, these individuals situate themselves, and are situated by others, as part of a sexual culture or community.

Obviously many, indeed most other people and groups in Australia have sex, do sex, consider themselves sexual—but do not regard those practices and identifications as so central. They do not self-consciously identify themselves and others like them through their sexuality, but through other social characteristics. Such characteristics matter more because it is these that somehow mark the individuals and group as different from a dominant social norm, as in the case of individuals who see themselves as lacking privileges or suffering discrimination because of racial, ethnic, class or regionally-based identifications. Put another way, because their sexual identity is not under challenge it can simply be taken for granted, as in the case of most heterosexuals. So the assumption arises that all members of minority groups are necessarily heterosexual, while all members of sexual communities are white and middle class.

Obviously, too, there are individuals within minority cultures or communities who identify along such other lines of difference but who also feel that their sexuality is marked and is more central to them than to their peers. Such individuals may experience a cultural denial of that centrality, as in the case of gay Koories or Greek lesbians or rural bisexuals. But as minority cultures currently operate in Australia, such individuals will necessarily feel torn between identifications, although there are increasing numbers of hybrid groupings that combine or bridge such double or multiple identifications. There are also groupings attempting to abandon the whole structure of exclusive identifications operating under the rubric of queer. Queer, which is discussed in a number of chapters, refuses definition; it identifies with only one negative—not straight; its positive substance is open-ended, multiple, playful. At this stage, however, most of its Australian practitioners, in the broadest sense of the word, are white, middle class and urban. Which returns us to the selectivity of this collection, and the decision to make a virtue of necessity.

As Fiona McGregor puts it, in an article published elsewhere:

> To me sexuality is like ethnicity. Being queer places me not just in bed with someone of the same sex, it places me within a particular culture. Queer culture has its dialects, dress codes, mating rituals, history and traditions . . . My sexuality is part of my cultural make-up and informs my writing as do my Australianness, my Celtic Catholic ancestry, my middle-class upbringing, the colour of my skin, my gender . . . As a writer, I try to eschew these fixed locations. I am not interested so much in the margins of a world I don't fit into as the centres of the worlds into which I do fit. I probably fit no one world completely—perhaps nobody does. Worlds overlap . . . (McGregor 1996, p. 32).

The concern of this book is precisely with those social worlds in which individuals and communities centre themselves in some sense through a positive understanding of sexuality. The contributors were asked to address sex as an element in cultural events and groups rather than to engage in a directly political agenda. They were also asked to approach their task with an eye to the pleasures of their subjects. So, in this book, although it necessarily wavers, the focus is on sexual cultures as providing some sort of a good time. This does not mean that the constraints and complaints against the pleasures of sex are not present. Indeed, Fiona Patten's discussion of the Australian sex industry establishes the precise boundaries of government regulation of at least the commercial aspects of sex, while Ted Gott and Elizabeth Ashburn both refer to the

INTRODUCTION

continuing censorship of artistic works. But rather than rail against these barriers and restrictions, the various authors are also interested in the nature of the lives and pleasures of groups within their own worlds. The key elements of their discussions are communication, identity, community and art.

In the early days following the sexual revolution, a number of politically self-conscious sexual communities came into existence, emerging primarily from within women's liberation and gay liberation. These groups engaged in programs of cultural and political activism that were based in the metaphorics of authenticity, visibility and resistance to oppression. Versions of such programs are still dominant in a number of the cultures and communities discussed in this book: political lesbian, Gay & Lesbian Rights Lobby, anti-porn feminist, Mardi Gras member. They still echo in current slogans: 'We are family', 'For women: born female, living as women, who identify as lesbian', 'Delivering the pink vote and the pink dollar'. They were defensive programs, and some form of such assertive defensiveness will continue to be needed as long as there is a hierarchy of sex that, by privileging heterosexual monogamous marriage, marginalises the lives of all who do not fit within its confines.

Yet for some time now there has been another way of telling the story of sexual culture. As recounted by Catharine Lumby, this is the story of appearances, fluidity and proliferation rather than visibility, identity and resistance. Her analysis of contemporary media culture traces the contours of desire and seduction that are dissolving the certainties on which the old sexual politics were based. Neither the out and proud, defiant identity which that politics authenticated in its adherents, nor the moral authority of the patriarchal order which it opposed, can sustain their integrity in the face of the flow between the media and its audience of a constantly shifting proliferation of images and the overwhelming desire to consume them. The media is flooded with competing and compelling images of gays and lesbians, of sexuality, of feminism. Lumby asks how any one specific sense of identity can be sustained in the face of this deluge. What sort of lesbian is a *real* lesbian: lipstick leso, feral dyke, leather butch, daggy swot, outlaw, wimminloving womyn? What community do they constitute, what is lesbian sexuality and what are its pleasures? 'The media is rendering the social body and its competing identities increasingly unstable. Images are not simply carriers of information, they are force fields which reorganise social relations in their wake.' To put that another way, 'our desires are increasingly modelled on the logic of images'.

Such multiplicity and unboundedness of desire and pleasure are pursued further in Barbara Creed's investigation of the medium of the Internet. Becoming other as well as interacting with other identities in the disembodied screen world of cyberspace induces new pleasures and sexual encounters. Central to Creed's analysis is a questioning of the place of fantasy in these pleasures. Freud argued nearly a century ago that the unconscious knows neither time nor stable identity, which are products of the social world. In curious ways, the Internet can erase this social world, the boundary between public and private realms dissolves; but 'someones' are still awake and keying in. What then happens to the meaning of pleasure? In particular, Creed asks, can Freud's primal fantasies of origins, sexual difference and sexual desire, which have been till now the staple terms of screen theory's understanding of the relationship between screen and audience, withstand the loosening of ties between body, desire and identity? 'Will the future consist of a new order of virtual erotics which is not based on body politics?' What is certain is that a lesbian in cyberspace can never be solidly guaranteed to be a 'woman: born female, living as woman, who identifies as lesbian'.

The media, of course, are not only a force field of disembodied desire, fantasies dissociated from the social world. Just as cyberspace needs people with bodies to be keying in their desires as writing and commands, so all the other media are composed of thousands of tiny elements, each of which has been crafted by an embodied creator, whether individual artist or publishing team. And though the author or creator cannot control the meaning of their works, nonetheless each creation is impelled by their specific desire for meaning. Moreover, while the new semiotic terrain or media process as a whole is unbounded, each singular element has its own boundaries. One's chosen medium or genre, one's craft, one's aesthetic and one's politics, each has its own history which moves at a different pace and rhythm, and all come into play in the process of creation. Sexual politics takes on new forms.

A salutary tale of such shifting modalities is told by Jenny Pausacker, for whom as a writer that play was initially a field of conflict between her specific feminist activism of the seventies and the more fluid desires of her readers in the nineties. Before becoming a highly successful teenage romance writer, she tried her hand with a friend at writing a Mills and Boon novel. 'We'd both been dedicated feminist activists in the seventies and we were moderately annoyed that no one had ever asked us to sell out, so we decided to arrange it for ourselves.' But those many years of political service had borne a cost. The feminist understanding of the dynamics of the world of gender relations and sexuality had remained somewhat frozen in time, mid-1970s. It no longer matched the world as understood by romance readers. These readers were the new audience described by Catharine Lumby. They had been drawn into the different 'dynamic of desire which flows between individuals and the social as it unfolds in the media'. Moreover, says Lumby, these new dynamics have been especially advantageous to women: '[i]f the accelerating symbiosis between contemporary sexual identity and the restless flow of images in the media has destabilised masculinity, it appears to suit women well'. The shift in the meanings of identity for this new audience was too much for the simple stereotypes of feminist parody: 'a heroine who cooked and a hero who was a cross between a saint and a rapist'. The consequence for Pausacker was a postmodern snub. 'To our dismay, Mills and Boon wrote back to say that we'd obviously done our research but that our novel was a bit old-fashioned.' Nineteen teen romances later, Pausacker has clearly got the various modalities of her writing into more comfortable alignment.

A very different personal and creative coming-to-terms with the identity shifts between old and new sexual politics is revealed in artist David McDiarmid's autobiographical sketch. A mixed tale of politics, art, sex and hairdressing, its exuberance in the face of death exemplifies both the anger of the old politics of authenticity and visibility and the joy of a queer culture of self-shaping and transformation. 'Having lived through an extraordinary time of redefinition and deconstruction of identities, from camp to queer; and seeing our lives and histories marginalised every day; we all have a responsibility to speak out. To bang the tribal drums of the jungle telegraph—"I'm here, girlfriend; what's new?" We've always created these languages, as we've created and shaped our identities. I hear our lives in many forms—coded, verbal, visual, physical and aural.' This is an identity politics that is defiantly queer, that will embrace, and probably fuck, everyone at the great pan-sexual party. It is not the politics of 'those sisters whose model for being gay was precious, alcoholic and European', and it certainly leaps the boundedness of McKenzie Wark's descriptions of 'the "gay community", or a private life in suburban Marrickville with a dog and a cat and a partner and a mortgage'. But nor does it refuse those identities, which it tumbles all together in an inclusive and undefined 'community'.

McDiarmid's chapter reveals the way in which life and art are intertwined in the creation of these new, fluid and proliferating sexual cultures. The utopian impetus of the old sexual revolution is being strongly revived by a number of artists like McDiarmid, who try to imagine a new community into existence both by recording its activities and dreams and by living them. Their art reveals a strong continuity with part of the agenda of the old sexual liberation movements of the seventies. What were marginal and despised sexualities have become proud and visible. Non-straight sexual practices have become embodied as identities, identities have merged into communities, and the social and aesthetic meanings of such identities and communities have been rescued from the condemnation of straight society by artists who have refurbished them and returned them to their own communities. Most particularly, the artists have attempted to return a joyful and positive expression of the sexualities of their people.

INTRODUCTION

For C.Moore Hardy, her practice as a lesbian artist has been an attempt 'to subvert the way the female body is seen' and thereby gain some control over the representation of lesbians in order to overcome both the invisibility of her community and its misrepresentation by outsiders. A similar goal is present for all the lesbian artists about whom Elizabeth Ashburn writes. Quoting the French writer Monique Wittig, Ashburn argues that 'the work of lesbian artists [and one could extrapolate to all queer artists] can change "the angle of categorisation as far as the sociological reality of their group goes, at least in affirming its existence"'. In the case of the photographer Marion Moore, as also with C.Moore Hardy, that affirmation has centrally involved celebrating the strength and diversity of their community, thereby also unsettling its easy stereotyping and condemnation by straight society. The process of changing the values and meanings of sexual representations inevitably has such a Janus-like effect. Not only are marginal sexual communities affirmed, the normality of straight society is undermined. Ted Gott shows how images of HIV sexuality and of gay sexuality can be subversive of what are deemed tasteful and normal understandings of sexuality: 'if homophobia and AIDS-phobia are to be truly combated, images both of HIV sexuality and gay sexuality must be *properly* targeted—at the whole country: otherwise the "dirty secret" tag remains. Every time the "general public" is "protected" from what may offend it, its own bigotry is allowed to continue unchecked'.

Lumby's discussion focuses on magazines, Creed's on the screen, Pausacker's on writing, while McDiarmid, Hardy, Ashburn and Gott address modes of artistic expression—media elements of the new semiotic terrain. It is more strictly as members of the audience in the force field of that terrain that McKenzie Wark and Rebecca Cox situate themselves. Wark finds himself up against the barricades of both the homosexual and heterosexual identities he calls monosexual/straight. Straightness, which constitutes itself by mapping a singular desire on to a certain identity and excluding all alternatives, is governed by the 'twentieth century logic of identity' which, like Lumby, he argues is crumbling in the face of media permeation and the insubstantiality of any boundary between public and private. While the form of desire he describes is named bisexuality by the monosexual police, in order to fix it as a solid identity, Wark's own understanding of it is open and fluid: a process, a movement that produces 'sexuality without identity, without the need to negate something to claim existence'.

Wark celebrates the fluidity of sexuality in abstraction; Rebecca Cox's story walks the more concrete beat of desire between surfer chick and fag hag, settling into her queer surrounds as a 'gay-identified girlie girl's girl who sometimes pashes off gay men' and who wants to have her gay lover's baby in a grief-driven fantasy to stop him getting sick. For her, as with McDiarmid, the dissolution of boundaries that Creed, Lumby and Wark address so positively comes from the effect of another positive—HIV. She teases at the strands of meaning that queer lets drop from its shroud, asking about the possibility of community. At the same moment as she 'long[s], almost melancholically, for a place where [her] libidinal fixations aren't read as stable and where [Judith] Butler gets misread so that gender seems voluntaristic', she also has another desire 'desperately to fix and stabilise this word [queer] so that [she] can become the identity that it purports to describe', while simultaneously having 'a presentiment that if queer could ever be the stable category that [she] imagine[s she] want[s] it to be then [she] would have to be something else'. Grief as well as the screaming queer/n's laughter run through the story, which seeks to play in the liminal space that is queerly constituted by both media and death, making its strongest argument against the 'normative and exclusionary rhetoric that circulates around the agendas of identity politics' and its most subtle argument for a space in which absolute difference is refused and desire and friendship are not policed.

The attempt to make such a space real and to live in it is the subject of Kimberly O'Sullivan's story of the emergence in the late 1980s of a lesbian sex radical underground in Sydney. Chafing against the denial of the erotic in the exclusionary politics of the dominant political lesbian feminist movement, a younger generation of lesbians, and some few disgruntled feminist pioneers, began expressing a fluidity of desire and practice that soon brought them into conflict with the old guard. This erupted into the Australian version of the sex wars that had been convulsing feminism in the United States since the late 1970s.[4] Explicitly 'politically incorrect' activities were set up in reaction to a censorious party line: 'public readings of sexual fantasies, demonstrations of vibrators and other sex toys . . . an SM demonstration and a night of dungeon play'. Soon Sydney nights were enlivened by a vigorous sub-culture of sex parties, contests, performance, exhibitions. The pleasures of such activity were palpable: cocking a snook at the old guard, breaking down walls of gender hatred and exclusivity and building a new and closer community through pansexual and gender-fuck performance, as well as restoring sexual joy to a lesbianism that had become merely a bitter expression of opposition to patriarchy.

Yet how real is this community of nighttime play among the inner-city grunge crowd? Who does one become in the daytime, and where does one belong? Can any community set itself up without boundaries, without definition, without exclusion of the not-like-us? Even the sex radicals deride the vanilla girls. Can the open community, sought by so many, only ever be a space of desire and longing, a nostalgia for what was promised but never became, the millenial dream of the sexual revolutionaries? As Rebecca Cox writes, 'Sometimes . . . it seems like this community only exists in its absence.' But perhaps all social groupings are essentially constituted discursively and in fantasy. In which case the nature of one's dreams matters. Barbara Creed quotes the American theorist Donna Haraway: 'a dream not of a common language but of a powerful infidel heteroglossia' (Haraway 1985, p. 101). Both

---

[4] The US sex wars are well discussed in the new introduction to Carole Vance (ed.) 1992 *Pleasure and Danger: Exploring Female Sexuality* 2nd edition London: Pandora; and in Lisa Duggan & Nan D. Hunter 1995 *Sex Wars: Sexual Dissent and Political Cultures* New York: Routledge.

these dreams, and others, coexist in the multiplicity of sexual cultures.

Lumby's queer postmodern story of media disintegration of boundaries and its dream of heteroglossia have clear resonance with readers, watchers, listeners, audience—as individuals—in their space of privacy. In the public realm, some sort of 'common language' remains the ruling fantasy. Perhaps the way Benedict Anderson (1983) configures the concept of nation can be used here as an analogy for those sexual cultures which self-define as 'not-straight' and somehow, sometimes, formulate themselves into a community, though not always a queer nation. Anderson writes of nations as communities, 'because, regardless of the actual inequality and exploitation that may prevail in each, the nation is always conceived as a deep, horizontal comradeship' (Anderson 1983, p. 16). Such nations, and communities, are also 'imagined . . . because the members of even the smallest nation will never know most of their fellow-members, meet them, or even hear of them, yet in the minds of each lives the image of their communion' (Anderson 1983, p. 15).

There are echoes of such communion in Gary Dowsett's delineation of: 'a burgeoning supra-national cultural formation, a kind of international gay community complete with travel networks and tour agents, accommodation and social/sexual activity guides, numerous information super-highway links on the Internet, and a definite political agenda on civil and human rights and HIV/AIDS recognisable from country to country. This international community is an astonishing achievement and it takes some time to grasp the complexity of the moves that have created this phenomenon in barely thirty years.' There are echoes of it too in the world of lesbian separatism, the Australian history of which is the subject of Judith Ion's chapter. Here, too, is an international cultural formation: expressed in women's lands, gatherings and festivals, based on a vision of separation from patriarchal society, and dedicated to preserving and enhancing women's energies and skills as individuals and for all women so as to end the oppression of women everywhere. In Australia, separatist land was bought in the early 1970s, with money raised 'by various women's communities throughout Australia and internationally and the land was considered to be "owned" by them all. It was run as an open women's land where *all* women and girls were welcome to live or visit'.

Nations and communities, as defined by Anderson, are intrinsically based upon difference and exclusion. They take their definition as much from what they are not as from any sense of what they are. In the past decade or so, difference has been receiving good press among feminist, gay, queer and postmodern commentators. Exclusion, however, is decried. Exclusion seems to connote a refusal to share access to goods, benefits and rights. Indeed, exclusion abandons rights in favour of privilege. But what if the community is one that constitutes itself specifically as a means of a collective strengthening to withstand the disadvantage and oppression that flow from its definition as the excluded other, the despised difference, by another, more powerful, community; if the first community has few resources and is explicitly denied rights? This certainly is what the Australian groups of both the international gay and the lesbian separatist communities understand themselves as being and doing. Exclusion here takes on another tenor. The dominant straight/patriarchal community, acting as individuals and as a communion, often responds to such expressions of collective strengthening by treating any demand for equal but separate rights as tantamount to the violent ripping away of its privileges, which it calls rights, but not universal ones available to the others.

McKenzie Wark comments on the relatively benign insistence on the right to belong wherever they choose that is manifested by 'the straight couples [who] wander around in the crowd—always holding hands' at the Sydney Gay & Lesbian Mardi Gras, which defiantly proclaims itself to be 'for ourselves', 'for our community'. More malevolent are the gay-bashers and the fundamentalist Christians and politicians who want the Mardi Gras to die, as individuals and collectively, and the well-meaning liberals who want it not to encroach upon their space of power and privileged humanity.

Analogous reports come from the women's lands: of local men who block access with 'chain-sawed trees across the road', of men who go 'on a rampage with a gun and an axe they took from the women's woodpile, destroying everything in their path, chopping down the orchard, killing chickens and terrorising the women'. The greater community responds to difference by attempting to assimilate it into the bottom of its hierarchy, or by violent suppression.

Clear-cut, black-and-white stories like these, of course, don't quite tell the whole tale—because the new, less powerful community, in attempting to strengthen itself against the dominant community, develops its own sources of power within the boundaries of its own ghetto or laager. A certain rigidity, an exclusiveness, even fundamentalism, comes to cling to the edges of such cultures which base their criterion of membership in some literal truth of being. This entails, by the binary logic each has necessarily constituted itself through, that it too exclude others. Such others are inevitably defined as being either of the dominant group, or its dupes and catspaws, if not its shock-troops. Wark identifies the feminist and gay argument that establishes 'bisexuality [as] the "clandestine" practice of the dominant group. It doesn't qualify for the high moral ground of the "marginalised"'. Kimberly O'Sullivan delineates the hostile division among women's movement lesbians, with the 'political lesbians see[ing] their decision to become lesbians as part of a revolutionary activism to overthrow patriarchy. They contrast their lives positively against those lesbians whom they judge to be oversexed, apolitical and ignorant. In extreme cases these other lesbians even get lumped in with heterosexual conservatives'. Political lesbians, she claims, held the dominant public position within the Sydney feminist lesbian community for some time, and excluded unwanted otherness by declaring it 'male'. 'Political lesbian minds snapped shut when anything was decreed to be "male", especially if it related to sexuality, and any such labelling was guaranteed to give the subject in question the lesbian kiss of death.' Under this regime, dildos, pornography and erotica, pansexual SM play, sex work, wet T-shirts, sex toys and sexual fantasy were all marked male and any woman who derived pleasure from them could not be a true lesbian.

These are extreme examples of the power of the logic of exclusion which is built into the very walls that constitute the haven of community. But let there be no mistake, there are very highly charged forms of desire and pleasure happening here. Facing outwards, there is the whipped fervour of purity, the passion of self-righteous blaming and condemnation; the pride of defence of citadel; the frisson of fear lest one be found wanting. Facing inwards, there is the intense, almost aching desire to belong, to be part of the communion; the embrace, the safety of home at last. The metaphors of military conquest and spiritual grace are key terms in the vocabularies of sexual cultures built on a hierarchy of difference and a logic of exclusion, just as they are in the vocabulary of the nation.

Curiously, however, whatever one may think of these stories of belonging and exclusion told by sexual communities, one consequence seems to be that stories of sex are also excluded from their standard accounts. Perhaps this is because, as the church and the army discovered hundreds of years ago, sex leads to indiscipline because its focus is on individuals (or small group at the most), against the collective. Yet perhaps this too is only another either/or story told in the voice of the old binary logic. Whatever the reason, when the stories of these collectivities are told, a certain sexual negativity or reticence returns to discursive dominance. A taboo against imaging HIV-positive gay sexuality is the central theme of Ted Gott's chapter. Only very recently, as late as 1992, did even the gay community begin publicly to produce and accept pro-joy expressions of HIV-positive sexuality. Gary Dowsett writes of the absence of sex from gay history and from sexuality theory. 'Even in the political histories of Gay Liberation there is little evidence of sex going on. It is as if gay men (and lesbians for that matter) did little else but attend meetings, rallies and demonstrations, and write political and theoretical tracts. In fact, there was a lot of fucking going on, and it is important to say so!' Judith Ion explicitly discusses why her history of women's land does not mention sex: 'these elements were not volunteered by any of the women I spoke to about their experiences on the land. Does that mean they didn't have sex? No. What it means is that talking about sex is not foremost in their minds when it comes to memories of life on the land . . . Sex was an integral part of life on the land but no more so than making sure you had enough to eat and drink. It was part of the fabric but it wasn't the whole fabric.' Jenny Pausacker identifies the same exclusion in the heterosexual world's attitude to love rather than sex: 'The books [are] now there but the climate, the discourse, the forbidden nature of romance writing [hasn't] changed . . . I've started to get the distinct impression that writing about love, especially love between a man and a woman, is one of the unacknowledged taboos of our time.'

There is no self-conscious sexual culture of heterosexuality as such. The dominant structures and discourses that proclaim heterosexuality to be normal are so overwhelmingly taken for granted that they do not need defence. Here indeed is a common language. To be heterosexual is always to belong, always to be at home and always pure. It is the other markers of difference attached to the heterosexual body that require explanation and collective defence: in Australia, not-white, not-man, not-middle-class, not liberal or agnostic Christian. But if Lumby, Wark, Creed and Pausacker are right, the very unity, certainty and unmarkedness of heterosexuality is now also becoming unravelled. Straights are being revealed as heterogeneous and quite queer. Fiona Patten's chapter presents a clear-sighted description and defence of that heterosexual world. If one needed concrete evidence of the curious mix of diffuse desire and fluid identity added to the politics of authenticity and civil rights, it is here. On all sides—government censors and regulators, sex industry workers, fantasy creators and performers, business entrepreneurs, consumers—they shift and slide.

But at least to a limited degree in the last few decades, within the sexual communities discussed here, there has been an increased talking about sex and concomitantly an increased taken for grantedness, openness, self-confidence, and lesser defensiveness about sexual differences. At this point the counterposition of lines, entirely out of context, from two prophetic poets will serve as well as anything else to summarise the range of responses and meaning between and within at least some Australian sexual cultures in the late twentieth century.

> 'Things fall apart; the centre cannot hold . . .
> The ceremony of innocence is drowned'
>
> W. B. Yeats (1921) 'The Second Coming' (1962, p. 99).

> 'I sing the Body electric;
> The armies of those I love engirth me, and I engirth them.'
>
> Walt Whitman (1855) *Leaves of Grass* (1945, p. 158).

1
Nothing personal: sex, gender and identity in the media age

CATHARINE LUMBY

So what *does* the modern man want? '... to lick your boots, suck your toes, lick your ass, worship your muscular throne, inhale your funk, to be spanked, whipped with cream.' Anything else with that, sir? 'A woman who just wants to shut the door on her worries and let her libido run wild, then calmly open the door and return to her proper world'; 'an honest trustworthy female with a flexible daytime schedule'; 'someone to take me out of Missouri'; 'a dominant lesbian who believes that the use of corporal punishment is a fine way to prove female superiority'; 'I'd like to know what really happens when you die'.

And for madam? '... no bisexuals, alcohol, drugs or head games'; 'I want to fuck a gay man silly. Bend him over and shove it in him hard'; 'two types. Fit solid hairless black body. Tall solid big dick white boy'; 'when she won't take no for an answer'; 'photos of ordinary people fucking'; 'a long conversation with an interesting gentleman of integrity and depth'; 'getting fucked basically'; 'a previously married music-loving, accomplished 50ish man who's self-aware, relaxed, sensitive, insightful, possessing a well-developed bicameral mind'; 'policewomen on duty'; 'being let down just before I'm about to come'; 'being in control'.

Think of the personals as a filter—a permeable membrane strung between everyday life and its representation. Images and information wash back and forth between these zones, leaving their traces, caught by the mesh. Here, at the intersection of the private and the public imaginary, the traditional trajectories of desire unravel. Uncoupled from gender and sexual norms, the standard binaries invert and reinvent themselves. Passive/active, straight/bent, feminine/masculine, subject/object. The personals are peopled with macho sluts, butch queens, twisted straights and straight queers. In a parody of the textbook fetishes of hetero normality, supplicants often nominate ridiculously specific objects and rules . . . 'hairy Italians with big hands and bald heads'; 'slim, clean-cut preppy boys with large feet'; 'non-smoking, vegetarian, black female top'; 'Ivy League essential'. Identity as a crazed laundry list.

In the contemporary media landscape John Berger's famous dictum, 'Men act and women appear', seems increasingly myopic. These days, everyone appears while everyone looks on. Or in Jean Baudrillard's manic depressive scenario: everything *disappears*. 'In matters of sex,' he writes,

> the proliferation is approaching total loss. Here lies the secret of the ever increasing production of sex and its signs, and the hyperrealism of sexual pleasure . . . When desire is entirely on the side of demand, when it is operationalised without restrictions, it loses its imaginary and, therefore, its reality; it appears everywhere, but in generalised simulation. It is the ghost of desire that haunts the defunct reality of sex (Baudrillard 1990, p. 5).

In Baudrillard's anaemic world, contemporary sexuality and the media have a lot in common. The media, Baudrillard suggests, dream of rendering everything transparent in an orgy of instant and ceaseless communication. The end result, however, is not the mere reproduction of the real world, but its simulation. The real, like sex, is simultaneously everywhere and nowhere. Both have disappeared in the overproduction of signs.

Against this masculine principle of simulation, Baudrillard

poses an abstract feminine principle of seduction, which must be understood in terms of play, reversibility and the strategy of appearances. The feminine principle in this schema does not oppose the masculine order, it seduces it.

Baudrillard's account of the disappearance of sex behind the promiscuous proliferation of its signs is tailormade for a flip, onanistic account of sex in the contemporary media in which the disappearance of the former is ensured by the obsessional pursuit of the latter. It's an easy mapping exercise, however, which evades the most subtle and valuable aspect of Baudrillard's argument: the complex resonance he gives the term 'feminine'.

As with all his terms, Baudrillard's references to seduction and the feminine are fluid. They slide about. Consistent with his critique of the instrumentalisation of knowledge, Baudrillard uses them to *seduce* the reader, rather than explicate his ideas or close an argument. The feminine is, on one hand, a kind of black hole characterising the viscosity of the media and its neutralisation of all meaning: 'the triumph of a soft seduction, a white diffuse feminization and eroticization of all relations in an enervated social universe' (Baudrillard 1990, p. 2). On the other it is simultaneously an ironic principle which subverts (or in Baudrillard's terms seduces) this quest for meaning and identity via artifice, indeterminacy and the play of appearances. The strength of the feminine, in other words, lies precisely in its indeterminacy, in its reversibility and its failure to produce identity.

Baudrillard quite deliberately leaves open the question of whether the implosion of meaning he detects in the contemporary world is ultimately an instance of this defiant seduction. 'All of production,' he concludes, 'and truth itself, are directed towards disclosure, the unbearable "truth" of sex being the most recent consequence. Luckily, at bottom, there is nothing to it. And seduction still holds, in the face of truth, a most sybilline response, which is that "perhaps we wish to uncover the truth because it is so difficult to imagine it naked"' (Baudrillard 1990, p. 181).

In a Wildean sense, then, Baudrillard wagers the sublime

power of appearances against the lust for overexposure which characterises the mass media. In another sense, Baudrillard can be accused of simply opposing an aesthetic order to the banality of mass culture. As Meaghan Morris (Morris 1990, p. 20) has pointed out, however, what makes his appeal more interesting is that these terms are reversible.

Female trouble

> You are now entering Heaven. Six pages of pure bliss. Claudia Schiffer bares her perfect breasts. Look inside and die happy (*People*).
>
> Wot's going down? Hot lezzo love-ins, that's wot . . . The Bisexual revolution has begun. "Lesbian chic" is born—and I can't tell you what GOOD NEWS this is for us. Consider: What's the Number One FURGLE FANTASY of the red-blooded rooters of Orstralia? Going the tonk with TWO gorgeous sheilas while they boldly bonk and boff each other's bushy bits (*The Picture*).
>
> Dr Bollard writes: I'm often stopped in the streets by strangers who ask me, 'Why do men like breasts?' These fools miss the point entirely. Men do not merely *like* breasts; they *need* hooters and funbags to ensure their very survival . . . Ambition is a vital part of modern life, and breasts play a critical role. It is my personal ambition to stroke the breasts hanging off the front of supermodel Kathy Ireland (*World*).

It would be hard to find magazines better designed to attract traditional feminist ire than the Australian tabloid weeklies *People*, *The Picture* and *World*. With their 'titfests', naked 'housewife' centrefolds, crude descriptions of female genitalia and introduction agency ads which promise bargains like 'join today and receive two kinky ladies for *free*', these publications are literally begging to be reprimanded.

A case in point is a 1993 feminist campaign to ban from the newsstands an issue of *The Picture* magazine which featured a woman on all fours wearing a dog collar on its cover. In the ensuing controversy everyone presumably got exactly what they came for. The woman-as-dog metaphor gave anti-porn feminists further grist for the outrage mill, while the largely blue collar male readership of *The Picture* got the sound maternal spanking they'd been spoiling for. In many ways it's a marriage made in heaven. With their brew of resentment, crude humour, exhibitionism and breast fetishism, the tone of *The Picture*, *People* and *World* is highly reminiscent of a virtuoso toddler tantrum designed to attract mum's attention at any price. And anti-porn feminists are at least willing to take the display seriously.

A cooler more contemporary response to all this moral posturing would point out that beneath the thin veneer of macho bravado *The Picture*, *People* and *World* are already sending themselves up. A typical example is the text which accompanied a recent photo spread of a semi-naked woman in *World*, detailing the model's unflattering views on men and sex. Asked what it was like to lose her virginity 'Julie' responded: 'Oh, God. It was really terrible. It was at the top of a building in the middle of Brisbane above a mall.' Of sex in general she opines: 'It's very dangerous and I'd rather not do it. There's too much to worry about with diseases . . . I'd rather play Streetfighter II . . . There's not much to say about sex. There's no sex. I'm not interested.'

This jokey, frequently ironic and self-puncturing tone certainly inflects much of the magazines' copy. The covers sport headlines like 'The Five Most Important People In History: Hitler, Darwin, Lenin, Erika Eleniak, Bert Newton' and 'Lost Lesbian Tribe In Combat With Dinosaurs! Can They Be Saved? (The Dinosaurs That Is)'. The methods and moral posturing of mainstream journalism are also a common target. One *World* columnist is referred to simply as 'the world's foremost expert' while another pledges 'in the tradition of Mike Munro' to 'ambush innocent people trying to make their way in a difficult world and publicly kick the living shit out of them'.

The problem with both responses to these magazines—the Bad, Literal Feminist reading which argues that the media train us to desire particular objects, and the Knowing, Culturally

Hip reading which credits the readers of *The Picture* with reorganising the media in line with their own desires—is that neither addresses the forms of desire which flow *between* the media and its audience or attempts to come to terms with the tension and continuities *between* contemporary gender politics and sexuality and its representation in the media.

While the traditional feminist position freezes its audience with a steely stare, the distracted populist gaze of the cooler response ignores the materiality of the text. Yet it is arguably at the intersection of this binary that the most profitable discussion of contemporary sex and gender as it is consumed in and produced by the media can begin—a discussion which acknowledges that the media is neither a mirror of reality nor reality itself—but an imprint of the traffic between the two. As John Hartley puts it in *The Politics of Pictures*, the problem 'is not a question of contrasting a real public with the illusory media (almost, vice versa in fact); it is a matter of showing how pervasive the textualisation of public life has become' (Hartley 1992, p. 2).

The important thing here is to recognise the dynamic of desire which flows between individuals and the social as it unfolds in the media. Making sense of this flow of images, like making sense of sexuality, involves a creative act. As readers and viewers we construct and reconstruct an imaginary subject position in relation to the social text. 'The pleasure of television is akin to frottage: a glimpse, a frisson of excitement provoked by taking private pleasure from public contact' (Hartley 1992, p. 91).

Yet while we speak back to the social as we encounter it in the media, we are simultaneously spoken by it. Audiences and readers are textual objects too. We are called into being by the media, and we construct our subjectivity in its shadow. This Moebius strip which runs between the media and everyday life doesn't lend itself to empirical dissection. But its contours can be traced.

Descent into the malestrom

> As Andy Warhol said, 'Sex is the biggest nothing of all time'. Just imagine everything you could accomplish if you eliminated that big nothing. From what I can tell sex is just getting worse and worse anyway. As my friend Laren Stover says, sex has become confused with narcissism in our culture. Placing an obsessively high value on image has made looking good seem to many people the path to happiness and good sex (*Details*, May 1995).
>
> Sexual harassment has turned the workplace into a minefield, where even an innocent remark can detonate a perfectly decent career . . . Time was when a kiss was indeed just a kiss, a sigh just a sigh, and suave men in fedoras would tip their hats to good-looking women and whistle as they passed. But no more . . . (*Men's Health*, September 1994).
>
> . . . the last guy I was with covered his naked penis with his hands and whined, 'Stop touching it' . . . We unanimously diagnosed this bizarre condition as postmodern performance anxiety (*Future Sex*, 1994).

In the 1995 Annual Sex Issue of *Details*, a contemporary men's magazine aimed at the twenties and thirties inner-city male market, a little bit of erotic pleasure comes out looking like a lot of awfully hard work. Good sex, according to an article on tantric sex, requires 'devotion, commitment and sacrifice', not to mention a couple of thousand bucks for an expensive course in how to do it. In the *Details* sexual IQ test, sexual competency emerges as a daunting array of knowledge about sexual terms, practices and devices. The lead article, a survey of 'the new landscape of sex and desire' warns that 'these days, no matter how you play, you pay'. And a forum on contemporary males poses a series of angst-ridden questions about the nature 'of that strange beast masculinity'.

In a contemporaneous issue, rival magazine *Esquire* (June 1995) considers the question, 'Do women actually love us or simply *tolerate* us?' The discouraging response was diplomatically summed up by Nancy Friday, who chaired a five-woman panel which considered the question: 'I would hate to think that the anger in that room represents women at large'.

Men's Health magazine, a leader in the burgeoning men's fitness magazine market, regularly raises the spectre of poor sexual performance and impotence in its features on sex. A recent article addressed to men in their late twenties and early thirties ran: 'Your early 20s are over, and those marathon lovemaking sessions are gone—along with the days off spent in bed that ended after your first promotion. It's easy to start wondering if perhaps the party's over, libido-wise. Well, we've a got a message for you . . .' The message is a rigorous and complex exercise regime aimed at 'getting fit for fooling around' and 'training your love muscles'. In case readers are thinking of slacking off after they've dominated in the sack, this guide to better sexual performance is buried between articles featuring spartan diets and exercise regimes designed to fight fat, as well as fashion how-tos and self-esteem guides.

It's a far cry from the superficially comfortable paternalistic world of *Playboy, circa* 1960, in which the major questions troubling men were 'the correct storage and serving of liquor in the urban apartment' and how to get hold of an unexpurgated copy of *Lady Chatterley's Lover*.

Anxiety about masculinity rises off magazines aimed at a young male market like steam off a locker room floor. From endless articles devoted to disciplining and beautifying the male body, to (sometimes hostile) articles examining the meaning of feminism and heterosexuality in contemporary society, the overriding message is that masculinity has entered an age of profound uncertainty.

Overt references to this anxiety aside, the most striking change in men's magazines of the late 1980s and 1990s is the explicitly erotic focus on the male body. While magazines such as *Esquire*, *Details* and *Arena* regularly profile attractive female celebrities, the great majority of naked bodies featured are male. In magazines like *Men's Health* and *Men's Fitness* women have all but disappeared. From ads for cologne and mineral water to the photo spreads accompanying feature articles, the focus is resolutely on the male form. These images cut across the essentialising grain of the text, suggesting that the truth of masculinity is simply a matter of appearances.

In Australia one of the first images to draw attention to this sexualising of the male body was a mid–1980s ad for Sheridan sheets, showing a muscled and tanned male torso emerging from a set of rumpled bedclothes. In the same era Bruce Weber's ads for Calvin Klein, featuring pretty, well-built adolescent boys, also caused a stir. Today toned and tanned nude male bodies are mandatory props in ads for a wide range of male products. The June 1995 edition of *Gentleman's Quarterly*, for instance, contains fourteen separate ads featuring naked men.

To understand the current mainstream eroticising of the male body as a purely homoerotic gesture, though, is to misrecognise the nature of the desire which flows between the media and its audience. The desire courted by men's magazines, whether they are pitched at a nominally hetero or homosexual market, is the desire to consume. For consumers it's a seduction which is increasingly mediated by the consumption of images. What is presaged by the new sexualising of men is not merely the extension and refinement of an existing market, but a new order of commodification. Originally carriers of the commodity virus, images have become desirable in themselves. Or to put it another way, our desires are increasingly modelled on the logic of images.

Blonde ambition

In 1994 a rival program finally knocked *Hey! Hey! It's Saturday* from its legendary dominance in the early evening Saturday night ratings. The show in question, *Man O Man*, relied on a simple formula: get a 150-strong all-female audience drunk on champagne and let them judge (read: ritually humiliate) ten semi-naked male contestants. The men have to jump through a series of set hoops—including singing, dancing, push-ups and chatting up a model. For their pains the majority wind up being pushed into a swimming pool in front of a group of cheering women.

A five-page *Cleo* article examining the immense popularity of the show among young women posed the question of what female viewers got out of it. The general response was epitomised in the following quote: 'It makes you feel like you can get back at the male of the species.'

If contemporary male magazines approach the subject of sex and gender with barely disguised angst, the same discussions in magazines aimed at a young female market are overwhelmingly characterised by defiance. While *Cleo* and *Cosmo* magazines remain committed to advising their readers on how to secure and hold together a heterosexual relationship, many of the articles are underscored by a sense of playful independence which was decidedly lacking from most mainstream women's magazines prior to the 1980s.

A new addition to the Australian magazine market, *Australian Women's Forum*, mates centrefolds of naked, toned men with advice to women suggesting they forget diets 'because some fool with a size eight mind has designed ludicrously small bathing suits' and refuse 'to declare war on our gorgeous girlie girths'. *Forum* consistently inverts the traditional male subject–female object axis, actively promoting female voyeurism and sexual aggression. In doing so it brings into the mainstream a feminist libertarian formula which has been tested on the media margins in magazines such as *Future Sex*, *On Our Backs* and *Wicked Women*.

If the accelerating symbiosis between contemporary sexual identity and the restless flow of images in the media has destabilised masculinity, it appears to suit women well. A brief consideration of the traditional symbolic role of femininity suggests why. As Baudrillard notes: 'in this society everything—objects, goods, services, relations of all types—will be feminised, sexualised in a feminine fashion. In advertising it is not so much a matter of adding sex to washing machines (which is absurd) as conferring on objects the imaginary, female quality of being available at will, or never being retractile or aleatory' (Baudrillard 1990, p. 26). Baudrillard's pejorative use of the term 'feminine' here buys into a long history of thinkers who have characterised the 'corrupt' aspects of mass culture in this way. But Baudrillard's own nuancing of the term also suggests a more profitable way of thinking about the relationship between gender, sexuality and mass culture.

The duplicity of women has traditionally been tied to their supposed mastery of appearances. Indeed, the history of aesthetics is crowded with condemnations of precisely this art. From Plato's distrust of the mimetic arts to Rousseau's hostility to the theatre and his desire to lift the veil of appearances and reveal an essential truth, conventional aesthetics has been troubled by the deceptive potential of artifice. In the twentieth century a related strain of iconoclasm has resurfaced in mainstream critiques of the superficial distractions afforded by the mass media. A number of feminist scholars have recently challenged this dumb blonde characterisation of mass culture and sought to unearth the gendered assumptions behind it (Landes, 1988; Fraser, 1989).

What has yet to be sufficiently mapped are the forms of knowledge embedded in the traditional relation between women and the debased aspects of capitalism—artifice and consumption; the sense, as Baudrillard has it, that 'there is no God behind the images, and the very nothingness they conceal must remain a secret' (Baudrillard, 1990: p. 94). In Baudrillard's schema, this knowledge offers women no comparative advantage bar a kind of aesthetic superiority. In his ideal world, women would simply shimmer on the shelf in a perverse parody of commodity fetishism. But if we set aside the fatalistic absolutism of his theory, his argument does suggest that femininity sits in a strategically knowing relation to the production of gender and sexuality in the contemporary media.

Future sex

Quim is for, by, and about dykes. Fuck the media hype. Society, gay/straight, male/female, black/white, will always suppress those who don't conform. We want queer dykes to have the opportunity to be ourselves for ourselves . . . We want out of trendy fashion tabloid middle-class okayed images of 'lesbianism'. *Quim* is about the real bad girls . . . (*Quim* 1994).

In 1993 the straight girl's bible, *Cleo*, ran a feature on lesbian chic which posed the following 'dilemma for the 90s woman': if you could sleep with Michael Hutchence or Helena Christensen who would you choose? The readers responded in a survey published the following month—63 per cent plumped for Hutchence's supermodel girlfriend.

Over the past three years lesbian chic has taken off in the mainstream media. No longer labelled fat, ugly, extremist, or more often simply ignored, the lesbian community has been flung into the limelight. According to *Cleo*, *Esquire*, *Vanity Fair* and a host of popular magazines and newspapers, lesbians are suddenly well-off, smartly dressed and, like their male yuppie counterparts, apt to hang around cocktail bars and nightclubs picking up women. British journalist Julie Burchill summed up the genus when she quoted the following ad from a personals column: 'Girl. Come around the world with me. I am a rich and beautiful lesbian looking for a young and pretty girlfriend. No butches, lefties or crazies.'

The appearance of the designer dyke phenomenon in the media is less interesting, however, than the concern it's engendered in the lesbian community. Australian author Fiona McGregor summed up a common response when she described media attention to lesbian chic as an example of 'this stupid notion that nothing exists until the media discovers it'. 'Lesbians have always been chic,' she told *The Independent Monthly* (October 1994), 'I have lesbian friends in their forties who have always worn lipstick and been pretty groovy. You think of people like Dietrich and Garbo in the thirties and that's just the tip of the iceberg.'

McGregor's comment reveals something more subtle than a simple distaste for media stereotyping: a fear of dissolving into the mainstream. After years of complaining about their invisibility, the lesbian community is discovering that media visibility comes with its own price tag, the chief cost being a loss of control over which images of lesbian identity circulate. Being out also means allowing the straight community in, and with this intermixing comes a more diffuse, less essentialist notion of lesbian identity. Debates in the gay and lesbian community over whether to allow straight and bisexual people to join the Mardi Gras organisation and attend the annual Mardi Gras party are a classic instance of this anxiety. A festival which began life as a protest march, the Mardi Gras illustrates the way the gay and lesbian community have, in one sense, become victims of their own media profile. The desire on the part of some in the lesbian and gay community to exclude straight and bisexual people points up the role that exclusion from mainstream society plays in founding a notion of community. Ironically, the accelerating representation of gays and lesbians in the press, on current affairs and talk shows, in television sitcoms and in Hollywood films, may do more to destabilise and fragment the lesbian and gay community than years of exclusion and hostility.

Feminists have had to face a similar dilemma in the face of persistent mainstream media coverage. Exposure has opened feminism to competing representations of what it means to be a feminist. Despite persistent claims on the part of some feminists that the media continues to oppress women and ignore feminist views, the opposite is demonstrably true. As the 1994 battle for women viewers between the prime time current affairs shows *Real Life* and *A Current Affair* illustrates, stories on sex discrimination, sexual harassment, domestic violence and internal feminist debates are now regarded as highly saleable. The current problem for feminism is not oppressive patriarchal misrepresentations of women, but how to maintain a sense of identity in the face of a flood of competing images of feminism itself. The media is rendering the social body and its competing identities increasingly unstable. Images are not simply carriers of information, they are force fields which reorganise social relations in their wake.

In *No Sense Of Place*, Joshua Meyrowitz argues that television assaults the dividing line between male and female worlds because 'it merges traditionally distinct gender information systems, blurs the dividing line between the public and private behaviors of each sex and undermines the significance of physical segregation as a determinant of sex segregation' (Meyrowitz 1986, p. 201). In this scenario, content (what television programs tell people their place is) is less important than what the medium itself allows (access to a vision of different places and cultural identities).

This collapse of boundaries is fuelling an identity crisis both within the traditional public sphere and outside it, among groups which have defined themselves by their marginalisation. In this volatile scenario it is fruitless to understand sexuality and gender as 'realities' distinct from their imaging in popular culture. It is no longer a question of opposing politics—the real—and the media—the play of appearances. It is a question of understanding the politics of appearances themselves. If these tangential explorations of slices of contemporary media culture tell us anything, it is that the proliferation of signs of sexuality and gender rapidly incorporate, reverse and exceed traditional or conventional valuations of, for example, the male body, the lesbian, the bimbo.

The contradictory, constantly shifting nature of contemporary information and image flows tends to erode the moral authority of any one social order, patriarchal or otherwise. It is this very collapse which has arguably fuelled social revolutions such as feminism and gay and lesbian rights, but which equally disrupts attempts by some to ground them in identity politics. While these movements have in turn benefited from the proliferation of mediated sexuality, then attempted to critique and control it, they have ended up being ever so subtly subsumed and incorporated into image culture.

To understand this process of the incorporation of the significance of bodies into media flows, it's not sufficient simply to juxtapose a 'naive' essentialist idea of gender or sexuality against a 'sophisticated' conception of gender and sexuality as floating terms. The idea that, semiotically speaking, 'anything goes' (or in apocalyptic terms 'everything's gone') is every bit as reductive as the idea that sex can be neatly mapped on to gender or sexuality can be mapped on to a series of acts. A far more interesting inquiry lies in the friction between these two fictional positions—between identity and its dissolution.

What the promiscuous flow of the contemporary image culture opens up, then, is an expanded and abstracted terrain of becoming. As some of the examples I've introduced here show, this emergent terrain works according to semiotic processes whereby images exceed, incorporate or reverse the values that are presumed to reside within them in a patriarchal social order. To argue this is not to deny dominant social constructions of gender and sexuality but rather to suggest that such social constructions compete with, and are incorporated within, another logic altogether: the logic of the production of appearances in the media space. A fair assessment of the possibilities and dangers of that space for projects such as feminism has to come to terms with feminism's own incorporation in media space, and also revise its attempts to critique the media as if 'from without'.

We can extend this line of thought with one further speculation: that the play of appearances in the virtual world of contemporary culture has a lot to tell us about contemporary gender and sexuality.

2
Screen sex: from television to teledildonics

BARBARA CREED

> I believe that organic sex, body against body, skin area against skin area, is becoming no longer possible . . . What we are getting is a whole new order of sexual fantasies (J.G. Ballard, 1984).

A pair of giant, slightly-parted lips pouts provocatively from a television screen, inviting the startled hero, Max Renn, to clamber inside. Max has discovered a secret television program which features torture, sex and death. The program is transmitted by a signal known as 'videodrome' which directly affects the brain, causing hallucinations and eventually physical mutations from which the addicted viewer will die. Directed by David Cronenberg, the film *Videodrome* (1982) was an immediate cult hit.

The videodrome signal has been devised by Brian O'Blivion, a scientist who hopes, through television, to bring about a union of human and machine—to create a technological subject—in preparation for a more advanced society. Viewers become addicted to videodrome because it offers pleasures associated with taboo topics such as sex and violence. As Max's hallucinations take over, reality blurs. Does Max really clamber through the woman's inviting lips? Is that a gun he keeps inside a vaginal pouch secreted within his stomach? Part of the pleasure offered by a film like *Videodrome* is that the viewer is drawn into the fantasy.

One of the main themes explored by *Videodrome* is precisely the nature of the pleasure generated in the screen/spectator relationship. What images do viewers find erotically stimulating? Is it possible to create a virtual reality in which the spectator is 'linked' directly to the visual experience? What kind of narratives seduce the viewer? What is the difference between reality and fantasy?

Cronenberg developed his script in the early 1980s when his ideas seemed like science fiction: today his scenario is a reality. Anyone with a computer and the right information can tap into the Internet world of computer pornography, without *Videodrome's* attendant dangers. While some warn of the addictive nature of surfing the net, for many, sex in cyberspace is a dream come true.

There are many ways in which the viewer can access a sexual encounter on the net. Most direct is the bulletin board system, accessed through a personal computer and telephone line. Thousands of people communicate via any one bulletin board, which is like a small neighbourhood of inhabitants with a common interest. There are boards devoted to almost every conceivable topic: religion, politics, media, sport, hobbies, *Absolutely Fabulous*, animal rights, feminism, literature and, of course, sex. The sex boards cover a range of interests, from straight to sado-masochistic sex.

While some use the bulletin boards to meet people, others simply talk. A more direct form of communication is 'Internet relay chat' (IRC), in which two people are on the system at the same time. The screen forms two sections; one person's words appear above, the other's beneath the dividing line. Users can find IRC channels that appeal to a range of interests—heterosexual, homosexual, lesbian, bisexual, etc.

Some users describe their sexual desires and fantasies in minute detail. Participants may change their identity in relation to name, gender, age, appearance, colour and sexual preference. Naturally, a medium that permits people to assume a completely different identity, without fear of disclosure, has strong appeal.

The enthusiast can participate in disembodied love-making by tapping out their desires and commands. Sometimes the unwary find themselves subject to abusive, sadistic messages. Sexual harassment on the net (Dibbell 1994) is already an issue. Other participants may eventually desire to establish actual bodily contact and arrange to meet. There have even been courtships through bulletin boards and IRC channels which have led to marriage.

Other popular cyberspaces are the MUDs, or multi-user dungeons. MUDs are imaginary or virtual communities set up by people who can assume a fictional identity if they wish. Members of a MUD, known as MUDders, must first create their new identity, then they can 'build' a house, chat with other MUDders, exchange intimacies, create whole new lives. MUDs are virtual stages on which every member is an actor. Communities may build a spaceship and take part in a science fiction adventure. Anything is possible. Once you have joined a MUD, you can be anybody—the world is in your net. Members of a MUD may decide to construct a community devoted to sexual exploration in which they might change their genders, describe their fantasies, engage in sexual encounters.

Cybersex travellers interested in erotica can—if they know the correct addresses—call up pornographic material. At the tap of a keyboard, viewers can salivate as cyberbunnies strip and wiggle, or quake in their shoes at the leather-clad, whip-wielding dominatrix humiliating her willing male slave. It all sounds like a case of *Penthouse* meets *Mission Impossible*. Viewers can then download whichever image arouses them most and use it for a masturbation fantasy or as a wall hanging. Studies indicate that the most frequently downloaded images from cyberspace are sexual. It is relatively easy to find written material (short stories, poems, jokes) on any form of sexual variation. The key word Zoophilia, for instance, opens up onto a world of 'interspecies sexuality, including animal role play, totemism, bestiality and zoophilia'. Some of the short stories are hairy and hoary.

Some authorities are alarmed because it appears virtually impossible to control computer pornography. The Internet does not recognise international boundaries. In Australia the Senate Select Committee on Community Standards Relevant to the Supply of Services Utilising Electronic Technologies, chaired by Senator John Tierney (and discussed by Fiona Patten in chapter 3), has changed the classification system for video games to introduce an X-rating to prevent certain games being made available to children. In their efforts to trace the sources of pornographic images, federal officials in America have listened in to private conversations and subpoenaed telephone records. Recently *The Advocate* (Morales 1995), a Californian magazine for gays and lesbians, ran a cover story which explored fears about State intervention in the virtual community. 'Cybersex: Is It Safe to Cruise in Cyberspace?' read the headline.

Compact discs offer a different range of sexual possibilities and pleasures, explored by Amy Harmon in her amusing article, 'Sex a la "seedy Rom"' (1995). Viewers can purchase discs and, through the CD-ROM facility, manipulate the visual and audio material to make their own erotic movies. In other words, sex is interactive or viewer-controlled. Participants can click their mouse on an alluring female or male image prancing on the screen and place it in a story which they create. By clicking on the relevant control the viewer can make the cybersex star perform—pout, pump iron, strip and lie down, legs spread. Already a book entitled *The Joy Of Cybersex* has appeared and a brand of discs called 'Interotica'. The majority of titles (such as 'Virtual Valerie') address the heterosexual male, but possibilities for niche markets are endless. According to Harmon the aim of the *Virtual Valerie* game is—unbelievably—to arouse the fantasy female; success is measured by a meter on the screen!

The form of cybersex that most resembles *Videodrome's* pleasure-drome is known as 'virtual sex' or Teledildonics, an unfortunately penile name. The term was coined by Theodore Nelson, the inventor of hyper-text, in 1974. At the moment it appears that virtual sex will evolve in two quite distinct but related directions. The first, which is possible now, involves 'sex' with a machine or virtual body; the second, which is predicted to be at least 30 years away, involves sex with other people who are not present.

Virtual sex is currently restricted to an encounter with a virtual body—an image of a well-known film star or a fantasy figure existing in a virtual space. The participant dons an eye helmet, with two small liquid crystal displays positioned directly in front of the eyes, and enters a virtual space in which she/he learns to 'travel' by moving the helmet. Having adapted to the artificial environment, which appears 'real', the virtual traveller 'moves' around the space, 'flying' and 'playing' with objects via head movements. Artificial sounds have been pre-recorded to accompany the traveller's movements and increase a sense of reality. The participant can also wear a special sensor suit. The sensors project an image of the participant's body before her/his eyes so that the participant can see her/himself within the virtual world. The user actually feels as if she or he is participating in a virtual world rather than simply observing it and can sexually interact with an artificial partner or manipulate the other 'person' in terms of a sexual fantasy.

The more futuristic form of teledildonics will involve sexual encounters between real people. The participant, wearing special glasses and a sensory vibrator suit, will enter a chamber and dial a partner—perhaps on the other side of the world.

> Embedded in the inner surface of the suit, using a technology that does not yet exist, is an array of intelligent sensor-effectors—a mesh of tiny tactile detectors coupled to vibrators of varying degrees of hardness, hundreds of them per square inch, that can receive and transmit a realistic sense of tactile presence, the way the visual and audio displays transmit a realistic sense of visual and auditory presence (Rheingold 1991, p. 346).

The couple, who control the entire scenario, will make love in cyberspace. Every caress and touch of the 'virtual hand' will be felt by the participants as if they were actually in intimate contact. The term for this kind of encounter is 'tactile telepresence'. What is actually happening is a form of disembodied sex. According to J.G. Ballard, the traditional form of sex, 'body against body', is becoming obsolete. 'What we are getting is a whole new order of sexual fantasies' (Ballard 1984).

Clearly, sexual experiences offered via the computer screen are vastly different in terms of form and structure—perhaps even in relation to pleasure itself. Virtual sex—available through bulletin boards, the Internet, MUDs—is very different from the sexual experiences traditionally available on television, video and in the cinema. Traditional spectator pleasure offered in the cinema or on television is like a consumer item, prepared and packaged, which the individual purchases. Player pleasures offered via the new technologies involve individuals in an active sense—they are able to play a more creative part in constructing their own pleasures.

Teledildonics, or disembodied sex, will be unlike anything ever experienced by human beings. In her fascinating discussion of cyborg imagery in contemporary cinema, Claudia Springer analyses the manner in which these changes are already being represented: 'Instead of losing our consciousness and experiencing bodily pleasures, cyborg imagery in popular culture invites us to experience sexuality by losing our bodies and becoming pure consciousness' (Springer 1991, pp. 307–8).

Pleasure and the new technologies

Voyeurism

Theoretical writings on screen pleasure have been mainly directed at the cinema, photography and television. All writers accept the view that the human being derives enormous pleasure from looking and that this can be a highly charged erotic activity. How will this change with the introduction of these new visual forms?

Freud used the term 'scopophilia' to describe the pleasure derived from actively looking at another. He was particularly interested in the behaviour of children (Freud 1905) and argued that for children, pleasurable looking is frequently associated with looking at taboo objects such as other people's private bodily parts, the genitals or the breasts. Boys desire to know how girls differ from them, and vice versa. Freud was one of the first to argue that such pleasure has a strong erotic component. In extreme cases looking can become strongly voyeuristic and lead to surreptitious looking. Pornography exploits this desire.

There is no doubt that the cinema appeals to a voyeuristic gaze. Audiences sit in the dark, cloaked in anonymity, watching as stories that reveal intimate details of characters' lives unfold. Films which contain large amounts of sex and violence, such as *Psycho*, *Blue Velvet*, *Fatal Attraction*, *Silence of the Lambs* and *Basic Instinct*, are guaranteed box-office success. Television programs such as those hosted by Oprah Winfrey and Phil Donahue, which lay bare the aberrant, salacious details of participants' personal existence, draw vast viewing audiences. Popular topics include everything from confessions of sexual abuse victims to adults living happily in incestuous relationships.

With the development of virtual sex, players/viewers will be able to construct their own voyeuristic scenarios to satisfy their individual desires. This may well lead to a decline in public forms of popular entertainment and pornography as individuals assume greater autonomy (and perhaps responsibility) for their erotic lives. It may also lead to the emergence of new narratives, fantasies and sexual scenarios, a factor I will discuss shortly.

A major change will concern the nature of pleasure itself. While virtual reality of course appeals to the visual, it also places importance on the tactile. Touch may come to assume the primacy now accorded to the visual. Some players may construct scenarios that displace voyeurism altogether as a dominant source of pleasure.

A crucial difference between present and future technologies is that the former are predominantly public while the latter can, although not necessarily, be carried out in private—enjoyed by a single individual in a personal space. One possible consequence might be an unwelcome sense of isolation. Perhaps one day we might see the advent of virtual reality cinemas in which an entire audience, snuggled into their special suits and goggles, experiences multiple versions of the same visual/tactile trip. The same may be true for television—nuclear families might share a large designer suit in which they enter the entertainment world together. The era of the virtual family is just around the corner. Such changes will also influence the architectural design of homes and auditoriums which will require both private and public spaces to accommodate players/spectators.

Identification

Drawing on Freud's theories, Laura Mulvey argued that the 'cinema satisfies a primordial wish for pleasurable looking' (Mulvey 1989, p. 17), particularly in relation to a sadistic male gaze: 'In a world ordered by sexual imbalance, pleasure in looking has been split between active/male and passive/female. The determining male gaze projects its fantasy on to the female figure, which is styled accordingly' (ibid, p. 19).

While Mulvey's thesis still appears to hold true for certain kinds of film (such as film noir, the detective genre, the slasher film), it has become clear that the gaze is not always active or 'male'. Since Mulvey first posited her theory of the controlling male gaze, other writers (e.g. Cowie 1984) have argued for the existence of a fluid mobile gaze which identifies across gender, and other categories such as class, race and age.

The new technologies encourage such fluidity. Today the majority of films and videos address a certain type of male and female viewer. Leading characters are predominantly young, white, good looking, virile and male. Leading female characters, although fewer, are also likely to be young and beautiful. This means that viewers are forced to make some kind of imaginative adjustment to identify with the screen characters. This situation does not hold for the new technologies. Players communicating with other participants will be able to create their own identity and assume the gender of their choice.

Apparently, in the early years of Internet interaction, so many men (Rheingold 1994, p. 166) adopted female identities that it was assumed that any 'woman' on the net was a male. (There were few women participants in the early years of the new technology.) Players can also change their age, colour, class—in fact, every aspect of their identity. At this stage, anything is possible. Donna Haraway argues for the possibility of using the cyborg concept to free women from the negative effects of gender conditioning by abolishing gender altogether.

> Cyborg imagery can suggest a way out of the maze of dualisms in which we have explained our bodies and our tools to ourselves. This is a dream not of a common language but of a powerful infidel heteroglossia . . . It means both building and destroying machines, identities, categories, relationships, spaces, stories (Haraway 1985, p. 101).

Some critics argue that cyberspace communication is inferior because it is a disembodied form of contact. Participants cannot see each other, read body language, tone of voice and countless other cues. They can only type words to express their feelings, describe their appearance, communicate their desires. Pryor and Scott argue: 'It is not surprising that the body, subject to vulnerability, pain and mortality, can become something from which it seems desirable to escape. Could you feel pain if you had no body? Could you experience racism or sexism?' (1993, p. 172). They conclude that virtual communication cannot replace actual bodily interaction and its attendant pleasures such as cuddling a baby.

Others argue that the freedoms associated with the new medium are so great they outweigh the disadvantages. Players are free to express themselves without the constraints imposed by appearance or face-to-face interaction. Moravec argues that his essential self lies in his brain processes, and that 'human thought [should be] released from bondage to a mortal body' (Pryor & Scott 1993, p. 172).

The potential of the new media to offer pleasures associated with a dissolution of boundaries is enormous. Not only can players blur gender boundaries, they can also place themselves in the shoes of the 'other' in terms of colour, age and race. 'Becoming' another is not necessarily a negative thing. Women may find pleasure in exercising behaviours normally associated with the male, and being responded to as male, and vice versa. It may also be that women, once familiar with the new technology, will voice their desires clearly and loudly in relation to interactive erotica or pornography. Crossing boundaries seems to be a general condition of the postmodern, and one which might prove a necessary step in the move to a more heterogenous world.

Narrative

Roland Barthes (1974) has argued that the pleasure of a text lies partly in the way in which the reader/viewer is positioned in relation to a knowing figure (the hero/heroine) by the text's narrative structures. For example, popular texts almost always commence with an enigma, delay resolution of the mystery through retardation devices, such as a subplot, then 'solve' the problem, thus creating in the reader a satisfying sense of accomplishment and closure. Open-ended conclusions, in which the ending is not neatly resolved, are found more in avant-garde and political texts. Clearly there is enormous scope in interactive video forms of entertainment for the viewer to play an active role in narrative development. Pleasure resides in the narrative possibilities open to a player; she or he can pursue divergent narrative paths and construct alternative endings, even open endings.

Primal fantasies and virtual pleasures

Critical discussions of viewing pleasure have centred around the way in which films frequently replay scenarios associated with the 'mysteries' of childhood. In *The Interpretation of Dreams* (1900), Freud first referred to fantasy in the context of daydreams. A daydream is not unlike a reverie, a moment of musing or rumination, in which the subject constructs a setting necessary to the fulfilment of a wish. The difference between a daydream and a nocturnal dream is that the subject can 'control' the shape and direction of the daydream. Not only does the subject shape the daydream through fantasy, there are, according to Freud, three key or 'typical' fantasies which are ubiquitous and which appear in all forms of dreaming.

These are the primal fantasies whose origins, according to Laplanche and Pontalis (1985), are explainable in terms of common infantile experiences. In other words, they originate in the child's attempts to unravel, or explain, certain key enigmas or mysteries. These are: the mysteries of (i) birth; (ii) sexual difference; and (iii) sexual desire. The three mysteries can be posed as questions: Where did I come from? Why is she or he different? Who do I desire? The three primal fantasies offer a 'solution' to these puzzles: 'In the "primal scene", it is the origin of the subject that is represented; in seduction phantasies, it is the origin or the emergence of sexuality; in castration phantasies, the origin of the distinction between the sexes' (Laplanche and Pontalis 1985, p. 332).

The crucial factor is that fantasy is not just a matter of imagining objects, but of arranging the objects and persons in a setting, a *mise-en-scène* of desire.

Freud's theory of the primal fantasies has influenced film theories of identification and pleasure. The primal scene, the scene of parental sex, which explains the subject's origins, exerts a strong fascination for the film viewer and is endlessly replayed in scenes in which we watch the couple making love. The spectator looks directly at the couple as they engage in sex, the act depicted in varying degrees of explicitness. So important is this concept that almost all filmic narratives contain reference to, or representations of, a sexual coupling between adults. Pornography, as a genre, is devoted almost exclusively to the representation of primal scenes.

Other film genres such as science fiction and horror, which represent unconscious fears and pleasures, construct bizarre representations of primal scenes. Here we can see woman or man raped by a creature or an alien and then give birth. In some pornography, women are depicted in sexual encounters with animals.

Awareness of sexual difference gives rise to the second primal fantasy—the castration fantasy. Such awareness also leads to representations of an erotically fetishised female body. According to Freud, the child's first knowledge of sexual difference revolves around the question of the presence or absence of the penis. A popular solution to the question of sexual difference, for boys, is that the girl was once just like him, but that she has 'lost' her penis.

The fetishist refuses to believe the female has been 'castrated'. The possibility of castration is so vivid and the fear that this could happen to him is so strong that he continues to imagine her as phallic. In order to avoid thinking of her so-called 'wound', he either overvalues other non-threatening parts of her body, such as her breasts, legs or hair, or he prefers to see images of woman decorated with phallic shapes. Pornography (Creed 1993) abounds with representations of the phallic mother: the woman whose body is adorned with phallic symbols—a whip, high-heeled shoes, leather, a gun.

Whether or not Freud's theory of the castration fantasy seems implausible, there is no doubt the cinema is obsessed with sexual difference. Almost all films construct visual representations of the sexes, not as different, but as opposites. Male characters are coded as 'masculine', female as 'feminine'. Films which explore sexual ambiguity almost always make this a source of humour (*Sylvia Scarlett*, *Some Like It Hot*, *Tootsie*), terror (*Psycho*, *Dressed To Kill*), or perversion (*The Crying Game*). Pleasure lies in abolishing ambiguity and in seeing the opposition between the sexes reasserted.

The third primal fantasy, closely related to the other two, is seduction—also a popular theme of many films. Although seduction is central to genres such as the love story and the musical, it figures in almost all films, from the Western to the boxing genre. Seduction takes various forms—passive, active, sadistic. It may be comic as in the romantic comedy, or frightening as in some horror narratives.

27

Cyber fantasies

While the three primal fantasies are endlessly replayed in film narratives, offering pleasure both normal and perverse through repetition of these key moments, it remains to be seen if participants in cybersex, or on the net, will continue to interweave these themes in the stories they create. As participants learn to think differently about their bodies (or lack thereof), they may come to evolve a different set of primal fantasies about origins, sexual difference and seduction.

Origins is a central issue in cybersex in that the participant can no longer be defined in purely 'human' terms. The cybersex subject is a technological being, a fusion of human and electronic. Cybersex offers the possibility of sexual fulfilment without bodily contact. In the past, various science fiction discourses (*2001: A Space Odyssey*) have assumed a separation between human and machine. In recent films (*Bladerunner*, *Robocop*), the two have been fused via the figure of the cyborg which, unlike the robot, represents the possibility of a perfect union.

A union between computer and human presents a completely different scenario from the above. Tactile telepresence enables the human to engage in disembodied erotic encounters. If sexual pleasure is no longer produced through the interaction of two physical bodies, but through a union of two electronic bodies, will a new set of sexual fantasies evolve? How might this transformation affect existing fantasies of the primal scene, sexual difference and seduction? Will the cybersex generation see birth as an electronic creation, gender as a completely fluid state and seduction as a meeting of strangers in space?

Will sex occupy a central place in the work day or will it continue to be relegated to leisure time? The dream of continuous sex has attracted many writers. De Sade even planned a 'phallic' machine (Barthes 1976), designed to offer continuous sexual pleasure to women, although perhaps he—like Freud—should have first consulted a woman to find what she might want. Will the world of teledildonics be primarily defined and created by men who make no attempt to explore the nature of female eroticism before launching their project into space?

In addition, given that the 'self' might become a union of the person inside the helmet, operating the encounter, and that person's image on the screen, will we need a new definition of identity? If participants in cybersex can construct themselves in any way they wish (represent themselves as physically perfect beings of any gender), what will this mean for notions of attraction? According to Howard Rheingold: 'If everybody can look as beautiful, sound as sexy, and feel as nubile and virile as everybody else, then what will become the new semiotics of mating? What will have erotic meaning?' (1991, p. 351).

A related issue concerns the 'double'. Almost all human cultures have been fascinated by the notion of the double, the twin, the doppelganger. According to Lacan, human identity is formed during the 'mirror phase' when the infant first recognises itself as a separate entity in a mirror or reflected in the eyes of another. In other words, identity is formed in relation to a mirror-image of one's self. The problem is that the infant imagines itself to be already like an adult, and in a more perfect stage of physical development than it actually is. Identity is formed in a moment of recognition and misrecognition. The human subject is forever haunted by an image of itself as an ideal.

Given the opportunity to create oneself in any likeness, will people construct their technological selves as perfect ideals? Will the future be a space, a screen, in which each human player—like Narcissus—gazes forever at an idealised image of itself which will remain forever out of physical reach? Given the enormous emphasis on the body in our culture, and the particular oppression of people through appearance (in terms of ethnicity, colour, gender, beauty), it may well be that subjects of the twenty-first century will use the new technologies to escape these oppressive influences. Will they design their new images in terms of existing ideals or will they explore new territories?

Jean-Francois Lyotard (1988–9) has already asked the

question: 'Can thought go on without a body?' If subjects are 'freed' from the tyranny of the body, and of the power of the State to control them through the body, will they think of 'themselves' differently? Will the future consist of a new order of virtual erotics which is not based on body politics? Questions such as these depend on the view that the body's power is, by definition, tyrannical. Will we control the cyberfuture or will it control us?

3
The economy of pleasure and the laws of desire

FIONA PATTEN

Sexual pleasure is the most judged, regulated and criminalised of all human desires. It is also the most political desire and its threads join tightly together to form a major industry of a diverse and complex nature.

The sex industry is subject to a disproportionately large body of law which costs both the taxpayer and the sex worker dearly. Its sectors are each subject to a bewildering array of federal, state and local government sanctions and regulations. These come in the guises of concern for law and order, censorship, taxation, zoning and public health, all implicitly justified to some degree by moral disapproval.

Sexual goods and services are provided in many ways to meet the many needs and desires of a cosmopolitan country like Australia. In structure and size Australia's sex industry is very similar to its main opponent—the religion industry. Both employ approximately 20 000 people, both have three or four major groupings with a number of independents in between, and both sell intangibles like 'fantasy', 'desire' and 'hope' along with an extensive 'spin-off' range of products.

The chief sectors of the sex industry in contemporary Australia are prostitution, adult or sex shops, erotic dancing and cabaret, X-rated or non-violent erotica videos, and other sexual media.

Prostitution

According to figures supplied by state sex worker organisations, Australia has approximately 16 000 sex workers currently employed in providing a wide range of sexual services. Each worker sees an average of fifteen clients per week with one out of every three visits ending up as a non-penetrative one. This translates into 240 000 client visits around the nation each week or 12 480 000 per annum—almost one visit per year for each man and woman in Australia's adult population of 15.5 million.

Allowing for varying prices and times, workers receive, on average, $50 per client while the brothel or 'house' gets the other $50. This gives the sector an annual wages bill of $624 million with a further $624 million of mostly corporate income. If governments legalised the prostitution industry in all states and imposed a fair taxation regime on it, the industry would return the federal government somewhere in the vicinity of $14 million which it currently does not get.

The number of brothels is difficult to estimate but, by including escort services, individual operators, bondage and domination establishments, and massage services that provide hand relief, they would number around 500. Sexual services are offered mainly for the entertainment and therapy of both gay and straight men with services for women still representing a relatively small area of the market. About 10 per cent of all sex workers are now male.

Because there are no federal laws covering prostitution there are currently seven different legal approaches to prostitution, discussed in more detail below. Many legislators still assume that women enter the sex industry due to the pressure of pimps or drugs. What they fail to realise is that the majority of sex workers make informed and rational decisions about sex work to meet economic and lifestyle needs. Many women report feeling empowered by the work and, often for the first time in their life, gain true economic independence.

Sadly, most states still maintain 'living off the earnings' offences, some introduced as far back as 1892 (Western Australia). Historically these laws were designed to protect the 'fallen woman', but these days they force women to work alone, secretly and in the most vulnerable of situations. Very recently there has been a marked change in some government attitudes to prostitution with regulation being recognised as preferable to prohibition. The main reason for this shift in opinion has been the recognition of the sex industry's powerful ability to corrupt police and politicians wherever it is criminalised. Associated with this has been a recognition that taxpayers' money is being squandered through trying to enforce prohibition on an industry that history and commonsense show cannot and will not be prohibited.

Adult (sex) shops

There are approximately 200 age-restricted adult or sex shops in Australia employing about 4000 people. Approximately half of these employees are female. A recent survey by the Eros Foundation (1995) showed that approximately 60 per cent of these workers were gay or lesbian. Sex shops, the retail outlets for adult products, can be found in all capital cities and some regional centres. The laws that govern the development of this highly specialised network vary from state to state and from council to council. Their locations are heavily controlled by local councils and in some cases by state legislation; in most areas, sex shops must have signs warning people that they may be offended if they enter.

There has been a concerted and market-driven shift in the style of sex shops and their products over the past few years. They now tend to be painted in pastels rather than black; couples account for the majority of customers; and entire shops, or sections of them, are directed specifically at women. As women increasingly acquire disposable income, they are choosing to spend more of it in adult shops, and women's nights and coffee groups are becoming regular features on such shops' calendars. Products like vibrators are no longer all the same. Once they were all realistic, skin coloured, large and rock hard. Now their colours complement any decor and come in the shape of humming birds, dolphins and smiling-faced mummies. Through a review of wholesale figures over the past five years, the Eros Foundation estimates that there are approximately 10 million vibrators in bedroom cupboards around the nation.

> Under the Classification (Publications, Films and Computer Games) Act 1995, the Office of Film and Literature Classification has issued the following guidelines for the classification of publications.
>
> - **Unrestricted**
> Publications can contain photographs of discreet male or female nudity but not if sexual excitement is apparent. Depictions of sexual activity between consenting adults are acceptable only where they are discreetly implied or simulated.
>
> - **Category 1**
> Sale restricted to people eighteen and over and must be displayed in a sealed wrapper.
> Publications can contain photographs showing obvious sexual excitement, explicit genital detail, simulated or obscured sexual activity between adults and touching genitals. Depictions of mild fetishes such as rubber wear and stylised domination are accepted. Images of sexual violence are not permitted.
> Illustrations and paintings can also be classified as category 1 if they are considered not to be bona fide erotic art works.
>
> - **Category 2**
> Sale restricted to people eighteen and over and must be displayed in a restricted publications area.
> Publications can contain photographs of sexual activity between consenting adults which include explicit genital detail. Depictions of stronger fetishes are permitted but not if non-consent or apparent physical harm are apparent.

It is odd that adult or sex shops attract such strong opposition from conservative councils and community groups when everything that can be legally sold in an adult shop can be sold in other shops like chemists, video stores, lingerie shops and even department stores. Non-sex shops in New South Wales sell Category 1 and 2 magazines (see box), lingerie, R-rated videos and sexual aids and toys, including everything from dildos to dolls.

It is, however, illegal to sell handcuffs in New South Wales and X-rated videos are prohibited from sale in all states. Curiously, Category 2 magazines which show the same images that are generally banned on X-rated videos are prohibited only in Queensland.

Erotic dance and cabaret

Table-top dancing venues exist legally in New South Wales, Victoria, the Australian Capital Territory and Queensland, although under different rules in each state/territory. Table-top dancing originated in the US; it basically involves women or men stripping and then performing erotic dances on a table or other raised platform. Customers sit around and put money in the dancer's garter belt or underwear for a closer or different view. They can also buy a private lap dance for about $30. This lasts about seven minutes with the dancer sitting on or about the customer's lap in a sort of 'wriggle-dance'. There is a strong protocol involved which means the customer cannot touch the dancer and it is seen as very bad manners to orgasm.

In New South Wales no alcohol may be served if the dancers are nude. All dancers at Sydney venues wear a sheer scarf, rolled and tied around their waist and must dance away from the bar areas. One venue in Sydney has been charged for allowing pubic hair to show out of the side of a G-string. In Victoria and the ACT dancers can legally show 'pink bits' during a dance routine (i.e. dancers can spread their legs so inner labia, anus and often vagina can be clearly seen), but in

Queensland they must place their hand between their legs to cover them. In Victoria dancers can dance nude and alcohol may be served.

Erotic dancing is very demanding work and dancers must be in good physical form and very fit. However, it can be very lucrative work and some dancers earn over $3000 per week. Some venues pay a shift retainer, particularly for less busy shifts, and some pay a small hourly fee, but the money the workers make is almost entirely from tips.

X-rated videos (non-violent erotica)

The X-rated (non-violent erotica) video industry has an annual turnover of approximately $25 million through legal mail order companies and retail outlets in the Australian Capital Territory and the Northern Territory. There are approximately 640 000 individual names and addresses appearing on lists held by six X-rated video mail order companies (*Good Weekend*, October 28 1995). Surveys show that 70 per cent of these individuals are ordering to share with a partner (Eros Foundation, April 1995) which, when added to the 85 000 adults who are able to buy X-rated videos over the counter in the Australian Capital Territory and the Northern Territory, means that there are nearly 1.1 million adults in Australia regularly and legally buying X-rated videos. This represents approximately 7 per cent of Australia's adult population. Industry executives believe this figure would be doubled if under-the-counter sales in the states were taken into account.

What is offered for sale under the X-rating has, like adult products in general, evolved in recent years to meet a growing female audience. People are more likely to watch a video with a partner than on their own. With current prices for X-rated videos ranging from $20 to $80 it is understandable that they often become a joint purchase.

Under the Classification (Publications, Films and Computer Games) Act 1995, the Office of Film and Literature Classification has issued the following guidelines for the classification of sexual images in films and videos.

- **G**—Sexual activity will not be shown, sexual activity may only be suggested in very discreet visual and/or verbal references.
- **PG**—Sexual activity may be suggested in very discreet, infrequent depictions. Verbal and visual references should be discreet.
- **M15+**—Sexual activity may be discreetly implied, and should be justified by the narrative. Verbal references may be more detailed than depictions, but if so, the impact should be reduced by tone and context. References to sexual violence must be discreet and must be strongly justified by the narrative or a documentary context.
- **MA15+**—Depictions should not be too detailed. Verbal references may be more detailed than depictions, but if so, the impact should be reduced by tone and/or context. Sexual violence may be discreetly suggested but only if strongly justified by the narrrative.
- **R**—Sexual activity may be strongly implied; the general rule is 'simulation, yes—the real thing, no'. Verbal references may be detailed but these should not be unduly exploitative. Sexual violence may be implied but only if justified by narrative sexual violence may be implied but only if justified by the narrative.
- **X**—This classification is a special and legally restricted category which only contains sexually explicit material. That is material which contains depictions of actual sexual intercourse and other sexual activity, including mild fetishes such as rubber and leather wear. It does not contain any depictions of sexual violence, sexualised violence or coercion, or grossly exploitative depictions. Such material will be refused classification.

The classification of computer games follows the guidelines for films but more strictly. Effectively everything goes up a classification. An image rated PG on films would be classified M on a computer game.

Most of the major censorship decisions in Australia since 1990 have been made by the Senate Select Committee on Community Standards Relevant to the Supply of Services Utilising Electronic Technologies—often dubbed 'The Morals Committee'. This Committee, currently headed by Senators John Tierney (Liberal) and supported by Senators Brian Harradine (Independent) and Margaret Reynolds (Labor) has recommended extremely conservative benchmarks for the emerging technologies of Pay TV, CD-ROM and On-Line services as well as for established ones like video and has severely limited the prospects of a legitimate adult industry in these areas.

The new sexual media

The criminalisation of parts of the non-violent adult goods and services industry has historically provided a catalyst for businesses to explore new technologies as a means of counteracting some of these laws. All forms of communication are used by the sex industry and with every new approach, the law is generally found to be a couple of steps behind. Sex has always assisted new technologies to get off the ground. For example, the transferring of hundreds of thousands of 'super-8' blue movies onto videotape in the early 1980s did more to launch video technology than any other single contributing factor.

There is now a plethora of sexual information on the newest medium, the Internet, but it still comprises only a very small percentage of the net's total information. Nonetheless, a high proportion of general media reports about the Internet discusses the availability of this sexual material. Similarly, government bodies and politicians are focusing on sexual material and trying unsuccessfully to grapple with the new technologies. A recent report by the Australian Broadcasting Authority on the regulation of material on the Internet (Investigation into the Content of On-line Services, 1996) recommends self-regulation with federal enforcement laws. In the past, governments have had one standard and instant response—to ban. The repercussions of such kneejerk reactions are, however, always uncontrollable. For example, former Prime Minister Paul Keating's ban on sexually-oriented computer games in 1995 has already backfired by giving rise to a huge black market. As with all black markets, games that show extreme sexual violence are now circulating alongside games that show exactly the same non-violent erotic images that are freely available in print from a newsagent and on video from a video store or adult shop. Any game containing any sexual depictions is now subject, effectively, to no labelling and no regulation. Because it is impossible for the police to grapple with the new technology and the high demand, there can be no real enforcement of the ban. Having come to terms with computer games and CD-ROMS in this way, politicians now see the ability to download sexual images via the telephone line as far more sinister and are insisting on the same inept solution.

Sexual media in Australia include both electronic and published material, although these lines are blurring as *Penthouse* goes onto CD-ROM and fetish magazines become available on bulletin boards. The most notable changes to the sexual publications market in recent years have been the increase in magazines with sexual content for women and small independent sexual-contact and relationship magazines. These magazines are comprised of ads from singles and couples around Australia seeking partners and other couples to have sex with.

Electronic sexual media is expanding despite the technophobic and proscriptive attitudes of legislators. Pay Television is still being discussed but, after extensive public opinion polls organised by the Australian Broadcasting Tribunal (later the Australian Broadcasting Authority) between 1991 and 1994 showing some 80 per cent support for adult restricted viewing

(ABT 1992; ABA 1993; ABA 1994), the federal government says it is still not sure what the community wants. But while the politicians prevaricate and patronise consumers of adult material, video-on-demand is being market-tested now and will supersede pay TV laws before the ink is dry on any legislation.

Telephone sex is another flourishing area of the new sexual media. Here, too, legislators have adopted an illogical scattergun approach based on censorship. Through the Senate 'Morals Committee', the federal government in 1992 banned any sexual content on 0055 recorded numbers. These phone messages are censored using video guidelines, which means we all must have great visual imaginations. It would have made a lot more sense to regulate this material using guidelines for the spoken or written word. As a consequence, one can say more on unrestricted AM radio than one can on a recorded phone message where there can be no mention of anything that can be construed as 'sexually titillating'. One phone message was prohibited because it mentioned 'Channel Nine's Sex Program', while another was cut for using the word 'erotica'. This has led to literally thousands of international phone numbers being advertised every week as a way for people to bypass these laws while still getting access to sexually explicit phone sex. These international services cost on average $3 per minute and the caller gets a recorded message that is totally unregulated. Live sexual discussion on the telephone is not regulated by government but rather by the service providers to ensure no minors are involved. However, the Victorian government is considering an amendment to its Classification Bill prohibiting these types of discussions happening on computer services such as e-mail.

Regulation

The sex industry is regulated by federal, state and local laws that cover almost all aspects of the business. These laws are different and constantly changing for better and worse.

Federal

Classification

Over many decades, the federal government has developed a classification system for publications, films and, more recently, videos and computer games, which it ostensibly deems suitable for all Australians. But the states still prohibit many of these, delivering the message to their citizens that Queenslanders, Western Australians and Tasmanians have a different morality from the rest of Australia. That part of the system that dealt with the classifying of publications has been a voluntary one for many years, but with the passing of the Classification (Publications, Films and Computer Games) Act 1995, any publication dealing with sex is now compelled to be submitted. This Act constitutes Australia's first national classification legislation. Until its introduction, the federal system had been operating under an ACT Ordinance.

The Act does not introduce many changes to the status quo except in the areas of advertising, some changes to customs regulations, and a user-pays fee structure. The Act allows for the classification of films, videos, publications and computer games. The new form of fee structure has the ability to increase the classification fees for all media fourfold over the next four years which will result in a form of economic censorship and has come under heavy criticism from industry groups. Much to the chagrin of morals crusaders in Australia, the Act still contains the controversial X-rated video category.

Taxation

The Australian Taxation Office plays particular attention to brothels all over Australia, both legal and illegal. Some establishments report weekly visits and mini-audits by Tax Department officers. Many brothels would like to operate in a similar fashion to serviced offices: for a fee they provide reception facilities, security, laundry, rooms and advertising if required. The Tax Department would prefer brothels and escort agencies to remain as tax collectors under the PAYE system. But this system does not reflect the flexibility of the service and work arrangements found in brothels—a problem commonly found in predominantly female industries. It assumes that sex workers work full-time and earn regular money. Nothing could be further from the truth. Approximately two-thirds of sex workers are mothers, while the majority do not see prostitution as a long-term career. Often it is a second job.

One of the major attractions of sex work is the flexibility of work hours. The downside for most workers is never knowing how much they are going to earn. For example, a worker may earn $2000 in a week, then take two weeks off for the school holidays. She is taxed at 48 per cent for that one week but if her earnings were averaged over three weeks the weekly gross would be about $660, with far less tax coming out. Some workers prefer working as employees, but income tax should in these circumstances be assessed over flexible timeframes. Other workers prefer to look after their own tax and business affairs as self-employed workers or as small businesses. They do not see the employer–employee relationship as appropriate or beneficial.

The Australian Capital Territory

The most liberal approach to the commercial sale of adult goods and services is found in the Australian Capital Territory where, with the exception of a couple of politically extreme Independent politicians, all parties that make up the ACT Legislative Assembly have decided that bipartisan regulation of the sex industry is less costly, more popular and more humane than prohibition. Canberra has in general taken a rational rather than a moral approach to the sex industry and its regulation.

The ACT decriminalised brothel and escort sex work in May 1993 (ACT Prostitution Bill 1992), by repealing all laws surrounding prostitution. As in all states and territories, it is still illegal to employ minors or to coerce someone into prostitution. Brothels in the ACT must register and adhere to health and safety guidelines. It is an offence to provide or receive penetrative commercial sex without a prophylactic (under threat of a $5000 fine) and, depending on how you rate cunnilingus, or how long your tongue is, dental dams are required for this service. The decision to contain brothels in industrial areas, while understandable in political terms, makes little sense in reality. Brothels are not generally loud, don't use heavy machinery or emit toxic wastes.

The ACT Prostitution Bill makes it an offence for a person with HIV to provide or receive a commercial sexual service. While nobody would wish HIV-positive clients or workers to be spreading the virus, this part of the legislation has been criticised as tending to promote the myth that HIV is more likely to be contagious if a sexual act is commercial, thereby further stigmatising sex workers.

Legalised sex work has brought with it compulsory superannuation, workers' compensation and formal conditions of employment. The ACT Anti-Discrimination Act was adjusted in 1993 to provide redress for people who are discriminated against because of their profession, occupation or calling. This was introduced in direct response to discriminatory acts against sex workers, and has given insurance companies a financial fright in relation to the provision of workers' compensation insurance. Not because they think that if they have to insure sex workers, brothels and adult shops that there will be a profusion of expensive claims, since, for example, in the nine year period 1986 to 1995 there were only two claims on Workcare from sex workers in Victoria. Rather, they are concerned that conservative shareholders in their companies, such as the churches, may be upset at insuring the sex industry and transfer their investments. This has been confirmed by insurance brokers and even in discussion with the Insurance Council. Insurance companies continue to discriminate against the sex industry although, when a major insurance company was threatened with an action before the ACT Human Rights Commission recently, it quickly reduced the insurance premiums on two adult shops by two-thirds.

The sale of X-rated videos is legal under the ACT Classification of Publications Act 1983. X-rated videos account for about 70 per cent of Canberra's adult shop trade. There are about six adult mail order companies which are confined to the industrial areas. The largest has a mailing list of some 235 000 regular buyers, which makes it one of the largest product lists in the country. Queensland is the largest per capita customer of all the states, accounting for one-third of all mail order X-rated videos. Approximately 10 000 videos per week are sold through the ACT's mail order system, with another 2000–3000 sold through its adult retail outlets.

New South Wales

New South Wales has had legal street and escort sex work since 1988, although it has always been illegal to have commercial sex or solicit in or from a vehicle or in view of a church, hospital, residence or school. In 1995 the New South Wales government repealed the Disorderly Houses Act 1943 and effectively decriminalised organised prostitution. This reform was a direct result of the Royal Commission into Police Corruption. The laws prohibiting brothels had generally been overlooked for years and the new amendments bring the law into line with current community standards. The new laws leave the control of brothels and other establishments entirely in the hands of local councils, which in the past have often refused planning approval. Appeals have generally been won in the Land and Environment Court, but only after considerable expense on the part of the owner and a considerable waste of taxpayers' money on defending morality-based council decisions.

New South Wales's Indecent Articles and Classified Publications Act (1975) provides that a Category 2 publication must not be sold or delivered to a person who has not made a direct request for it, and when sold it must be contained in an opaque package. There are no restrictions or classifications applying to the sale of sex toys or lingerie apart from general hygiene. In New South Wales such products could be considered as indecent articles, but there is nowhere to have them classified. The Office of Film and Literature Classification refuses to classify novelties, or anything other than films, videos, publications, computer games and discs. Wearing a strap-on dildo or a sexual message T-shirt in public is not an offence under the above Act, but may put the wearer at risk of breaching more generalised 'obscene behaviour' legislation.

Western Australia

Western Australia boasts the oldest prostitution laws in Australia, with sex workers still subject to the morality and language of statutes passed in the days of Queen Victoria (1892). In some situations these laws are overlooked in favour of a police policy called 'containment'. This allows the police to run the industry and to decide who will be involved in it and where brothels may be situated. Most businesses are run by women, as is preferred by the police, although corruption seems to be tolerated or expected. Workers must be over 21 to work in a brothel, but only 18 for the far more risky business of escort. In Kalgoorlie, the control of the industry is even more draconian. Women wanting to work in Kalgoorlie must register with the police and have photos and fingerprints taken. They can be subject to a dawn to dusk curfew and, like lepers, may be banned from pubs, swimming pools, local parks and other public areas.

No changes are likely under the present conservative government as Western Australia is the only state that doesn't have prostitution on its agenda. However, the Western Australian opposition and the Western Australian police commissioner have both come out in favour of decriminalising the industry.

Western Australia has also opted out of the federal system for classification of publications, adopting instead an approach that allows only for 'unrestricted', 'restricted' or 'refused' classifications, with no options in between. There are no definitive guidelines for these categories—only an adjudicating board comprising a church official, a health professional and a representative from the Attorney General's office. Not surprisingly, decisions from this group often mean that publications allowed by the Chief Censor are banned in Western Australia.

Queensland

Queensland under Premier Wayne Goss boasted the most draconian censorship legislation of any state in Australia—even harsher than under his predecessor, Joh Bjelke-Petersen. All sexually explicit and sexually simulated books, magazines and videos are banned.

The history of censorship in Queensland is intimately caught up with the anti-porn campaigns of ex-Queensland Labor leader and federal Member for Capricornia Keith Wright. His campaigns against sexually explicit material, on the grounds that it could 'corrupt the morals of young people', were widely taken up by local councils, church groups, state politicians and morals groups, many of whom still successfully petition governments with Wright's arguments and rhetoric. In September 1993 this creator of the well-known 'Porn Free Zone' and 'Save The Children' campaigns was convicted of the rape and sexual molestation of young girls, one as young as eleven.

1992 saw the the complete prohibition of organised prostitution in Queensland, notwithstanding the findings of the Fitzgerald Inquiry, which were to legalise the industry, and a survey by the *Courier Mail* newspaper in 1991, which found that 70 per cent of Queenslanders would prefer a decriminalised system. While New South Wales's approach to police corruption in the sex industry was to decriminalise brothels, Queensland's response was to give the police greater powers. Sex workers must now work alone from their own homes, except where local councils have banned this also. This government-imposed style of operating is the most dangerous and risky way for sex workers to operate.

Goss promoted the new prostitution laws as necessary to catch the 'Mr Bigs' of the prostitution industry. So far the Queensland police force has charged over 70 people with offences under the new laws, and all but three of these have been struggling sex workers or clients. During the same time, there have been at least three deaths of sex workers that can be directly attributed to the prohibition of organised prostitution. These women have been murdered by their clients because standard systems of protection cannot be implemented. Many workers are now completely isolated from peer support and education. They cannot employ someone to screen calls or visitors as this could be construed in a court as 'living off the earnings' and thus evidence of organised prostitution. The number of robberies against prostitutes has increased dramatically, as has the number of assaults, many of which go unreported. Safe sex education has become harder to provide, increasing the risk of HIV infection for both worker and client. Sex workers in Queensland are discouraged from seeking regular medical treatment for fear of being incriminated.

Tasmania

Tasmania's government recently funded a study to ascertain whether prostitution existed in the Apple Isle. After the laughter subsided, many people remained shocked to find such ignorance about basic human sexuality at a government level. Many of Tasmania's sexual service businesses have been set up to service Japanese fishing boats and US naval ships. Interestingly, the first organised prostitution in Tasmania was introduced to service the visiting British Navy around the turn of the century. It is the historical and current belief of most Tasmanian officials that only people from the mainland work in or use the sex industry. Consequently, Tasmania has the most insane and illogical laws to regulate sex.

It is an offence for a man to live with or accompany a sex worker but not for another woman to do these things. In practice, this means that husbands, lovers and male children of sex workers can be charged with 'living off the earnings'. As the industry is kept so underground, there are a number of unscrupulous operators and little control on safe sex or underage workers. Recent media coverage of sex workers in Tasmania has introduced some pressure to reform the laws, but legalised homosexuality and prostitution may be too much to hope for in this century.

South Australia

South Australia's prostitution laws have been reviewed and inquired into almost continuously for nearly 20 years. The industry is heavily policed and workers may be busted more than once in one night. In June 1994 police decided to axe down the doors of a number of establishments instead of knocking. South Australian police never close down brothels—they simply charge workers and owners so they are fined or jailed; most eventually make their way back into the industry. It is simply a way for the city of churches to raise revenue. Police put strong pressure on clients to give evidence in court against the women they have had sex with. If the client is required to go to court, under Witness Compensation legislation the sex worker may be forced to pay the client's salary for the day, as well as copping the fine. The question is frequently asked by the sex industry: 'Who is screwing whom?' The South Australian police prohibit safe sex information being distributed to sex workers and their clients by threatening to use it as evidence in prosecutions. They have also started to use safe sex tools, such as condoms and rubber gloves, to incriminate workers or establishments.

The Northern Territory

The Northern Territory's prostitution laws were reformed in 1992. Under the new regime, escort is the only legal form of sex work, although it is more dangerous and harder to regulate than brothels. All agencies except single operators must register with the police and the escorts must also register their lovers, husbands and dependants. If any of these people are seen as unfit to associate with a sex worker, he/she will be refused permission to work. Commercial sex in one's own home is illegal under these new provisions—a precedent that has not been followed by any other state and is bound to be challenged in the courts in the near future. At its most extreme, this part of the law could technically render a person's partner guilty of a prostitution offence if they paid for a meal before going home for sex.

Along with the ACT, the Northern Territory is the only

other jurisdiction that allows the sale of X-rated videos. Unlike the ACT, the Northern Territory government bowed to the peculiar political muscle of the Top End's video shop owners by allowing them to sell and hire X-rated videos from ordinary video shops as long as they have a restricted area within them. To assure church leaders that the Northern Territory was not about to become a mecca for X-video mail order companies, the government made it an offence to sell or possess more than ten copies of the same X-rated video.

Victoria

Victoria has had a partially legal prostitution system for a number of years. Under town planning legislation, brothels can operate legally but with ridiculously strict controls. For example, if the proprietors of a brothel want to change the wattage of an outside light bulb, they must apply for permission. Unfortunately, under the present system only 60 of the estimated 180 brothels are legal. Independent workers cannot operate without local council approval. How this approval is given seems to be a mystery but the potential for corruption seems obvious. At the time of writing, Victoria's prostitution laws were under review.

4
Grief and the lesbian queer/n: a love story

REBECCA COX

> 'Queer' seems to hinge . . . radically and explicitly on a person's undertaking particular, performative acts of experimental self-perception and filiation. A hypothesis worth making explicit: that there are important senses in which 'queer' can signify only when *attached to the first person*. One possible corollary: that what it takes—all it takes—to make the description 'queer' a true one is the impulse to use it in the first person (Sedgwick 1993, p. 9, emphasis in original).

Thus am I queer. Or should that read: thus, am I queer? Is this impulse to use it in the first person merely a rhetorical compulsion? Or is it more like a pulse, pumping through my veinness like a fluid inside my body. Beating, quickening, stopping and starting. Constant but not consonant with what might pass as my identity. Am I passing, or merely parsing? Who is speaking this 'I' as though it is somehow self-evident? My eyes glaze over and I want to say, as though I have misread queer, 'Thus, am I a queen.'

I never knew that I was a queen. I swear I didn't know until my analyst asked me 'Why are you a queen?' And it made me wonder why it is that I'm not a fag hag, although of course I am. But I am something else as well: a gay-identified girlie girl's girl who sometimes pashes off gay men at the

Taxi Club.[1] And it makes me think of Sydney (because this is where the Taxi Club is, just off Oxford Street) and of the convenient narrative of the coming out story. But there isn't a story to tell. Or at least there isn't one that lends itself to the telling. Instead there are fragments of grief and grandeur, rubbing together and producing fiction. This kind of rubbing (and I'm not only speaking figuratively) and I'm burning up. Memories singe and blur the edges and my inner queen screams feverishly.

I grew up in Sydney with the dictates of a harbourside geography: Bondi Beach to the east or Oxford Street straight ahead. Bondi beckoned in my fifteenth year for a summer. A season spent on the beach with the girls, waiting for the boys to get out of the water, smoking unsatisfactory cigarettes in the wind and checking out each other's tits. Firm and teenage we were, firm bodies and firm sexualities. Our bodies were so tightly bound in our gender roles, configured as opposite and separate, and only to be fitted together in very few and specific ways. Back then I knew for sure which of us were boys and which were girls. I would never be as sure of what these discrete definitions meant again.

I was always a girlie girl. High-heels and make-up were/are my clear markers of femininity. Back then I had a heightened awareness of the nature of this masquerade. I knew I didn't have tomboy appeal because I wasn't sporty or good at rough-housing with the boys. Nor was I ever a fresh-faced beauty like the surfie girls were, with no adjuncts to their

---

[1] I have no idea why this place is called the Taxi Club. Any connection to taxis is elusive, or purely allusive. I spend a lot of time in the toilet when I'm there. I am fascinated by the patina and patter of drag queens and they seem to have a likewise interest in me. We swap lipsticks and beauty tips. They tell me what a hassle it is to shave every day, and I talk about menstruation. One time when I was there I needed a tampon desperately. I asked everyone who came into the toilet. One girl I asked was just that, a mere (slip of) a girl who hadn't started having periods. The next woman I asked retorted with 'well Love I've got a cunt but it doesn't bleed'. Last time I was there I was almost disappointed to see that they have installed a feminine hygiene dispenser next to the Silent Partner vending machine.

bodies other than eating disorders and the peroxide bottle. I took to the bottle only years later.

My girlish body was an intensified moment of femme role-playing. And although it is only now that I can look back and call it that, at the time I was massively implicated in the performing of my version of correct and verifiable feminine signifiers. I knew my cunt was for boys' fingers and not my own. My tits were felt-up over clothes and bras. I was always so worried about my lipstick that I never sucked cock, but my mouth was fucked dumb by tongues and fingers. My body may have been the site of the performative, but I wasn't putting out.

> Is 'the body' or 'the sexed body' the firm foundation on which gender and systems of compulsory sexuality operate? Or is 'the body' itself shaped by political forces with strategic interests in keeping that body bounded and constituted by the markers of sex? (Butler 1990, p. 129).

As that summer faded the beach palled as I realised that I didn't tan and it was more fun waiting with the girls for the boys than it was when they actually arrived. Literally turning my back on the beach I travelled westward, towards a street where make-up and humour were highly exchangeable currencies and everything else became sweetly shaky.

I narrativise a false distinction here—the choice was never so clear-cut. I hung around the perimeters of the suburban east, fascinated by both cultures and unable to see how to make a choice that would make living possible. But in the tale of the journey from Bondi to Darlinghurst all the subtleties disappear and the story lies and tells itself as a seamless text without internal contradictions or external fictions.

Every day on the way to high school I would traverse what were then the dispersed beginnings of Oxford Street as I now know it. I would stand at the bus stop at Taylor Square, reading my *Dolly* magazine, rubbing the pages for secret signs that would tell me how to make boys like me, never suspecting (but always knowing) that the boys I would want to like me would be gay.[2]

I was about to tell you about my teenage job at a supermarket on Oxford Street, Darlinghurst, but as I write this I remember something; before this I worked at McDonalds on Oxford Street at Bondi Junction. (This story makes more and more sense as I tell it, revealing evidence of a linearity I never realised was readable before.) I was the only person who worked at this hamburger restaurant who didn't have blonde hair. Almost every shift would end with me in tears as yet another teenaged surfie boy would ask me why I had a moustache. I finally quit and started the journey up to the other end of the same street. All that remains of this lesson in fairness is a residue (like the sand I no longer find in my swimsuit): my own fantasmatic desire for blonde-haired-early-adolescent-real-gone-surfer-boys.

The archetypal gay man of the early eighties, when this story takes place, was a far cry from this. In those days I was drinking a lot and ending up in the bed of a very good (but at that stage new) friend, Sid. If we were at the same place at home time (usually dawn) we would go home together and have drunken and unsatisfactory sex.[3]

One night after a protracted drinking session at the Taxi Club, I found the world spinning and, taking the key to Sid's house, I left to curl up in his bed. Hours later I woke up, rolled over and found him lying next to me, eyes closed and his cock in some boy's mouth. I turned over and went back to sleep. But something kept waking me up. Finally I sat up, made eye contact with the cock-sucker, realised the bedside light was shining in my face, turned it off and returned to my alcohol-sodden

---

[2]   My analyst tells me that I discovered early that the sexiest people I knew were gay men, and that most women find that their earliest memories of sexy people are of other women. She says I have an extra wrinkle of perversion. I love her for telling me this. It's like I forgot to iron my degeneracy before I came out which speaks volumes about the state of my closet.

[3]   It is only with astigmatic hindsight that I can characterise the sex in this way. At the time it was fine, if a little hurried and genitally focused. Besides it was 1983, I was only nineteen, and sex was neither good nor bad.

slumber. The next day, when Sid and I woke up, the other boy was gone leaving only a note which read 'Who WAS that girl?' Sid has no memory of this. This was how I found out that he was gay or, as he puts it now, in his bisexual period.[4]

After this experience I made a conscious decision not to have sex with him again. I didn't care that he was having sex with men, but at the time there were starting to be articles in the gay press about a disease that was affecting gay men and I thought that avoiding sex with a gay man was probably sensible. Now sensible rings in my ears and seems a nasty antidote to love. When I found out that he was HIV-positive I felt that if I had never worried about him contracting the virus he never would have; that it was somehow my fault. Guilt and narcissism converged to make me ashamed of my own fear. I have secretly felt this in my heart-of-broken-hearts since 1988 when he told me.

'When he told me'. I say it as though it was a simple exchange of information. As though he told me and I said fine and we had another cup of tea. It wasn't like that. It was awful. He told me as though I should already know, and I heard it and disavowed by asking who gave it to him. He told me that it didn't matter. And it didn't and it was the perfect wrong question to ask but I didn't know this. I truly didn't know. I have spent a lot of time trying to make up for the wrongness of this question. But it is only recently that we are able to talk about his T-cells and whether he should go on anti-retro-virals or not.

It would hurt every time someone who didn't know would

---

[4] My analyst and I had some very difficult sessions around what this story means. I told it to her at the height of my transference, wanting very much to please her, and hoping it would make her laugh. She didn't. She burst into tears and cancelled our next two sessions. When I saw her again she wouldn't speak about it. Finally she told me what should have been obvious to me all along. She said 'of course he wanted you to wake up; in more ways than one.' The light was on to show me something I'd been disavowing until this session; his desire for me was not heterosexual. I was witnessing the primal scene—the mistaken watcher of a scene whose content is always directed at/to you. After she told me this I couldn't see her for a while.

bring up HIV and say, 'It's the children I feel sorriest for,' and I would cringe and worry about what I might have said before I knew, and about what I thought after I knew. I had a conversation with him, drunk, in a bar in Melbourne. 'How do I have ambition?' he asked me. And I said (and I am ashamed of this), 'But I could be hit by a bus tomorrow.' As though these two things were the same, that I could conflate the difference and make it disappear. And he cried and I felt inadequate, and it was horrible.

After this I started to set myself tests—infection tests—jumping in front of stationary buses. I remember standing in the shower at his house after a night out, holding his toothbrush in my hand and daring myself to use it. Telling myself over and over that HIV is a fragile virus. And then brushing my teeth, and telling somebody later, and them saying to me that I was stupid, that I was putting myself at risk. And me saying, 'Well, if I have to be so vigilant to avoid this virus then I'd rather get it.' But I didn't, and although I continued to use his toothbrush for many years, now when I spend the night at his house I put toothpaste on my finger.

Then I fell in love with him.[5] After many years of being

---

[5] There is a precedent for this love of gay men in my family. The only grandfather I ever knew was your basic Viennese nightmare. He told me that he had studied with Freud, and that the whole Oedipal thing had been his idea. He often talked about the beauty of his glamorous aristocratic mother. We who are still alive often wonder when she turned into the dumpy, plain, peasant woman in the photographs. He opened the Centre for the Human Condition in London in the fifties, where he objectively studied the misery he inflicted on the people around him. My aunt tells a story of how she had sex with one of his assistants. Apparently the man laughed as he said to her, 'This is just what I was doing with your father last night'. My grandfather had that hubris thing down to an art. My aunt, instead of poking out her eyes, drank until she was blind and insightful and left home. My grandfather stopped speaking to my mother when she fucked one of the homosexuals he was researching for his book, *The Invert in Society: A Dispassionate Look*. He died slowly not so long ago and neither my mother nor my aunt would go to his death-bed. My father has told me that he doesn't like having sex with men. He's tried it, he assures me. Is my crush on Sid the logical patrilinear destiny in this story of men wanting men? Am I merely fulfilling genetic desire? Have I got the gay gene? I am the only grandchild, there are no sons. For the first time in my life I almost yearn for a penis of my own.

his friend I developed this enormous crush and I couldn't leave him alone. I rang him every day, often more than once. If we were in a room together I had to touch him, lie on him, sit close to him. He knew and he didn't mind. One day at the Oxford Hotel we were drunk and I asked him what he was thinking (I had to know everything, colonise every moment of his life, get in between him and the virus, you see), and he told me that he was thinking it was nice to have me in love with him. He warned me first that it was corny, and it was, but it made me happy and both of us got embarrassed so we drank some more and forgot.

Then all I wanted to do was have unsafe sex with him. A part of me knew that this desire was an attempt to stop him from getting sick; that my grief was manifesting as love and vice versa. But I felt like if I could just have his cock inside me everything would be okay. I started looking into the possibility of having a baby with him. I still want to more than anything. And I told him.

How is this not a story of How I Became a Silent Straight? Of how I miscast heterosexual desire for my gay friend as my becoming a queen? There is something going off. Not off the boil, but getting ripe. This casting is fishy. This lust is queer. But what of my wish for the baby? This is not, I tell myself, the naturalised progression of normative het love. It is a totally camp wish to stop death: the homosexual desire of a lesbian for a gay man, such that if I were a man I would have to be a faggot.[6]

I would spend every night at his house. Sleeping in his bed. Sometimes, in his sleep, he would push up against me and moan and my heart would fill and rupture. I would listen to him have sex with his boyfriend and pretend it was me. He would tell me

---

6   When I was in the thick of this incredible operatic desire I talked about it to my analyst whose boyfriend is positive. I asked her if she ever wants to have unsafe sex with him. She told me that she loves him, not the virus, and that she has always been incredibly clear about differentiating them. It made me weep because of her strength, but I couldn't understand it and I still can't. I would love to hate the virus but I have a strange ambivalence towards it. I can't see it outside myself enough to hate it. And I can't see it as part of myself enough to hate it either.

of his infidelities, blow by blow-job descriptions of nights spent in toilets and saunas. I could never understand how he knew who wanted to have sex with him and I would question him incessantly about the signals, asking him again and again, 'But how do you know?' So he tried over and over to explain homo-eyes to me. He would look at me in that way—the slight narrowing of the eyes, the imperceptible raising of the eyebrow—and I would pretend to myself that he was making eyes at me. Then he would glance around wherever we were, slip into the toilets and come back with a tale of trade to tell.

Fuck. I hate the way I write about him in the past tense. It makes me stiffen up (not engorged with blood). He is still here but in another city and I miss him, and I almost decided not to come here because I didn't want to leave him. But this type of relationship doesn't get counted by anyone, except us, as one that you make sacrifices for. So I left.

Does this story then become one of distance; a matter of propinquity and proximity, of merely being in the right place at the right time? Well, I am close, but not close enough. Not just near but akin to, approximate, almost. I am related, not by blood, not yet. This story starts in blood and ends in tears. Venal not carnal. My love is not of the flesh but in the body. Although my blood runs cold I can feel my heart beat. Like the punch line of a bad joke. Boom boom.

But the joke falls flat and my love, like a girdle, firms and flatters. I can never tell jokes. Instead I affect a kind of archness, a snide superiority that is the vernacular of camp. In this dialect I discursively construct a space that I am trying to constitute as a place, a community. Sometimes, when I'm being sentimental (which I've come to realise is most of the time), it seems like this community only exists in its absence. It is a place where those present (like in high school role call) try to answer for those who are away. Our presence is fleeting and the missing are body-doubles for the dying. This is a community founded on shifting grounds, on a double fault line. How has a disease that ravages these bodies produced this body of queer? Such an unverifiable body; a leaky, splashing thing that leaves traces in beds and psyches. Queer as fuck, angry and sad.

I have a fantasy, when I'm not being figurative. In it, the queer community is reifiable and ontological. I know it's not real or possible. Somebody said to me not long ago, 'Oh fuck, I am *so over* queer,' and although this seems an impossible thing to say, in her head it was something that could be gotten over. In other words it was. Or maybe it still is but has simply gone out of fashion. I want to fashion a rude community but, style queen that I am, if it doesn't look good will I want to be part of it?

It is this shift from the proclamation 'I am queer' (and remember all it takes is the performative statement) to queer as having other discursive enactments that I want to make a claim for. I long, almost melancholically, for a place where my libidinal fixations aren't read as fixed or stable and where Butler gets misread so that gender seems voluntaristic. What does queer mean when I don't use it in the first person?

When I first heard queer being reused in the early 1990s it seemed to offer the opportunity for disturbing the fixed positions that gay and lesbian identities had, on the whole, been assumed to have. It was a distinctive nose-thumbing term that was a useful destabiliser for the polemics of the politics of liberation. Queer had promise as a position that could cross identities and make fluid the differences that previously were spoken of as though they were immutable. It offered the possibility of multiple confluences of identities rather than a singular point of contact between lesbians and gays which figured around same-sex desire.

One of the earliest academic theorisings of queer was by Teresa de Lauretis (1991), in her introduction to the Queer Theory issue of the journal *differences*. For her, queer is a useful way of looking at the conflation of differences that happens around the 'and' in 'gay and lesbian'. It also, she claimed, opens up a space for a coalition politics that recognises both the differences already demarcated and acknowledged between the identities 'gay' and 'lesbian', and those across and between these identities that configure around culture, ethnicity and colour. This of course makes me want to ask about the *similarities* and identifications between the couple 'lesbian/gay'? 'What about Sid and me?' I plead, and if it sounds like I'm whining it's because I am.

For others queer was and is an unproblematic statement, a term expressive of a genre, or a generation and/or a positionality to signal perversity in style. This usage enfranchised previously marginal sexualities such as S/M practitioners, fetishists, bisexuals, transgenders and sex-radicals. What this deployment of queer assumed was that someone somewhere had already defined queer and that this definition was simply being referred to. But queer is not simply a citation, it is also iterative. The word still smacks to some of painful derogation and closets, of not being quite right. (She's a queer one, they say, and it's not me or Eve Sedgwick who is saying it.)

To assume that the strategic redeployment of a vilificatory term erases its history is to assume that to be queer now is not made possible by being queer then. This transparency assumes that identity is a *tabula rasa*. In the attempt to come to self-evident identity we lose the very thing that identity is contingent on: the history of the term. Queer is always a re-inscription, and although in this rewriting there is some loss, it is not total. In the recoding of the word, the excess of its already substantial prior meanings is not lost. Queer would not have such discursive power if it wasn't always referring to what is being said as well as to what has already been said. In this calculation the term becomes synergetic, escaping the laws of addition and negation.

These most common definitions of queer (either as a modern synonym for or as a marker of the differences between lesbians and gay men) are predicated in a number of ways on identity-based notions of 'same-sex desire'.[7] There is a mean-

---

[7] Is my desire for Sid same-sex desire? Does this somehow make us the same sex? If this question seems absurd, I ask it because I wonder sometimes whether we have the same sex. In 1983, Pat Califia (1983 pp. 24–27) announced that sex between lesbians and gay men was gay sex. This was a tremendous move in terms of the politics of the times and predated queer by many years. When I read her statement, years after she made it, I wondered why it is she characterised the sex as gay and not lesbian. When I thought about it I realised the answer was obvious; lesbians don't have sex. I on the other hand have, on the very odd occasion, had lesbian sex with straight men.

meaning in this definition's refusal of other differences. This lack of generosity is most apparent in the normative and exclusionary (although sometimes strategic) rhetoric that circulates around the agendas of identity politics. There are resistances in and to this definition of queer, that start to rub up uncomfortably against the word itself.

Queer in this way has also come to stand as a metonym for (a) shifting identity politics. It signals the shifts but refuses definition and definitive positionality. But in this refusal things are being said. Meanings are being read into this apparent silence. Loud statements are being made about ambiguity and confluences. Sentences are being constructed inaudibly about identification and slippage. It makes me want to scream. I want desperately to fix and stabilise this word so that I can become the identity that it purports to describe. As usual this desire attaches itself to ambivalence and I am glad that there is no way to know precisely what queer identifies.

In the space that queer claims as a challenge to identity politics it becomes clear that the absences and silences, like the definitions, still don't shift the debates nearly far enough. A refusal to define queer can be read as a strategy of defiance but it is a petulant and furious pose. We can't be naive about our refusal. Our anger is returning grief and we are in danger of being disingenuous if we deny this.

This anger enacts itself in a number of ways under the rubric of queer. One of the early reclaimings of the term was by a group of activists who met in 1990 to discuss the bashings of gays and lesbians in the East Village in New York City. They named themselves Queer Nation and began a campaign of radical action, stencilling slogans on the footpaths which read, 'My beloved was queer bashed here. Queers fight back' (Smyth 1992, p. 17). This slogan's second use of queer ('queers fight back') directly interpolates the queer in 'queer bashing' and illustrates an awareness of the complex history of the term. The Australian version of this would have to read, 'My beloved was poofter bashed here. Poofters fight back.' The sanguinity of the second sentence is complex but also starkly clear. It makes a number of points. First, it is a declarative. It is saying we are not easy targets who are fearful and incapable of inflicting harm but that we do fight back and we will when bashed. Second, it is a performative statement. The saying/reading of 'queers fight back' is the fighting back of queers. The writing of the slogan on the footpath is doing the fighting back. Third, it is a call to arms, a convocation. It is telling us to fight back.

This radicalness, although assumed, is not always evident. For instance, in 1992 the local chapter of Queer Nation, like its American counterpart, staged a demonstration outside the Village Cinemas in Sydney to reveal who the murderer was in *Basic Instinct* in an attempt to stop people going to the film. This political action, with its queer association, was assumed to be a radical intervention into a representational system that denotes all lesbians as killers. What this demonstration in fact demonstrates is the conservative impulse of queer. It shows how little the debates have shifted the term out of the mire of same-sex desire as the only true marker of our difference. Revealing the identity of the killer in the film assumes that the only pleasure that lies in the text is in finding out whodunnit.[8] To make this assumption buys into all of Hollywood's own assumptions about a homogenous public, and ignores the possibility of other pleasures that are to be found in films. If this were the only pleasure in film (in this case to find out who the killer is, or in other cases to see whether the boy gets the girl), gays and lesbians would have stopped going to the movies years ago and of course we didn't. In our viewing we have found other sites of pleasure that do not necessarily reside in the narrative, or in a notion of identification, which isn't to say that pleasure in narrative closure is only possible if you somehow 'believe' a movie, or if you can 'relate' to it. There is much pleasure to be had in suspending disbelief, and in entering into the hermetically sealed world that a film pro-

---

8   In fact, as Linda Hart points out in her book *Fatal Women* (Hart 1994. pp 124–135), there is no narrative certainty in this film that Catherine Trammell is the killer. Hart makes a lovely queer argument about this uncertainty and the comedy of heterosexuality that it makes clear.

poses. In Queer Nation's account *Basic Instinct* can only be a movie about lesbian psychopaths, and that is that.

Sometimes I wonder why, given the ease with which the term queer can be and often is a simple reiteration of many of the old problems of identity politics, I am still attracted to it; why it is I still try and work with it. The answer I come to is that it is illustrative rather than definitive. Queer allows the very act of writing that I am attempting here. Through its entry into the academy particular performative practices and textualities have become permissible. This form has led many to both academic and pleasurable play (not that they are in any way mutually exclusive) with pain, fetishism, misidentification, pornography, butch/femme, and other modalities of sex and text.

What is opened up is a liminal space, one that is comfortable and terrifying. Some nights, as I cry over the ravages our bodies and psyches have endured to get us to this point, I mourn sentimentally the nostalgia of a lost moment in history that never was. Other nights I can't believe that queer is anything but a desire to rage together.

> My friendships with a handful of men and women have had an importance for me that friendship doesn't seem to have for most straight people. I've known one of my best friends since I was sixteen, and I still see her constantly. My old lovers have become close friends. I have loved one man, another writer, for seven years with an almost romantic passion although we have never been to bed together. Such loving, chaste devotion would strike many straight people as adolescent; at least, I've been told it is adolescent. If so, I can only be grateful that I have never outgrown it (White 1977, p. 35).

And so am I. Grateful and grief-full. I have a presentiment that if queer could ever be the stable category that I imagine I want it to be then I would have to be something else. This something else that I already am. I am a screaming queer/n who screams with laughter as well as pain; a girl who does girls and will always be in love with gay men.

5
Bisexual mediations: beyond the third term

McKENZIE WARK

I'm up at Gilligan's, a bar overlooking Oxford Street, having a few drinks with the boys. A woman I know, or used to know, launches herself across the room at me.
'Dahrling!'
'Sabina!'
She drops into my lap and gives me a friendly kiss.
'So good to see you!'
And so it is. We're about to catch up, reaffirm a friendship, when a waiter comes over.
'Excuse me! This is a gay bar. Would you mind not doing *that* here.'
My friends look away, embarrassed.
'Um, sorry,' I offer.
'Really!' says Sabina. But he's gone. I can see his point. But nobody wins here. Offence, embarrassment, a spontaneity contained. Another reminder that *I have no place*. It's like the time my boyfriend drives me to the airport. Will he kiss me outside the departure gate? A moment's hesitation. I look directly at him:
'Come on, kiss me you faggot!'
And he does. That place doesn't feel like 'ours'. In Gilligan's

he wouldn't hesitate. He belongs there. But I don't. My 'clandestine' life.

The bisexual 'problem'

These bisexuals: where are they hiding? Their identity is either a mystery, a problem, or of strictly marginal interest. Psychological and psychiatric authorities debate how many axes on a 'dynamic scale' might render the variability of these versatile agents of hydra-headed desire. The social and medical institutions ponder how to prevent them from couriering HIV/AIDS between 'high risk' and 'low risk'. Gay and lesbian folk bitch about bisexual infidelities and betrayals, while their 'community leaders' and cultural spokesfolk ignore them.

And yet, for all that, bisexuality refuses to either settle into an identifiable kind of agency or to go away. Bisexuals remain, if not exactly spies in the house of love, in Anaïs Nin's phrase, then at least double agents in the institutions of sexual discourse. Not to be trusted. Not even they know who they really are. Maybe they like it that way. Or maybe they don't feel like they have any choice.

The early 90s saw many of the tensions bisexuals experience privately within gay and lesbian communities break out into public discourses. I have the membership form for the Sydney Gay & Lesbian Mardi Gras in front of me. Joining obliges me to tick a box as to my 'orientation'. Gay, straight, lesbian, transgender, bisexual. Tick whichever box you fancy. It wasn't like this the first time I joined this organisation. The prominent 'community leader' who eagerly signed me up and took my money didn't seem to care. I've heard a lot of biphobic nonsense from him since. Now I'm obliged to conform to somebody else's kinky fantasy—namely that sexualities come in neatly dividable identities that can be assigned and aligned by the bent world as well as the straight.

Then there was the refusal of the Gay & Lesbian Rights Lobby to widen its charter to include advocacy for the rights of bisexuals and transgender people. An ugly stoush in the gay press ensued, which spilled over into one of the Stonewall forums. Things weren't helped by the youth and inexperience of the bisexual activists who pressed their case. I don't consider a young man and a young woman kissing passionately in front of a gay and lesbian crowd a 'political act'. I consider it bad manners.

Whatever bisexuality 'is', its singularity isn't helped by aping the rhetorics and strategies of the gay and lesbian communities, as happens in some of the literature of the emerging 'bisexual movement' (Hutchins & Kaahumanu 1991; Off Pink Collective 1988; Weise 1992). To openly declaim an identity nailed fast to the gender of one's object of emotional and sexual investment is a fine and noble thing. I think most people who consider themselves bisexuals support that. But perhaps 'we' are someone else; perhaps what 'we' are is something else.

Bookmarks

I'm cruising books. I'm interested in Connell and Dowsett's *Rethinking Sex* (Connell & Dowsett 1992). But it's not interested in me. In an otherwise excellent paper on 'AIDS and the Discourses of Sexuality', Dennis Altman mentions the B-word once, in passing. Then he talks about men who have sex with men. Then he makes a useful distinction between the pretty useless notion of 'risk groups' and the more definable 'risk behaviours'. So far so good: behaviours and identities have complex and shifting relationships to each other. But then he goes back to talking about homosexuality again. One finds this again and again: a glimmer of interest, a hint of recognition, then it's gone, displaced or misplaced between the categories.

Same again in Connell and Dowsett's paper. They critique various ways the categories of sex are produced in history, and show how they are in return constitutive of our perception of history itself. Dazzling stuff. And yet . . . hetero, homo, transexual. But no bisexuality. It woud appear that I have lost my place in this book.

Liz Grosz's *Volatile Bodies* is a brilliant book on the production of bodies as a material practice, but . . . let me see now . . . four mentions. Two to stigmatise bisexual men for putting straight women at risk. For example:

> One must assume that in the era of AIDS, it is still the sexuality of marginalised groups—gay men, intravenous drug users, prostitutes—that is increasingly administered, targeted, by public health policy, while the sexuality of the reproductive couple, especially of the husband/father, remains almost entirely unscrutinised, though his (undetected) secret activities—his clandestine bisexuality or drug use—may be responsible for the spread of the virus into hitherto 'safe' (heterosexual) populations (Grosz 1994, p. 153; cf. p. 197).

Oh, right. Bisexuality is a 'clandestine' practice of the dominant group. It doesn't qualify for the moral high ground of the 'marginalised'—and so Grosz marginalises it, ethically and actually.

This 'clandestine bisexuality' is actually a major focus at present of publicly funded sociological scrutiny and media phobia (Davis et al. 1991; Dowsett 1991; Jackson & Lindsay 1991; Bartos et al. 1994; Kippax et al. 1994). If the point of a corporeal approach to theory is to affirm the powers of the body to produce itself in all its glorious singularity, then why this reactive othering of bisexuality, as belonging always and only to the bad patriarchal other?

Grosz later glosses Deleuze and Guattari, theorists of a self-production of fluid, molecular, creative desires, as arguing that 'they are not advocating the cultivation of "bisexuality", which is simply the internalisation of binarized sexuality . . . without actually stretching or transforming them' (Grosz 1994, p. 176). And that's correct, as far as it goes. But I find it hard to see how one could 'stretch or transform' those polarities without passing *through* them—both of them. How is bisexuality any more bound to the poles than either of the 'monosexualities'? Surely it is potentially less so. Whether it is in the space of the city or the space of the text, monosexual logics collude in sustaining their identity in relation to each other, but at the expense of an other other, at the expense ultimately of other conceptions and productions of sexual selves.

Monosexuality

'I suppose *you'd* call me bisexual,' says JM, a 38-year-old teacher, when he is asked by a sociologist with a clipboard to put a label on himself (Bartos et al. 1994, p. 28). Good on you JM! Why give in to the satisfaction *others* might take in putting you in your place? Why is it that monosexuals, gay and straight, so want to identify this other category according to the logic by which they define themselves?

From a gay or lesbian perspective, the way straights stigmatise and render homosexuality *other* is a major concern, not least because of the ostracism, discrimination and violence that follows. Straightness defines its boundaries by excluding its other, but conceives that other according to the same monosexual logic: to what Monique Wittig calls the 'straight mind', if you fuck with people of the same sex you are a faggot or a dyke (Wittig 1992). This is a reactive, negative construction of sexuality, defined by what it excludes, by its limit.

But as Anna Munster sees it in 'hateness of straightness', the same logic can affect gay and lesbian thinking as well:

> straight does not discriminate on the basis of sexuality. straight is not heterosexual or gay. straight crosses into both worlds. straight is the fact that a lesbian tells me I'm straight because I fucked a man for money or sport or whatever, that makes me straight, does it? I'm open to a variety of actions and a million possibilities when it comes to sex, but I still call myself gay; that makes me straight does it? (Munster 1993, p. 11).

Seen from somewhere else, from somewhere outside the logic of identity discovered as the negative image of its limit, its other, then both straight notions of gayness and gay notions of straightness amount to much the same thing. I wonder even if the popularity of the Sydney Gay & Lesbian Mardi Gras with a straight–straight crowd is that a visible homosexual world, contained in space and time, is such a great image against which heterosexuality can define the nothing that it is. I wonder about this every year as the parade goes by, and the straight couples wander around in the crowd, always holding hands.

Seen from elsewhere, from this somewhere else, then bisexuality is a category that the straight–straight and straight–gay worlds tacitly police together. By identifying the slippery supplemental third term between them, they police the boundaries of the twentieth century logic of identity. A logic that I would want to join JM in refusing. What do the Gay & Lesbian Rights Lobby and the Festival of Light have in common? An agreement on the presence of a boundary defining two kinds of monosexuality, one affirmed against the other.

I come at it this way: gay and lesbian communities and identities do the straight world an enormous service, precisely by presenting to it an other pole—safely labelled and removed. Like the famous Kinsey scale:

heterosexual <————————> homosexual

'Pure' homosexuality presents itself at the opposite pole—only now it no longer needs sexologists, psychologists, sociologists and the police to identify it. It has taken on the burden of bounding the category of straightness by identifying itself. That's a position from which some reform of the socio-sexual order can be proposed and defended—precisely because it affirms that order. It also gives homosexual identity a stake in suppressing ambiguity between the poles. The poles collude in suppressing, ignoring or repelling the middle. But there's nothing natural or given about this construction. What if we looked at it another way:

monosexual <————————> bisexual

This diagram isn't equivalent to the first. It transcends it. The dynamics of the first diagram is included within one pole of this second diagram, which at its other pole proposes . . . something else again. Something that stands at the limit of the binary logic of an identity that can only exist negatively, as defined by its other.

Beyond monosexuality

Perhaps it's not enough to refuse the bounded constraints of straight or gay, where each holds a mirror of otherness to the other. Beyond that lies a third term. One that holds a mirror up to both. One that both straight and gay would want to manage and limit as a point of negation that exists solely for the benefit of the identity of either monosexuality.

What comes next is the affirmation of this third term in its own right. In making this affirmation, bisexual activists repeat the shift from negative to positive otherness made by gay and lesbian activists, but like them remain trapped in the game of otherness, of identities always defined in terms of the mirror of another term.

Beyond that lies something else again—a *vector* to the production of sexuality without identity, without the need to negate something to claim existence. A vector is a line of movement that neither leaves from, nor expects to arrive at, a predetermined point. It's a movement without a logic of otherness (Wark 1994a). A way out of the binds of identity-policing lies through what is defined as bisexuality in this logic of otherness, but which in practice exceeds and eludes this nightmare hall of mirrors, because it doesn't need to define itself in relation to or against a grid of oppositions. So when we draw the next segment of the diagram, it looks like this:

monosexual <————————> bisexual <————————> X

Rather than a mirror relation, what lies beyond bisexuality is an open vector, by which I mean any possible relation that does not depend for its existence on the terms it relates in mirror opposition to each other, but which could head for the unknown, the unnamed. If there is an ethical goal that lies along these vectors to unknown pleasures, it is what Felix Guattari describes as 'a way of life where people can circulate freely not only in space, but in ideas, emotions, desires, even sexes . . .' (Guattari 1995, p. 45). There lies what performance artist Virginia Barrett calls 'subject X': X for that which needs no identity to produce itself in relation to who and what it choses.

Bunburying

In a delicate and seductive reading, Eve Kosovsky Sedgwick teases a curious sexual logic out of Wilde's *The Importance of Being Earnest*. She talks of 'the play's *resistance* to homo/hetero scientism: in this case, by appealing to the pre-modern (though by no means obsolete) understanding of sexual nonconformity in terms of *acts* (e.g. sodomy) rather than types (inverts, homosexuals) or even relations (pederastic)' (Sedgwick 1993, pp. 67–68, emphasis in original). This at first appears to contain the same difficulty. Tasmania's equally premodern law proscribes sodomy, not homosexuality. Why position one's sexual self in terms of the legal institution's coercive line between acceptable and unacceptable acts rather than in terms of the psychological institution's coercive line between acceptable and unacceptable identities? Because at least one can conceive of an infinite number of acts via which a self produces its self, in the act, as whatever. Not as a love that 'dare not speak its name' but as a love that has no name, and hence does not constitute a self-identical category to be managed by legal, psychological or cultural coercions that straighten up the boundaries defining the them that makes us 'us'. Or a love that makes a place for itself by making its own name, like Wilde's fabulously elusive practice of bunburying. Does that mean, in the slang of the time, 'to bury the bun'—sodomy? Or something else, always something else, out of reach of 'identity'?

To return to *Volatile Bodies*—Grosz doesn't want to pass on through the category that monosexualities erect at their limit, the 'bisexual', on through to the infinitely volatile bunburyings that bodies might produce out of themselves, might make out of themselves. Not to mention the bodies beyond the body they might make of themselves, when they exceed the inscriptions placed upon them from without and find their own multitude of connections (Deleuze & Guattari 1984, pp. 232–309). And not to mention the infinite and varied ensembles bodies make with images and things outside of themselves. For what Grosz does not quite relinquish is a normative phenomenology of identities. It is not enough to revalue the poles of such a phenomenology, however tempting that might be as a short-cut to a certain limited kind of power for the gay and lesbian 'communities'.

It is not enough for bodies to become 'volatile'—the notion of identity must be held to the heat until the myth of it explodes. As Felix Guattari asks:

> Should pleasure be registered and recorded upon the body, or should pleasure call into play parts of the body, of social sequences, of machines, of words? It is clear that there are thousands of ways of making love: with a look, etc . . . we can easily imagine a perverse, polymorphous economy where, clearly, there are bodies, although it is unnecessary to inscribe under the phallic dichotomy the results of a text and a social practice. This is a completely different vectoralisation (Guattari 1995, pp. 157–8).

Grosz's is a theory intent on getting away from binary relations, where the image of the other guarantees the identity of the one, bounding it, providing the external measure for its self-policing. And yet it has to pick the least binary, least stable, *almost* most marginal thing to stigmatise as its bad other. As for the most marginal thing, in this discourse, it's female bisexuality. Bisexuality is either male or unmarked in Grosz's book. Never female.[1]

---

1 In Grosz's subsequent collection of essays (Grosz 1995), the female bisexual does put in an appearance. Grosz uses her as a question mark in the margin of Teresa de Lauretis' attempts to construct a lesbian psychology. She appears tactically as the negative limit to such a project.

If one wants to celebrate fluid desires, then one has to head in the direction of those who mark sexuality as neither a binarism nor a monism: not hetero, homo or androgynous. One of the roads going that way leads through this mysterious category of bisexuality, to the secrets those marked by it might be keeping quietly to themselves. This is not a question of seeking the truth of gender in the body, but of producing bodies, connections between bodies, and connections between bodies, images and things, irrespective of any originary form—bunburying. This entails an ethics of the production of new and singular connections, rather than an ethics of the reduction of the body to any supposedly normative law of 'behaviour'—be it that mandated by scientific 'experts' or the moral authority of the 'community'.

Taken to its limit, what lurks within a bisexual practice is something that turns the solid body of thought that might compose, for example, a specifically gay or feminist knowledge to sticky liquid. As such it exposes the complicity of such knowledges with their unacknowledged models—the management and maintenance of stable identities by the disciplinary apparatus of the State.

The politics of polyvalence

I was in the audience at the 1993 QueerLit conference when Robert Dessaix copped a verbal lashing for omitting prominent Sydney gay writers from his anthology of Australian gay and lesbian writing (Dessaix 1993). It's a book of acts that defy description, ascription. Surely this is what literature is for? Do we read Proust 'because he was gay' or because he so captivatingly describes what seethes beneath the orders of sexuality (Deleuze 1977)?

It's a sad irony that it takes an epidemic to see that while gay and lesbian communities are fine and legitimate and wonderful things for some, they are not coterminous with the acts that ground their identities. The identities produced and maintained by these communities, like those produced by all communities, are false. That is their value—they provide a space in which the bunburying flux can be bounded and contained, such that it can shape an image of itself for the world and a self-consciousness of itself for itself.

But it's in the act that one finds the juice. I can imagine much more fun anthologies than Dessaix's falsely named one. How about *The Oxford Companion to Cunnilingus* or *The Little Golden Book of Showers*? It is out of a series of acts that one composes a body's sexualities. But does the choice of the series of acts have to determine a point of identity? Why not a curve or a spiral or a zig-zag to and fro?

As much as I sympathise with writers like Charlotte Wolff, attempts to psychologise bisexuality into a category of self-conscious identity must be judged a failure (Wolff 1979). Wolff's interviews and questionnaires add up to nothing more than a fuzzy set of beings who bonk across the great gender divide. They did not all have any particular kind of childhood. They did not all experience the same traumas. Their childhoods and traumas don't seem too different from any 'control' group. Unable to say how these 200 people *were made* this way, Wolff can't quite come around to saying that they *made themselves* that way. Made to feel unwelcome in, but supportive of, gay and lesbian organisations, and/or married with kids, these folk don't form a whole that you could pass a rope around.

In the United States there is a movement among some bisexuals to put the rope around themselves. The magazines *Frighten the Horses* and *Anything That Moves* give expression to its libidinal and political urges respectively. But if there is an attribute of what monosexualities call bisexuality worth celebrating, it is precisely its *refusal* to come out, to share its secrets, to accept its place in the negotiations, via State and community, in the order of things.

So far I've tried to provide an opening for an ethic to emerge out of the space mapped by others as 'bisexuality', without requiring of it that it 'position' itself in relation to its others in the grid. What lurks within that category challenges the grid itself. But while that might define an ethic of refusal in relation to identity, it doesn't say much about a politics that would allow one to act in and through the communities defined by the monosexual grid.

And yet there is a need for such a politics, when bisexual men are stigmatised as the 'clandestine' vectors of disease, when the Lobby won't accept its responsibility to defend the rights of bisexuals but remains instead a narrowly defined monosexual (self) interest group, when the Mardi Gras requires you to tick a box and wants to segregate its spaces along monosexual lines. So perhaps one has to adopt the mask and speak through it, but without for all that legitimising or naturalising the mask. But I'm sure it is clear by now why I would like to take some critical distance from the emergent notions of bisexual activism modelled on gay liberation.

Bisexual chic

'GIRLS WHO LOVE GIRLS: Hollywood's sexy swinging secrets.' The cover of the supermarket tabloid *New Weekly* with this headline shows the ubiquitous Drew Barrymore, in luscious white underwear, demolishing a wedding cake with a rather large knife (*New Weekly* 1995). The story beats out 'OH NO! Brad Pitt to Marry' for prominence. And so it should, too.

The fabulous Sandra Bernhard. She refuses to be called a lesbian yet writes in loving detail of her sexual and emotional life with women (Bernhard 1993a; 1993b). What's more important: containing the acts in the label, or letting the acts proliferate in their places and senses, flowing through and between all the orders of sexual discourse? Sandra Bernhard: *out* as a *spy* (Wark 1994b).

Sharon Stone, in *Basic Instinct*—she has the girl, gets the boy—and gets away with it. She embodies the myth of the bisexual as having powerful access to secret knowledge. As the camera creeps up on her and her pals getting it on in a nighclub toilet, they slam the cubicle door straight in our face. While those around her turn jealous, obsessive, murderous, or make the fatal mistake of falling in love, the bisexual remains elusive. She is the only character who at the end of the day has not been reduced to an identity. Is she or isn't she implicated in murder? Will she or won't she settle down to 'fuck like minks and raise rug rats'? The ice pick lurking under the bed in the last shot is the answer.

Marjorie Garber quotes *Time* and *Newsweek* on the latest thing, 'Bisexual chic'—from 1974 (Garber 1995, pp. 18–19).[2] Bisexuality, it seems, is always a coming fashion—but never becomes a classic. When it manifests in the media, it winks and hints at what the vectors of media and the vectors of sexuality have in common. Just as Sandra Bernhard or David Bowie appear to fashion a sexuality out of freely chosen images and 'object choices' that manage to evade an easy categorisation, so too does their fans' investment of desire in them—or indeed in any appearance. 'Bisexual chic' is one of the signs of a new terrain of desire that traverses the boundaries of normative sexual identities and places. Which is why there is not and never will be a 'bisexual community', other than as a poor and derivative mirroring of how the straight and gay mind would have the world, if only the world would present itself exclusively in their image.

Bisexual vectors

I'd like to conclude this chapter, not by circling back to its beginnings, but by pursuing the vector of thought it inscribes just a little bit further, into a speculation on the reconfiguration of the relations of desire of which the bisexual 'problem' might be a symptom and a way out. I don't want to arrive at the point of identifying a new subject position, but rather to open up *subjective trajectories*: terms which by definition don't know in advance where they terminate.

The rhetoric of being either 'out' or 'closet' still defines a

---

[2] Garber's book, *Vice Versa: Bisexuality and the Eroticism of Everyday Life*, is reviewed, predictably enough, as 'Bisexual Chic' by John Baxter, Weekend Australian, 20 January 1996, p 30.

social space of boundaries and partitions. One comes out of the closets imposed by the boundedness of family and community, of public and private—yet one ends up retreating into another boundedness: the 'gay community', or a private life in suburban Marrickville with a dog and cat and a partner and a mortgage.

These bounded spaces are steadily transgressed by flows of a peculiarly modern kind. Once the patriarchal order ruled both the public space and the bounds of private space, yielding only a corner of moral authority to a matriarch within the confines of the household. The neat division of roles, in public and private, in the domestic arena and the public arena—all that has been challenged and partly changed by social forces that make possible such things as a gay public identity, or a lesbian private realm. But what else has changed?

The neat bounds of public and private space come increasingly to be permeated by media vectors. First the radio, the telephone, then television: revealing images of the private in public, bringing images of the public into the private. No wonder representatives of the old social order—family and church—feel so threatened by something like the televising of Mardi Gras. Both the Festival of Light and the organised gay and lesbian communities spend a lot of energy debating exactly the same thing: the policing of the rhetoric of the televised image of sexuality. For the same thing is at stake: the inability of social forms premised on the old divide of public and private spaces to partition the slippery ambiguities and spatial transgressions of the media vector. While gay and lesbian rhetorics and politics seek to reform the structures of public and private spaces, the proliferation of vectors *across* public and private boundaries is making that an obsolete project.

Perhaps it's no accident that the rhetorics embodied in bisexuality, and those carried via the media vector, both appear as threatening to the boundable identities and communities of gay and lesbian. Once outside the law of desire, whether policed by the patriarchs of public space, the matriarchs of the private realm, or their contemporary successors, the psychologists and social workers, then sexuality is free to compose itself along the line of a flow of images that in themselves can't prescribe a limit on what is acceptably desirable (Wark 1993). The proliferating flow of images, freed from the ability of any social apparatus to limit interpretation, makes possible an abstract, virtual field of possible desires.

6
Sexual conduct, sexual culture, sexual community: gay men's bodies and AIDS

GARY W. DOWSETT

It captured immediate attention—so prominent, so provocative. With its blue-grey tones, its very size drew the gaze, and the recognition of its possible meaning drew gasps of delight. It was February 1995 and in the well-sited display window of a men's fashion shop on Oxford Street, Darlinghurst in Sydney, one of Australia's best known professional Rugby League players had bared it all for the Gay & Lesbian Mardi Gras.

For footballer Ian Roberts, like Sister Mary McKillop, 1995 marked his beatification—but in his case it was by the Sisters of Perpetual Indulgence, an order of gay male nuns. This was not Roberts's first strip routine. A nude photo essay in a new, up-market gay photography magazine, *(not only) Blue*, had earlier in the year launched him into gay culture nationally as a major icon and superhunk. His attendances at the 1995 Mardi Gras Community Fair and the Gay Community Awards Night during the same month have assured his eventual canonisation and placed the question of his sexuality (yes, a professional footballer) on the mainstream media's agenda (*Weekend Australian*, 15–16 July 1995, 'Review', p. 3).

Roberts at that time wisely refused to discuss his sexual interests, noting only that, 'Being part of a different group, being labelled as an outsider because you live your life in a different way to the "norm", has put me in a position to look at things laterally and to think about them objectively' (*(not only) Blue* 1995, p. 56). But for the gay community in Sydney, Roberts was offering another moment in the major re-situating of 'gay' in Australian social life.

It was no secret in Sydney's gay communities that Roberts was gay. But as part of an unwritten rule in gay community life, one does not 'out' other gay and lesbian people without good reason. He has since 'come out' of his own accord in the United States press, and this story was picked up in the Australian sporting press very soon after. But before this, the intense speculation about Roberts' sexuality throughout 1995 had another agenda, and it was quite clear that his media agent was handling the whole issue with immense skill. Roberts soon appeared at many other gay events, always carefully avoiding a declaration of his sexual interests. He and other celebrated professional sportsmen offered an expensive fitness and training workshop to gay men, and he began providing a regular fitness column for the national gay magazine *Outrage*.

Throughout the year speculation about Roberts' sexual interests intensified, with carefully worded articles in the *Weekend Australian* and other media, all spurred along unwittingly by Rupert Murdoch and his acquisition of Roberts for Super League. Roberts' body, again nude or semi-nude, began to appear in various advertisements, always sustaining that ambiguity. Three ads for jeans exemplify this ambiguity. In the first, Roberts and another man, both wearing the jeans, offer exposed and straining torsos as they pull at another pair of jeans in a playful tug-of-war. The second ad featured the two men standing in the jeans, again bared to the waist, with a young woman sitting at their feet, suggesting a possible competitor for Roberts's attention. In the third ad, Roberts and the woman are standing completely naked, pressed face-to-face and body-to-body. The wording says that if you cannot get these particular jeans, then no jeans will do. Or does it also imply that only then will the woman do?

This kind of ambiguity about men has blossomed in advertising over recent years, but I would like to situate the Ian Roberts issue within a different frame—that of the changing position of gay men and gay communities in Australian culture, one with which gay academics, activists and researchers have yet to grapple.

Australian culture has for a long time been regarded as deeply anti-homosexual, despite a colonial history in which sex between men seemed almost compulsory (Hughes 1987; Fogarty 1992). Sydney in particular has always had a vibrant, if hidden, homosexual subculture (Wotherspoon 1991), but no one could have foreseen in the early 1970s, as the Gay Liberation Movement got under way in Australia, the speed and breadth of the social change that would occur.

The re-situating of 'gay' can be seen best in law reforms that legalised adult male homosexual activity in all states of Australia bar one (Tasmania, whose laws were overridden federally in 1995). There has been an enormous increase in political support for, and courting of, the gay communities in electoral politics nationally and in New South Wales in particular. The Prime Minister, various state premiers, leaders of the state and federal opposition parties, and other politicians each year offer congratulations and issue statements of support in the Mardi Gras Festival Guide. Indeed, former Prime Minister Keating even offered his official support for the Australian gay communities' bid to host the 1998 International Gay Games.

Yet Mardi Gras itself was born in the late 1970s as part of the Gay Liberation Movement's struggle for civil rights. Street demonstrations, multiple arrests, raids on gay commercial venues, two or three failed attempts at law reform: these are just some of the events indelibly etched in the memories, not of some previous generation, but of those men and women who made and are making the Sydney gay and lesbian community. These changes in the re-situating of 'gay' have been very rapid and have taken just a little more than a decade. The contrast to the situation for gay men and lesbians in Britain and much of the United States cannot be greater.

Meanwhile, the Australian gay communities have weathered the devastation of the human immunodeficiency virus (HIV) epidemic for thirteen years now. That epidemic and its consequence, Acquired Immune Deficiency Syndrome (AIDS), have dominated the lives of gay men in particular, and of the lesbian and gay communities in general, to such an extent that they have obscured this re-situating of 'gay' to all but the keenest eye. HIV/AIDS has been accompanied at times by the worst of homophobic discourse and discriminatory practice all over the world (Watney 1987; Crimp 1988; Mann et al. 1992). Yet the Australian response to the epidemic in large part has been marked by an even-handed, cooperative, less strident and, it appears, more successful approach than has occurred in many Western countries with similar epidemics. Most importantly, this approach includes the Australian gay communities in government public health policy formation, and in day-to-day program design and delivery. It also gives to the gay communities the major burden for stopping the epidemic—an enormous responsibility that represents significant trust on the part of government.

HIV/AIDS has had a profound effect on the sexual behaviour of gay men. In the West, gay communities have produced a sustained and far-reaching alteration in those sexual practices that facilitate the transmission of HIV. Anal intercourse is the most effective HIV transmission mode, although transmission has been recorded through fistfucking (Donovan et al. 1986) and fellatio, although the proven cases are few in number (Lifson et al. 1990). For gay men the centrality of anal intercourse to HIV transmission created a strategic problem in the early days of the epidemic. To that time, the struggle to legalise sexual activity between men in many industrialised countries (particularly those without the legacy of the Napoleonic Code, which had decriminalised homosexual offences) had centred on anti-sodomy laws. Beyond these narrow legal issues, the symbolic nature of sodomy as the definition of homosexuality produced a politics focused, *inter alia*, on a defence of sodomy by the Gay Liberation Movement in the 1970s. HIV/AIDS has produced a crisis in that politics, played out in public health debates such as that over the closure of gay saunas and bathhouses in the United States (Shilts 1988). No such closure occurred in Australia, although there were calls for it to happen. This is often forgotten, and is emblematic of the different relationship between gay communities and government in this country noted earlier.

Gay men's fight for sodomy within the frame of HIV/AIDS was also instrumental in producing what became known as the safe sex strategy (Callen 1983). The very ubiquity of the exhortation to have safe sex in the global fight against HIV/AIDS obscures the fact that the invention of safe sex was premised less on a scientific analysis of sexual transmission of the virus and more on gay men's accurately judged adjustment to (homo)sexual expression, based on a keen understanding of the choreography of male-to-male sex—how it is done, how to read it meaningfully, and how it has been experienced to date by gay men individually, and articulated collectively, within their growing critique of sexuality itself. In this sense, safe sex is as much a product of sexual practice as it is of sexual politics.

The costs of the HIV epidemic to the gay communities have been enormous. Over 3000 gay men have died in Australia so far, accounting for 84 per cent of the deaths from AIDS, and it is known that at least 10 000 gay men have been infected with HIV since the epidemic began (National Centre in HIV Epidemiology and Clinical Research 1995). About half of these deaths have occurred in the Sydney gay community and at times the obituary page in the *Sydney Star Observer*, the local weekly gay community newspaper, is so full as to wrench the heart unimaginably.

There is no doubt, however, as to the success of the gay communities' efforts to stop this epidemic. Australia can rightly be said to be one of the few countries to have made real progress on this issue, and much of the tribute for that success is due to the gay communities and to the governmental processes in this country that have taken these communities seriously as partners in this public health crisis. In this sense, it is of no surprise to note that the re-situating of 'gay' owes some of its construction to the fight with HIV/AIDS.

This is not to say that HIV/AIDS has had good effects on the gay communities—this is an absurd and thoughtless contempt. But it is to indicate a complex entwining of the fight with HIV/AIDS and the development and growth of gay communities over the same period, and to suggest that the success of both are interdependent. Whatever else has happened, it is clear in 1996 that the gay communities have emerged as larger, more vigorous and growing, if depleted of their early gay liberation leadership.

The Gay & Lesbian Mardi Gras may be the brightest moment in an assemblage of dynamic activity. But there is also flourishing publishing, film, drama, dance and performance of various kinds. Significant gay commercial development in the Oxford Street area of Sydney and to a lesser extent in Melbourne has occurred, marking definite gay and lesbian precincts. Openly gay candidates run in local and state elections. A considerable inclusion of gay ideas (for want of a better word) has occurred in mainstream culture—reviews of gay writing, both fiction and non-fiction, and feature articles on gay culture in mainstream press and television. Significant gay and HIV/AIDS exhibitions in major galleries have their origins in the courage of gay curators and artists (e.g. Gott 1994), but draw strength from the seriousness of HIV/AIDS overwhelming residual homophobia in many artistic and intellectual circles, where the loss of creative performers, writers, musicians, producers, editors, painters, poets and academics has been alarming.

While the Mardi Gras and some of this magnificence in gay cultural life is uniquely Australian, there is an evident internationality that speaks of something else: a burgeoning supra-national cultural formation, a kind of international gay community complete with travel networks and tour agents, accommodation and social/sexual activity guides, numerous information superhighway links on the Internet, and a definite political agenda on civil and human rights and HIV/AIDS recognisable from country to country. This international community is an astonishing achievement and it takes some time to grasp the complexity of the moves that have created the phenomenon in barely thirty years.

One set of approaches has attempted an understanding, dominated by the notion of gay communities as cultural formations to be explored through historical and political frameworks (e.g. Altman 1979; Duberman et al. 1989; Weeks 1990). Others situate the recent rise of gay communities within more complex analyses of the history of sexuality in the West (e.g. Foucault 1976; Greenberg 1988; Weeks 1985). A third strand of investigation traces the West's fascination—nay, obsession—with homoeroticism through literary and cultural heritage, and postulates an almost structural continuity in representation (e.g. Goldberg 1992; Koestenbaum 1993; Saslow 1986; Sedgwick 1990; Woods 1987). These perspectives are all fascinating and have ended the silence that has surrounded homosexuality (as it came to be known in the late nineteenth century). Although, as Michel Foucault has taught us, that silence was in fact a very loud unyielding scream.

That said, there remains an absence in this remarkable documentation of modern gay life: the absence of sex itself. By this I mean that there is a sense gained in reading these remarkable intellectual accounts that no one actually fucked with anyone else. While a pornographic history can be found in writing and in representation, hugely expanded by the invention of photography and all that followed from that, these more academic accounts would appear to have homosexuality and, more recently 'gay', being generated in heads rather than beds, in intellectuality rather than intercourse, in semantic manoeuvre rather than seminal emission. The old quip used against early gay activists about being 'gay from the neck up' stands unchallenged.

My argument here is for a stronger recognition of sex itself in the construction of gay and of gay community—indeed, of sexuality itself. This is not to gainsay the emphasis on discourse and identity that has dominated the field of inquiry for so long; nor is it a call for a return to the conservative sexological tradition of, say, Masters and Johnson, which has received a significant boost with the onset of HIV/AIDS and the need to monitor sexual behaviour change among gay men. Rather, the argument to centre the action of (homo)sex is a call for a practice-based analysis of sexual identity and gay culture, that is, a notion that in the sexual encounters of men, within their bodies and the sensations they produce, can be found a deeply formative or constructive moment, one that is not merely experienced individually, but is deeply socially and culturally mediated by 'gay' as a collectivity with a historically formed sensibility.

> I was at [a beachside park] late one night. It was warm and the moon was really bright over the headland, and it made the beat look just stunning. I walked round for a bit checking the place out. I always make sure it's safe. There were a few guys around and I saw one really cute one wearing nothing but board shorts and a singlet, bare feet. And I kinda let him know I was interested . . .
> (What exactly did you do to let him know?)
> Well, I walked past once and just briefly looked at him, you know, out of the corner of my eye. Then I walked back past him again and looked for longer and waited to see if he looked back. He did, for just that little bit too long, you know.
> (What do you mean?)
> If they look away quick, you know they're not interested. But if they look a bit longer and meet your eyes and stay looking for a few extra seconds, you know you've got 'em.
> (What happened next?)
> I headed off down the rocks. There's sort of rock steps leading off the path to under where the rocks overhang. You can't be seen by anyone unless they know where to look. I've had sex there before. I checked back to see if he was following and waited to see him move to come after me. Then I went to this part of the overhang where there's a flat rock you can sit on. I sat on it with my hand sort of just holding my crotch and waited. He came down and stood a bit away near the overhang and looked at me for a long time and I looked back and sort of rubbed my lunch a bit, as a signal, you know.

85

(What happened then? Can you tell the rest of the story?)

Well, we did this a bit and then the guy slowly opened his fly. It was Velcro and you can always tell when they open their flies when they're Velcro [laughter]. It's a dead giveaway. Anyway, he slid his hand inside his pants and started playing with himself. He had a hardon, you could see that as plain as day. I did the same and changed position on the rock so he could see me, you know, opened my legs a bit, sort of face on. You're enjoying this, aren't you?

(All in the name of science. Do go on.)

Well, I played with myself and then slowly pulled my cock out of my pants and started rubbing myself a bit. He could see my dick easily. But he still didn't come over, you know, he sort of waited there, playing hard to get, sort of, and I thought: 'Right, you bastard, let's see how good you really are.'

(What do you mean?)

Well, he was playing poker. You know what I mean? Upping the stakes, making it more, sort of, not just exciting, ah, more tense and more titillating by holding off and going slowly. Fine by me!

(What did you do?)

Well, I thought I'd see just how far he was prepared to go, so I slowly took my shirt off. I was only wearing a tee shirt and jeans and thongs. No jocks. I never wear jocks to the beat; too hard to get them on again if you need to in a hurry. Anyway, so I took off the shirt and he then did the same a few minutes later, all the time playing with himself inside his pants. Me—I'm waving my cock around like it was semaphore, you know! [laughter] Then he undid his shorts and let them drop, stepped out of them and stood there stark naked in the moonlight. I was on the rock; it was under cover a bit, you see, but he was still out in the open a bit. And he just stood there and stroked his thing slowly in full view and looked at me. Fuck! By this time I was really hot and ready for anything, so I stood up on the rock and stripped off and we faced each other naked like, I dunno, like um, like not boxers, but like, shit, who knows? Anyway at that point he walked toward me and I slid off the rock and we did it there and then in the middle of the rocks.

(What did you do? I warned you I was going to ask explicit questions?)
Yeah, you did, didn't you. We fucked. (Straight away?) No. We kissed first, and rubbed and wanked, and then we sucked each other for a while, and then I fucked him until he came and then he fucked me until I did. It was great; a long, smooth, slow fuck, me bending over the rock. And then we kissed, again real slow and deep, you know, and he got dressed and took off up the rocks and disappeared. I got dressed and left. Never seen him there again.
(Did you ask him his name or anything?)
No, we never spoke. (Not a word?) No, didn't need to.

This account comes from a much larger study of gay men undertaken during the HIV epidemic in Australia (Dowsett 1996). At first glance the tale may affront. Gay men invading public spaces for sexual encounters often arouse anger and fear among the non-gay and occasionally provoke police intervention. It seems to prove all that is meant, but not always directly said, in terms such as 'anonymous', 'casual' or 'promiscuous' sex. But a second reading reveals that this so-called anonymous or impersonal sex is anything but emotionally cold and uninvolving. There is a real connection between these men: they kiss 'real slow and deep'. The relation may be different from what is conventionally expected from sex between lovers; but are these men less than lovers for their silence? A deep reading of one's partner is required for this kind of pleasure. A shared knowledge and awareness underpins the choreography of the encounter, a sharing between all men who pursue such pleasure. The engagement in such sexual moments speaks of a multi-textured mutuality, a joint pleasuring that contrasts with the more common accounts of men's selfishness in, say, heterosex. This mutuality extends to the physical. The very reciprocity of the sodomy available only in male-to-male sex demands a different reading of penetration from one where the penis by definition dominates.

The sexual satisfaction available in such encounters is not simply a direct product of orgasm, although that counts a fair bit. Such encounters are sexually fulfilling for both partners.

Each is sexually validated by their success in performing well physically and emotionally. The moment is a highly charged one, and the elaboration of the ritual carefully draws on previous experiences and recognised processes and elements. But the *frisson* derives from the overall event, not just the sex itself. The possibility of such complex satisfactions becomes a central feature of such sexual adventuring, an adventuring that requires considerable skill and determination.

Learning these skills is part of the training sought and received by almost all gay men, a training secured in gay men's familiarity with the pleasures available in their own bodies. The significance of such sexual training and skill-building lies in producing sexually proficient men in sexually vital bodies. Successful encounters such as that just described demand men not only proficient in mutual pleasuring but also skilled in negotiation beyond sexual technique. There is a significant lore to be learned about male erotics, the sensuality of the specifically masculine, the similarities and differences in sexual pleasure between men, the seeking of the self in another and recognising the other within.

In this sense, homosexuality is made in sex, in the endlessly recurring encounters of men exploring in many different contexts the unique possibilities of male bodies-in-sex. The uniqueness is not confined to the penis, that much berated and over-scrutinised sex organ, but also includes a more dispersed eroticism, involving the anus, the hands and the lips. Indeed, in the encounter just described the whole body, the gaze upon it and the choreography of the encounter itself contribute to the success of the event.

In reading much contemporary gay history and sexuality theory, the reader could be forgiven for thinking this concupiscent collision of men's bodies was a figment of a demented sexologist's mind. Even in the political histories of Gay Liberation there is little evidence of sex going on. It is as if gay men (and lesbians for that matter) did little else but attend meetings, rallies and demonstrations, and write political and theoretical tracts. In fact, there was a lot of fucking going on, and it is important to say so! What's more, there were all those other gay men who weren't in Gay Liberation anyway . . .

In such bodies-in-sex, identities are also formed: knowing the sexual self is also recognising one's body-in-sex. Knowing others as gay is as much about a recognition of what their bodies can and might do or have done, as it is about a sense of belonging, a solidarity, or commonly shared understandings. In this sense, it has to be realised that the ongoing project of making gay identities, of making gay communities, is also occurring in and on the bodies of gay men.

This is no simple claim about sex. Rather, it seeks to place all that sex and all that other overtly sexual activity—cruising for partners, seeking brilliant encounters in parks and public toilets, visiting saunas for maximised pleasures and partners—squarely at the heart of the construction of gay community. Add to that all the sex happening in what would more readily be identified as gay relationships and a larger picture emerges. This collective formation of sexual culture can be explored at many levels, and there is no dispute here with the discursive, the theoretical, the historical or the cultural. Yet experience can often reveal much more about, and different modes of, that formation than theory can tell us on its own. Accounts of sexual experience do offer an opportunity to examine social processes, and yet so few accounts exist outside biography and fiction in the now-mammoth literature that documents gay community. In the era of HIV/AIDS, by virtue of the consciously pursued changes to (homo)sexual practices that it has demanded, these once secretive and privatised processes of sexual construction of culture have become readily available to scrutiny. It is time to go back and rewrite gay history—this time with the sweat, bump and grind in it.

Sex must be added to gay history's notion of the construction of gay community as a sexual community, and rather more literally than in John D'Emilio's original formulation (1983). This addition is not merely an erotic icing on the cultural cake; it argues for a sexual construction of sociality and culture. It argues that bodies are central to the structuring of gay life, not as scripted actors or as recipients of discourse, but as sensate flesh, smeared and imbibed body fluids, yearning and sweating limbs, orgasmic genitals and shattered psyches creating the collectively produced possibility of endless pleasure that is gay community.

When Ian Roberts' glorious body inserted itself wittingly at the centre of Australian gay men's representations and fantasies in early 1995, he again claimed men's bodies as beautiful and played at the leading edge of a growing if confused discourse on the male body as desirable. Roberts could do so unambiguously as a professional footballer, as that exemplar of hegemonic masculinity. But in revealing his nude male body to the world he shifted that body from desiring to desirable, *passively* letting it be gazed upon. With his sexual interests undeclared at that time, and by offering his body first to a gay magazine, Roberts placed his passive body at the centre of the gay community's active gaze. In this, Roberts publicly sanctioned gay men's gaze on all men's bodies, re-situating it at the direct centre rather than on the furtive margins.

This has changed the stakes in 'gay', which to date have deployed declarations of gayness as difference, as distinction. Roberts's deliberate sexual ambiguity at that time embodied the (homo)sexual possibilities in all men's bodies. He suggested that gay bodies were not *other* at all; they might be right next to you in the showers after footy, or clutching at your shorts in the scrum. When he finally 'came out' as gay, the gay community could notch up one for its side and, with delight, watch the squirming sports commentators accommodate a hero turning over, as it were. But it is not just Roberts' homosexuality that unsettled their boys-own game of masculinity; his coming-out simply finessed a sequence of events in which he repositioned the very concepts male, man, masculine, and gay. During 1995 Ian Roberts not only newly embodied the potentiality of *being* gay, but increasingly intimated that he might also be *doing* gay, declaring that when push comes to shove, it's the body that counts.

7
A short history of facial hair

DAVID McDIARMID[1]

I'm a visual artist, I'm middle class, I'm a pervert, and I was diagnosed HIV+ in 1986. I grew up in Melbourne, but came out in Sydney in the early seventies. I was part of the Stonewall generation—consciousness-raising groups, zaps and bad haircuts. I moved to New York in 1979 in search of men, art and sex. The city I left nine years later was a nightmare. The acronyms in our discourse went from NSU, MDA, PCP, THC, F/F and V/A, through GRID, to aids, CMV, PCP and KS. I'd like to talk about my life as a sick queen, with and without facial hair.

In 1965 I had sex with a man for the first time. It was a Saturday night, I was thirteen and I was horny. I walked around the Fitzroy Gardens for hours until I got into the front seat of a blue Valiant driven by a man with a hairy chest wearing Aramis. My first hand-job, and the first time I'd ever shot a load. I got crabs the next year. I had a Mod haircut.

In 1972 I was involved in organising Sydney Gay Liberation. We ran a drop-in centre, held demonstrations, kiss-ins, conferences and dances in municipal Town Halls. We were

---

1   This piece was originally written as a speech for the forum 'HIV: towards a paradigm' at the Positive Living Centre, Melbourne, 19 April 1993. David McDiarmid died in may 1995. 'A Short History of Facial Hair' is reproduced here with the kind permission of the executor of his estate.

cousins of the Women's Liberation Movement—we believed that 'the personal is political', and that to 'come out' as proud lesbians and gay men was central to our liberation. I got gonorrhoea. I had a curly Afro and a terrible beard. I worked as a community artist—designing posters, badges, flyers and banners.

In 1976 I began exhibiting in galleries. My work was concerned with questions of identity, culture, history and homosex. It celebrated and critiqued the flowering of gay consciousness as we knew it then. It was both personal and political. If my work was reviewed in the 'mainstream press', they would often refer to the 'novelty' of a 'gay artist', both marginalising and fetishising in one flourish. A lot of curators who were gay would privately support my work, yet felt publicly compromised by the fear of association. The notion of a 'gay mafia' was born to discredit, divide and conquer. I was accused of producing ghetto art for a specialised audience. I replied: 'So what?' I also washed dishes in a gay disco in Sydney. It had an illuminated dancefloor like the one in *Saturday Night Fever*, and the queens wore body shirts and flares. One night I noticed a cluster of men dancing together who wore check shirts, 501s and military haircuts. They were Sydney's first taste of clones, and they were members of a gender-fuck troupe from L.A. called the Cycle Sluts. Sydney would never be the same again. 'Haughtiness' was replaced by 'attitude'. The politics of butch had begun. I got syphilis. I had my hair cut short.

In 1979 I was living in New York, working as a hustler to pay the rent, and having a ball. A typical week began with a job fucking a closeted Texas oil baron at the Plaza Hotel, followed by a trip down to the waterfront for some recreational sex, followed by a few hours dancing at the Anvil which opened at 4 am. I was living in the West Village, in a community of men that took cruising for sex very seriously. I got NSU, amoebas, hepatitis and gonorrhoea. I grew my first moustache.

In 1981 I met a black guy called Robert in a straight porno theatre where men went to have sex with other men. We were lovers for six years. He introduced me to his world of privileged white bourgeois gay men—summers on Fire Island, dancing at the Saint and Studio 54. I introduced him to my world of the street—summers in the East village, dancing at the Paradise Garage (a black and Hispanic club). Our friendship networks—our families—started to overlap. Through Robert I met two gorgeous men—Enno Poersch and Paul Popham. Their lives are described in Randy Shilts' flawed book of the early years of the aids epidemic, *And the Band Played On*. They were part of a group of gay men who formed the Gay Men's Health Crisis in 1982, which published the first guidelines to a new concept—'safe sex'. Enno and Paul had both lost lovers and friends in those early uncertain years of the 'gay plague'—their grief was tangible when I would see them on that Street of Dreams called Christopher in the summer of '83. Yet they refused to be defeated by the unknown. They grieved, but they also organised, they questioned, they raised money—they were an inspiration to many others like myself. And the history of our tribe was in their blue eyes. They were love-gods in the truest sense of the word.

In 1982 my first friend died from aids—Herb Gower. I visited Australia several times and saw gay communities that were similar to those in large North American cities. Queens had travelled, and acquired a taste for big city pleasures—we all turned into porn stars, we took lots of clever drugs, we dressed down and dirty for sex, and dressed up to go dancing—often confusing those sisters whose model for being gay was precious, alcoholic and European. Yet something was vastly different. Gay men in Australia felt aids was an American phenomenon. The epidemic had not touched their lives. None of my Australian friends knew anyone who'd got it—it happened 'over there' to queens who used poppers and lived in the fast lane. I felt traumatised, and alone in my grief. I shaved off my moustache.

In Australia there was a great deal of misinformation and denial—I can remember getting rejected several times in bars when they discovered I lived in the 'Plague city'. Safe sex meant not fucking with an American. I grew another beard. In New

York at that time, safe sex meant no sex. There was a new 'condition' discovered, known as sexual compulsion. Men who'd previously been perfectly healthy sluts like myself were suddenly labelled 'sex addicts', ripe for 12-step programs. Cruising became a quaint historic activity. Manhattan became like Geelong in the '50s, with little eye contact, lots of guilt, but some fabulous haircuts. I was blond'.

Around 1983 I started painting images related to the aids epidemic. Those first images were sombre, sentimental and full of yearning. I often used a traditional Valentine's Day message: 'Hand and heart, shall never part, when you see this, remember me.' My friends and fuck buddies were dying horrible deaths. I was convinced I would be dead within two years. I was calm and rational. I felt sad for two years. Then I had an HIV antibody test. I was positive. I grew a moustache.

Despite the probability of getting it—the who, when and where of it—I was shocked. It was one thing to assume I would be positive, and another to hear it from a doctor. My relationship with Robert had finished the year before, my chances for a green card were very doubtful, I had no health insurance, New York was a graveyard, and I had a heavy cocaine habit—real Sally Jesse Raphael material. So I kept doing coke for another year, and *then* I moved back to Sydney to die. That year I grew four moustaches, three beards and started growing my hair.

In 1988 I started work at the Sydney Gay & Lesbian Mardi Gras as a workshop artist and art director. One of my key functions, apart from attending too many tedious meetings, was to work with community groups in developing a public profile for the annual Parade in February. Typically a gaggle of queens would arrive wanting to print some T-shirts, and leave wearing tutus, fired up with visions of gigantic swans made out of shopping bags. I worked with just about every group associated with aids in Sydney, each with different priorities.

In 1990 I designed a concept which combined all the disparate groups from ACON (the aids Council of New South Wales). The theme colours were white and silver, with giant umbrellas on poles, each with a white shirt hanging from it. The umbrellas and shirts were inspired by African funeral processions. These were interspersed with banners identifying the individual groups such as the beat outreach, the needle exchange, women and aids, etc. Placed centrally in this group, which spread for two blocks, were two floating structures, lit from within and inspired by a scene from Fellini's *Juliet of the Spirits*. The procession suggested an image of the dead being sheltered and celebrated. Everyone participating carried percussion instruments, and invented their own rhythms. The effect was a sort of tribal Vegas disco funeral.

In 1990 I had an exhibition of watercolours and mosaics entitled 'Kiss of Light'. I felt worn out by the past two years as a community art slave, and wanted to process my feelings, alone. The work came out spontaneously over a period of months. I had started taking AZT, Ketaconazole, Zovirax and Bactrim, and felt oppressed by the medical process. I went to a public hospital clinic in Sydney, disagreed with the doctors and made friends with some nurses. Looking around the waiting room each fortnight, I watched the other men deteriorate. I had two bouts of shingles, and felt I was on a continuum of infections that would finish in my death. I grew a goatee and long sideburns.

In 1991 I was commissioned by ACON to design a series of safe sex and safe use posters aimed at the gay male community in Sydney. These posters received a lot of attention around the country, and worked in a number of spheres—aids education, pornography, art and community bonding. Despite their apparent success, I feel that the nuances of emotion and language achieved with the Kiss of Light work had been diluted within the confines and imperatives of the aids industry. However, this is more than compensated for by the access that has been achieved by the campaign. The audience for a gallery exhibition is extremely small and privileged.

In 1992 my most satisfying experience as a community artist was with the HIV Living group from ACON, a bunch of HIV+ men and women, who wanted to be fabulous (who doesn't?). It almost didn't matter what we created—our public coming out as HIV+ was inherently exhilarating. But I wanted to push it further, as usual. I was inspired by a puppet created for the Trinidad carnival, the skeleton from the Mexican Day of the Dead. But in the context of aids, it became an empowering icon. Death controlled by a rowdy menace of beauty contestants wearing sashes that read Paula Pentamadine, Doris Dementia, Kathy Karposi. Our group became divided about using this idea, but those who liked it really liked it; because of their passion and commitment we went ahead. It was an extremely confronting experience for everyone, including the 400 000 unsuspecting suckers who watched the parade that year. I wore a moustache.

This year I published a book called *Toxic Queen*, which is like a cultural history of fagdom. It's also a textbook of '90's attitude. As Kenny Everett said last month when asked by a journalist if he had aids, 'Yes, I'm HIV+, isn't everyone?' I wanted to move the work out of the art temples and galleries, and into a different, more accessible arena.

My priority as an artist has always been to record and celebrate our lives. Having lived through an extraordinary time of redefinition and deconstruction of identities, from camp to gay to queer; and seeing our lives and histories marginalised every day, we all have a responsibility to speak out. To bang the tribal drums of the jungle telegraph—'I'm here, girlfriend; what's new?' We've always created these languages, as we've created and shaped our identities. I hear our lives in many forms—coded, verbal, visual, physical and aural. It might be the anticipation and release of hearing Sylvester's voice on the dancefloor at 7 am while the best tits in Sydney work your very last nerve. It might be the language of the fierce divas in *Paris is Burning* as they 'read' and 'shade' their sisters into oblivion. It might be seen in the sublime gaze of the gods in Tom of Finland's drawings. Or the ACT-UP T-shirt that says, EARN YOUR ATTITUDE. Or an obituary that reads, MOODY BITCH DIES OF AIDS.

We just have to trust our inner queen's instinct. *Oh*, and I shaved off my moustache last week . . .

8
Degrees of separation: lesbian separatist communities in northern New South Wales, 1974-95

JUDITH ION

Across the centuries the question of what is female sexuality has produced a wide range of responses; the pendulum has swung (and occasionally paused) between 'woman as nymphomaniac' and 'woman as frigid'. What has remained constant across time is male control of female sexuality and the treatment of 'woman as object' (Jackson 1984). In theory, the sexual revolution of the sixties shifted the emphasis of sex from procreation to enjoyment. In practice, some feminists have argued, the 'revolution' merely freed up male access to women—it was a revolution for men (Morgan 1978; Steinem 1980; Wagner 1982). Women began the monumental task of redressing this imbalance throughout the sixties and seventies as the Women's Liberation Movement came into its own. Second wave feminism witnessed women organising explicitly on the basis of sex and sexuality. One strand of the diverse agenda which typified seventies feminism was a merging of feminism and lesbianism that was based in a vision of a separatist utopia. The seventies saw an explosion of lesbian separatist communities throughout the Western world as women sought to create and live in such utopias.

This chapter takes a fleeting look at the separatist ideology that emerged in the seventies and tells the story of three interconnected women's lands in New South Wales: the Mountain, the Valley and Herland.[1] It is based on my own experiences of the separatist culture, and on several conversations I had with a woman who has devoted many years of her life to the land(s).[2]

Separatist beginnings

In many ways separatism has always existed as the hidden underbelly of respectable white middle-class feminism. Separatism is a source of embarrassment referred to in hushed or contemptuous tones by non-separatist feminists; it is a term that is frequently and unconditionally aligned with man-hating, hairy-legged, overall-clad lesbians; it is a position criticised for its perceived long-term impossibility in terms of population regeneration; it is a strategy criticised for its perceived racist, classist, ageist, lesbianist, able-bodiest underpinnings. In short, the notion of separatism has acted as a useful scapegoat for mainstream feminism since the early seventies (Hoagland 1989, p. 56). And for 25 years separatists have generally accepted that position. They have chosen to turn their focus inwards instead of engaging in a direct battle with respectable feminism. And yet, even among separatists, there is no consensus on what separatism means (Atkinson 1974; Hess et al. 1980; Hoagland 1989; Frye 1983; Treblicot 1986). Add to that the fact that many women who do not consider themselves separatist lead lives that others may label 'separatist' and the complexities surrounding the issue begin to unfold.

US lesbian theorist Julia Penelope offers one definition of separatist as:

---

[1] Named after the utopian novel *Herland* written in 1915 by US feminist Charlotte Perkins Gilman.

[2] Throughout the chapter this woman is referred to by the pseudonym Wicca. Any direct quotes attributed to her come from both verbal and written interactions between us. While I have tried to be accurate in presenting Wicca's story as she told it to me, I am ultimately responsible for any errors, oversights, or misinterpretations presented here.

A Lesbian (virtually always) who believes that men, individually and collectively, oppress women, that every man benefits directly and indirectly, from birth, from the oppression of women, that the rule of men, patriarchy, is a social structure designed to perpetuate the subjugation of women and the dominance of men, and that all females must withdraw their energies from men and cease to nurture and take care of them if women's oppression is to cease (Penelope 1986, pp. 39–40).

US lesbian philosopher Marilyn Frye approaches the question of separatism from a more fluid perspective, analysing it as a multitude of actions and behaviours based on a conscious separation by women from men. According to Frye, all acts of separation constitute a threat to patriarchal society: 'When women separate (withdraw, break out, regroup, transcend, shove aside, step outside, migrate, say no), we are simultaneously controlling access and defining. We are doubly insubordinate, since neither of these is permitted' (Frye 1983, p. 107). By shifting the focus of definition from identity or beliefs to actions and behaviours, Frye creates the potential for a multiplicity of separatist positions. She provides a useful means by which to classify as separatist a range of women, actions and behaviours that would usually fall outside its narrowly perceived scope. For the purposes of this chapter, I accept Julia Penelope's qualifier that separatists are virtually always lesbians and I also use Frye's continuum theory to include: self-identified lesbian separatists who live on the land and who consciously have no contact (or as little as possible) with males; those who refuse the term 'separatist' for themselves but who live and embrace a politics based on the separation of the sexes; as well as those in either group who welcome contact with specific males (boy children, brothers, fathers, neighbours, etc.).

In the US a vast amount of material has been published by lesbian separatists for lesbian separatists. Occasionally that material has slipped into the feminist mainstream, but for the most part the separatist tradition has flourished within its own context. Separatist events, women's lands/lesbian lands, women's gatherings and festivals that have been discussed, debated and documented in the US have been devoured by separatist lesbians worldwide. All too often this has meant that the histories of lesbian separatist culture outside of the US have not been written: there is very little written on the history of lesbians in Australia and next to nothing specifically documenting separatist lifestyles. Yet separatist lands do exist in Australia and have done so for at least as long as their American counterparts. The multi-faceted stories of these women and their culture remain hidden, stories they themselves have had little desire to tell those outside the separatist web. And with good reason.

Take for example the *Sunday Telegraph*'s sensational story in 1987 about the northern New South Wales women's land. Entitled 'The Garden of Eden where men are banned: haven from abuse where the male is feared more than nuclear war', the article is reminiscent of that unfortunate style of wildlife reporting where 'civilised man' discovers a new and rare species:

> It was from a grassy cliff on the edge of the mountain rainforest that we first spotted the Amazons . . . we were now in Amazon territory. We had been warned they would be unfriendly, that this mountain tribe fiercely protected its territory and carried guns and knives. The locals said they would be naked, and filthy. But most of all, they stressed, don't trespass on their land in the company of men (*Sunday Telegraph* 1987, pp. 16–17).

With the tone thus set, reporters Candace Sutton and Linda Duberley do an admirable job of misrepresenting every aspect of the land and the women who inhabit it. Complete with photographs (including the feature shot of a group of so-called Amazons, none of whom has ever been seen on the land), this is a superb example of inaccurate and libellous reporting. It is certainly a good illustration of why the women usually steer clear of telling their stories. More accurately, rather than supporting the headline that the women fear men more than nuclear war, the article actually goes a good way towards illustrating the fear men have of sexually independent and politically motivated groups of women.

Women's land, New South Wales: the Mountain, the Valley and Herland

About five years ago I visited the women's land in New South Wales for the first time. The land was isolated, the road little more than a muddy, winding track. It was rugged, it was beautiful. Being on the land provided me with a glimpse of the utopia that inspired it, of a world that could exist. I was awed by the environmentally sensitive architecture hidden across the land: the beauty of wood and glass next to nature; the originality of design; the fact that women and women alone had designed and built every house, hut, lean-to, yurt, tepee. I was touched to see the horses, rescued from a glue factory fate, running wild. I was impressed with the orchard and the expansive (if a little wild) vegetable garden.

But my strongest memory of the land has little to do with the landscape. It was my first inkling of an existence not hedged with fear. I discovered what it was to step beyond the knowledge that the stranger in the bushes, the loud footsteps behind me on the street, the heavy breather on the telephone and the bogeyman of my childhood are all variations on a single theme: man. I experienced how it felt to walk and sleep alone at night without fear of the (bogey) man. Whatever this secret land was about, it wasn't solely about hating men or exploring sexuality or allocating blame; it wasn't solely about a future based on separation; and perhaps most importantly, it wasn't about being a victim.

The mountain women and the locals

Over the past two decades, many hundreds of women have visited and lived on the land. They have been variously ridiculed, despised, harassed, tolerated, admired, liked and sometimes even respected by the local population who refer to them as 'the mountain women'. The constant stream of mountain women through the local town has seen the place come to terms with all manner of things usually outside the

101

realm of small country town living: mohawks, shaved heads, dreadlocks, unusual body-piercing, all manner of clothes and the open intimacy of women for women.

In the early days of the land(s) many women claimed social security benefits which necessitated regular visits to the local town. Receiving unemployment payments enabled the women to devote their time to working on the land (building, growing vegetables and fruit, clearing lantana, etc.). As the years went by and the harsh reality of life on the land took its toll, more and more women chose to work part-time in the nearby towns. This led to houses being rented and bought in town and to larger numbers of women becoming part-time rather than full-time land dwellers. In addition to this, in the late eighties the Department of Social Security (DSS) attempted to get as many mountain women off social security as possible. If their mission was to rid the local area of the women, they failed miserably. The women flooded the local job market and came to hold a number of key positions in the community as doctors, radiologists, nurses, carpenters, sexual assault officers, disc jockeys, even within the DSS itself.

Today, the Mountain and the Valley have been paid off and only a couple of thousand dollars remain owing on Herland. The lands together total close to 2660 acres (1077 hectares), making it by far the largest women's land I have heard of. It is a substantial area and that a fluid community of women, in spite of their many differences, have for over twenty years lived, loved, fucked, played, worked, survived, celebrated and purchased this land with one another is a truly remarkable achievement.

The Mountain: also known as Amazon Acres, Kennedy's Mountain and Mount F.[3]

Amazon Acres, as it was first known, was described in an advertisement run in the *Sydney Women's Liberation Newsletter* in early 1974:

---

[3] Full name is abbreviated here and throughout the chapter at the request of Wicca.

Amazon Acres, Mount F.
Amazon Acres is 1000 acres of red fertile earth, the undulating plateau of Mount F. . . . It has permanent water rising in natural springs, and these feed several creeks, one of which runs across the plateau, and two of the creeks have beautiful waterfalls. There are two shacks, fairly strong and OK temporarily. Other huts will probably be built soon, including a large round stone house. About 40–50 acres have been cleared and a few vegetables have been planted in hopeful anticipation.

The price is $30 000—the owner wants cash and has agreed on $15 000 at the end of February and the other $15 000 at the end of March. Sisters in Sydney and Melbourne have already promised most of the first $15 000 and a deposit of $3000 has already been paid.

What we want to do is have a women's farm, to be increasingly as self-sufficient as possible, a place where women can go to get stronger, as a break from the struggle with male culture. The mountain is good for farming, very beautiful and very remote. No through road, it lies at the top of the mountain, and the road is fairly rough.

The farm is open to all women (and no men) who want to live there or just to visit.

If you want to be part of Amazonia—if you want to contribute money (very important), equipment, ideas or your presence—come to a meeting for Amazon Acres at the Women's House on Saturday 9th February at 1pm (*Sydney Women's Liberation Newsletter* 1974, p. 5).

Three women signed Amazon Acres' original lease but between thirty and forty women actually lived there. The money for it was raised by various women's communities throughout Australia and internationally and the land was considered to be 'owned' by them all. It was run as an open women's land where *all* women and girls were welcome to live or visit.

The Mountain had two old loggers' huts on it where the women lived in the early days. They later built a giant hexagonal structure which functioned as a communal space and an assortment of caravans and shelters appeared where women slept. Communal living was a high priority with the women, who came together to prepare food, to eat, to celebrate, to make music, to plan, plant and tend vegetable gardens big enough to feed them all. It was an idyllic time, especially in the light of what was to come.

The period around 1981–83 marked the beginning of the first major division among the women on the land, the main issue revolving around degrees of separatism/separation. The big question was whether boys and men were welcome as visitors on the Mountain with restricted access, full access or no access. The ultimate split coincided with a prolonged period of hardship where access to the mountain had been purposely blocked by locals who had chain-sawed trees across the road. This meant that the women were often forced to carry in heavy supplies on foot. The physical strain of this wore a lot of women out and the conflict over 'the man question'[4] proved to be the final straw for many of them. Some of those women who were politically opposed to male access were too tired to fight the issue; they either left the land for good, dropped their 'women-only' stance and stayed on the Mountain, or fled to the nearby Valley which had in the meantime been purchased by a new group of women.

The Mountain sent out word on the Australian and international women's grapevine (by word of mouth and in various women-only publications) that it was 'closing its doors' for twelve months in order to attempt restructuring. In many ways the Mountain never fully recovered from this turbulent time. After the proposed restructuring, which eventually saw the

---

[4] My use of the term 'the man question' is meant as a tongue-in-cheek reminder of times past where men debated and sparred over 'the woman question'. The separatist/separation issue on the land often came down to 'men' versus 'no men'—and the ensuing debates were not totally removed from those conducted over the years by men as to whether women should have access to the (male) public realm and those activities pertaining to it, such as the right to education, to the vote, to jobs, etc.: 'women' versus 'no women'. On the land, women who advocated no male access whatsoever were the separatists and those whose approach was more flexible (access for specific men, access for any man trusted and vouched for by a woman living on the land, access for male neighbours . . .) were the non-separatists.

introduction of shareholders and a collective structure,[5] only one woman out of the original thirty or so remained on the Mountain.

The Valley

The Valley is 660 acres (267 hectares) of land with a creek and an orchard. An influx of women from the Melbourne Powerhouse Women's Theatre Group began squatting in the Valley in the late 1970s, making use of the existing structures which included a house, a dairy and a feed shed. Gradually they were joined by others: women who wanted to escape city life; women who were outlaws; women from the US, Europe, Australia, New Zealand; women escaping domestic violence; women with children; women who had no place else to go; poor women; Aboriginal women; anarchist women; environmentalists; peace activists. Most of these women did not call themselves separatists.

Given that the fight about male access to the Mountain did eventually spill across into the Valley, it is useful at this point to refer back to the earlier definitions of separatism given by Penelope and Frye. By momentarily side-stepping individual self-definition as required by Penelope's definition of a separatist, and by utilising Frye's continuum theory, it is possible to classify the actions of these women as separatist while remaining respectful of their non-separatist self-definition. Such a distinction is useful in understanding how it is possible to have a separatist vs non-separatist division in what is, according to the continuum theory (as well as mainstream society), a separatist culture.

The Valley was purchased for $30 000 by the women sometime around 1980, soon after the owner of the land and his mate had tried unsuccessfully to evict them. The two men went on a rampage with a gun and an axe they took from

---

5   This was after Herland had earlier set up successfully as a co-op with shareholders despite the onslaught of criticism levelled at them for such an elitist and patriarchal system.

the women's woodpile, destroying everything in their path, chopping down the orchard, killing chickens and terrorising the women they had cornered.[6] One of the women managed to get away and went for help. The police eventually arrived and removed the men. While the women had been content with squatting the land, after this violent incident they decided it was too dangerous and set about arranging to buy it.

The actual purchase of the Valley saw few changes in the day-to-day lives of the women living there. The main house functioned as a communal area for eating and gatherings and, in the rainy season, for sleeping. Days were spent on subsistence, creating and community building: tending massive vegetable gardens, building horse yards, horse riding, digging shitters (toilets), carting water from the creek, walking, visiting other women, meditating, talking, healing, celebrating solstices, making music, getting high, fucking, sleeping, fixing cars, reading tarot, preparing meals, writing, going into town for supplies, eating, doing astrological charts, building makeshift shelters, washing up, swimming, organising dole payments, chopping wood. There were around thirty women living there permanently with any number of transients, travellers and international visitors. Most women slept outside by choice but some put up temporary tarps and shelters while others slept in the dairy and the feed shed.

A fundraising event was held to meet the first payment for the Valley. It was a week long drumming and healing celebration which was attended by a great many women from the local area, interstate and overseas. Among them was Wicca who, living in nearby Nimbin, was finding herself increasingly starved of the company of lesbians and the communal lifestyle she craved. Fed up with the all-too-often misogynist alternative lifestyle, and after hearing rumours of a women's band called Clitoris and a six-foot (180 cm) Amazon musician on the land, Wicca decided to hitchhike there. When she eventually walked out into a clearing, seemingly in the middle of nowhere, she

---

6 Over the past 21 years sporadic violent attacks on the women have occurred, something I was blissfully unaware of on my visit there.

was met by the sight of a huge bonfire surrounded by women drumming and dancing. The drumming did not cease for the whole week, night or day. After years of searching Wicca had finally found what she was looking for: a spiritual community of women free from men and male values; a space where women could work towards gaining control of their lives; where they could interact with one another, help each other, be alone but safe; where they could live a self-sustained country life as part of a lesbian community. Returning to Nimbin, she packed up her stuff and headed back to the land. While little remained of the gathering she had so recently witnessed, Wicca remembers this period as joyous: 'Little remained of the tribe and high energy, however other womyn returned and times were good for a year until the debates and fights up the mountain started . . . At this point there were still lots of women around and lots of great things happening. I was still idealistic and visionary and this didn't fade until some years later.'

Throughout this period the Valley had been fairly structureless but inevitably 'the man question' did rear its ugly head and a firm decision on the issue needed to be made. According to Wicca, most of the original women squatters 'wanted boys and some men to be able to come and were upset when all us separatists, who arrived from 1980 onwards, out-voted them and *No Males* became the new status quo'. Despite this outcome, Wicca remembers the decision as being more of a 'numbers game' than a secure decision. Eventually, after it became clear that the dissension was irresolvable, she and two other women decided to break with the Valley and to establish yet another land elsewhere.

Herland

The primary aim of these three women, who all identified as separatists, was to establish a farm for women and girls only. They found land nearby and began organising meetings for interested women as well as negotiating for the land and fundraising. About thirty women became involved in the new project which was to be run as a co-op based on $1000 shares. Herland, of 1000 acres (405 hectares), was purchased for $75 000 in 1982, along with a flat-top 4WD truck, bringing the total to $80 000. A great many of the women who bought shares in the land did not live there, including some German women who had never even been to Australia. After purchase, thirteen women lived permanently on Herland, all of whom had previously been involved in the Valley or the Mountain.

Soon thereafter the construction of a house on Herland marked the beginning of a building boom across all three lands. Building began in 1983 at the beginning of the rainy season which, true to its name, rained on for some eight months. It took close on twelve months to complete the first house. Herland was the least accessible of the lands and getting building materials there proved to be very much a labour of love. Sometimes women trekked to Herland from the nearby lands to lend a hand. They wanted to learn how to build and cherished the opportunity to learn in a supportive women's environment. Eventually the house was finished and the women dispersed back to the Mountain, back to the Valley, in some cases back to urban life. Their newly acquired skills and inspiration saw more women building their own houses (always helped by other women).

Two years after the original Herland house went up, Wicca decided the time had come to build her own place. She had lived under a tree until this time. Her much loved tree spot became her kitchen and her room, a yurt, she built a little way up the hill. In remembering the isolation of her chosen spot, Wicca recalls thinking that, had she screamed as loud as she could no one would have heard her. It made for a hard slog lugging all the building materials over two creeks and up a hill. She put hundreds of woman-hours into building her yurt, helped along the way by many other willing women. Like so many of the shelters across the lands, Wicca's yurt contained the passionate commitment of these women to a different way of life.

Wicca remembers this time as peaceful and fulfilling in every possible sense, but it also marked for her the beginning

Wicca's yurt from a distance © Judith Ion

Wicca's yurt hidden in the rugged terrain of Herland
© Judith Ion

of the end. She considers the building boom and its aftermath mark a shift from the communal lifestyle to one more focused on the individual. When women began to cook for themselves in their own kitchens and sleep alone (or with a lover) in their own structures, the sense of community somehow shifted. Eventually, without the regular (impromptu or otherwise) communal campfire gatherings, music making and sense of togetherness that had existed in the early days, life on Herland became an isolating, lonely experience for many women. Many began to question why they were there and, unable to mend the rift, began to drift back to urban life.

From the outset Herland was the most controversial of the lands. The Herland collective was often accused of elitism due to their shareholder co-op structure and their 'women and girls only' stance.[7] In Wicca's words:

> Attacks/criticism of us came mostly from the fact that we were separatists and because we were the first on the land to set up a co-op structure and ask women to pay shares of $1000 each (the Mountain did it after us). And asking women to pay shares was seen as 'Oh! You can't go there unless you pay $1000; how mean' when the reality was quite different. Some women lived there for years and never became a member/paid shares.

According to Wicca, the collective of Herland was mostly made up of working-class women, poor women, and also included at least five women who had parented boys. As self-identified separatists, these women were all passionately committed to the theory and practice of women-only space. The women who had boy children did not treat their male children as surplus baggage to be adopted or fostered out (as reported in the *Sunday Telegraph*). They were often no less committed to their sons than their daughters. They simply wanted the land as a place to retreat to; as a place to create a women-centred community to which they had access when they needed to step away from male-defined culture. Separate

---

7   For a US based account of separatist land accused of 'Nazi' politics by anti-separatist lesbians, see Copper 1981, pp. 320-322.

space did not necessarily equate with a belief in the male as parasite or as mutant (although these views were held by some women). It was in many instances quite simply the desire for a space outside of male culture and male influence. No woman who wanted to stay on Herland was ever turned away for any reason except on the basis of that one cardinal rule—they were expected to respect the land as being for women and girls only.

The Mountain, the Valley and Herland in the mid–1990s: an overview

In the cold light of the mid–1990s, the early vision(s) of these women have faded. The world has survived the seventies: a time when the 'newness' and 'vastness' of nuclear war was overwhelming and the end of civilisation seemed close at hand. Certainly the threat of nuclear war, after the horrors of Vietnam, was what initially inspired many of the women to make connections between men and war and women and the environment and to think about alternative lifestyles more in harmony with nature. This, combined with the thriving Women's Liberation Movement, led many to view the land and other women as the only direction forward. Today, despite the all too numerous signs of the earth in revolt against human interference, 'civilisation' continues to thrive. The urgency of the seventies, the belief in the imminent demise of male-defined civilisation and culture, has somehow lost its edge and its immediacy. This, combined with emotional and physical burn-out from trying to live a utopian vision, has taken its toll on many women.

The realisation that women cannot escape patriarchal conditioning overnight has been a hard lesson to learn. That women in a women-only environment are capable of violence, stealing, and alcohol and drug abuse has been disillusioning and has certainly contributed to the breaking down of a sense of communality and community on the lands. But these have not been wasted years. Women have exchanged skills, have grown in confidence, in strength, in themselves as individuals,

111

in themselves as relational beings. Those who have left the land do so with this hard-earned knowledge and it necessarily feeds into their more recently chosen lifestyles. Many women have chosen to return to an urban life; others have left 'the land' to buy other smaller pieces of land with chosen financial partners, with lovers, by themselves. And a few women remain living full-time on the land. At the beginning of 1995, according to Wicca, there were four women living full-time in the Valley, one on the Mountain, and three on Herland; as well, there are visiting part-timers who have shares in or connections with the land(s) but who live elsewhere (of whom Wicca is one) and the usual stream of local transients and interstate and international travellers.

Regardless of the internal conflicts of each of the lands, regardless of how the different visions turned out, the very fact that this land, open to *all* women, is paid for is an incredible achievement. Many of the lands in the US that have broken down (often for similar reasons to the ones mentioned in this chapter) have not remained in female hands (Cheney 1985). That the Mountain, the Valley and Herland do remain women-owned is cause for celebration. Geographically, the three lands do not border one another but are separated by state forest as well as some land owned by a local woman farmer. As the crow flies, though, they are only a few kilometres apart and despite their different paths over the years they all hold one thing in common: the importance of a space where women can be with women in a variety of ways for a variety of reasons.

It may seem odd that in a book ostensibly about sex there has been little mention of it in this chapter. It's true, there has been no explicit mention of the physical acts of woman-to-woman fucking, only implicit references to woman lovers, to women living, loving and fucking together. No grit. No dirty details. No sweaty bodies, arched backs, sensual mouths. No erotic soundtrack. No discussion of the health risks attached to dirt-filled fingernails. No comments about SM sex, safe sex, vanilla sex. Why? Because these elements were not volunteered by any of the women I spoke to about their experiences on the land. Does that mean they didn't have sex? No. What it means is that talking about sex is not foremost in their minds when it comes to their memories of life on the land. The land was not a fuck-bar where you went to get laid (unless you had totally exhausted all other avenues). Getting to the land was no small feat and there were certainly more accessible places to get a fuck. Sex was an integral part of life on the land but no more so than making sure you had enough to eat and drink. It was part of the fabric but it wasn't the whole fabric. Girls gossiping over breakfast would comment on how noisy so-and-so was last night; some found that an incredible turn-on, others delighted in hearing the moans of other women echo across the valley, others were shocked. In the same way that choosing to live on the land was for many women a decision grounded in escaping patriarchal culture, sexual relations on the land were often about challenging normative heterosexual behaviours, in particular that of monogamy. One women I spoke to who had spent time on the land in the late eighties remembers monogamy and jealousy as being two of the thorns women were trying to remove from their conditioning. She remembers one year a sexual celebration was planned on May 1 for Beltane (an ancient Celtic festival). In celebrating the harvest and fertility about twenty women took part in group sex on the side of the mountain. The theory behind the practice was that on this occasion you could have sex with whoever you liked with no strings attached. The practice was, of course, another story.

Do these women, their lands, their utopian visions, their commitment to the earth and to one another, constitute a sexual culture? Well, if a sexual culture is about fucking and fucking alone, if it revolves solely around having a pool of potential lovers of the same sexual orientation in the same place, then I would say no. However, if the term can be used to describe a culture which implicitly (or explicitly) is built around a common sexuality as *one* of a multitude of diverse, shared commonalities, then I would say yes. The lesbian culture that inspired and led to the creation of women's lands and the multitude of other separatist gatherings and events that continue to exist even now in the 1990s does indeed warrant the label 'sexual culture'.

9
Dangerous desire: lesbianism as sex or politics

KIMBERLY O'SULLIVAN

Within a shared identity as lesbians, women can drastically differ from each other in sexual attitude and sexual practice. Sexuality is complex and often contradictory. Rarely is it acknowledged by lesbians as a whole that our variations of sexual pleasure and desire are as diverse as any other group's.

Until the early 1990s it was rare for a lesbian subject to make it into even the gay press. Intra-lesbian debates, furores and controversies of any kind, particularly about sexuality, remained unreported. The goings-on of that curious foreign species, the lesbian, remained out of male sight and mind, whether in the gay, the straight or the straight alternative (although still largely heterosexual) press. Unreported or not, sexual controversies raged in the lesbian communities where passionate and often bitter ideological battles were fought over dyke hearts, minds and, most of all, bodies.

'Seventies lesbian feminism' has become a nineties shorthand for a conservative, many would argue reactionary, political stance, bogged down in a rose-coloured view of feminism's political heritage. The 1970s has been often glorified as a sort of feminist golden age. This was the era, its protagonists argue, when political purity reached its pinnacle, when women became lesbians as part of the struggle to overthrow the patriarchy and not just to get laid. To such women feminism has been on a grubby downhill slide ever since.

Although the lesbian feminist mantra 'lesbians are everywhere' was regularly recited in the 1970s, the period was in reality a time of great intra-lesbian division within the broad women's movement, with lines firmly drawn and identities strictly defined. The initial split was between those who chose lesbianism as a political position (the 'political lesbian'), and those who believed that their lesbianism was an emotional and sexual state. This position was first articulated in 1970 (Radicalesbians 1971, p. 81), but remains a major division in the 1990s.

For self-described political lesbians, the choice to be a lesbian is based on a political commitment to other women. This is seen by them as a far superior reason than to be a lesbian because one had an overwhelming desire to get another woman's clothes off. Political lesbians downplay the importance of sex in lesbian relationships, with the erotic secondary to the challenge to men's power over women that their lesbianism symbolises. In addition, sexuality is almost universally seen among them as the core of the subordination of women. These political lesbians see their decision to become lesbians as part of a revolutionary activism to overthrow patriarchy. They contrast their lives positively against those lesbians whom they judge to be oversexed, apolitical and ignorant. In extreme cases these other lesbians even get lumped in with heterosexual conservatives.

> It is necessary to address lesbianism as a lifestyle—what has for many come to be a sexual preference without a feminist politics. For one thing, this lesbian lifestyle is preoccupied with sex. Not lesbian sexuality as a political statement, that is, as a challenge to hetero-reality, but lesbian sex as fucking—how to do it, when to do it, what makes it work—in short, how to liberate lesbian libido. Lesbian lifestylers and hetero-conservatives agree on one thing—that for women sex is salvation (Raymond 1991, p. 7).

115

There was, however, another important strand to 1970's feminism which is now rarely acknowledged, a feminism which was sex positive, anti-guilt and where a lot of lively discussion about sex, desire and fantasy took place. Women's sexual fantasies were widely discussed at women's liberation meetings, in feminist collectives, in the feminist press and at conferences. Rape fantasies were a hot topic which initiated numerous passionate discussions. It was particularly brave for women to admit, in a feminist setting, to having what is one of the most frequent, but most taboo, female sexual fantasies. Many women were concerned that such a public admission could be used as an excuse by men to rape women. This was extensively processed in a collective seventies kind of way and a number of interesting positions emerged.

There was a clear acknowledgment that rape fantasies do not mean that women want to be raped. There was an acceptance that, as women's sexuality is so suppressed, the only way most women can fantasise about what they want sexually (without crippling guilt) is to set up scenarios of 'force' where they are absolved of responsibility for whatever happens. Women already felt enough guilt about sex, it was argued; they should not be made to feel any more. Sexual contradictions were recognised as a product of living under patriarchy and, as women certainly weren't to blame for their own oppression, they weren't to blame for their own fantasies, however 'unsavoury'.

Leichhardt Women's Health Centre, a Sydney inner-city feminist clinic much frequented by lesbians, used to run evening courses on women's bodies and sexuality. These consisted of intense discussions about bodies and sexual self-images and always included a genital self-examination. Lying on your back with a mirror between your legs, you'd learn to insert a speculum and, using the light of a torch, look at your own cervix, for most women for the first time. The Centre also printed a leaflet on tips for reducing painful periods, one of which was to have an orgasm. It cheerfully advised that if you don't feel like sex with a partner, use a vibrator, which was strongly recommended for the sexually self-sufficient woman.

The feminist classic, *The New Women's Survival Sourcebook*, urged us:

> Orgasmic sex is an end in itself in contributing to the health and well-being of the individual woman . . . But politically speaking it is a critical means to an end . . . we do believe that a woman who feels strong and powerful rather than vulnerable and powerless is more likely to have the drive and energy and confidence to undertake the tasks which will end her oppression in other dimensions of her life (Grimstad & Rennie 1975, p. 54).

The 1970s also saw great debate around the words 'frigid' and 'nymphomaniac'. There was universal agreement that these derogatory words had to go. Out they went, to be replaced by 'pre-orgasmic' and 'sex-loving'. These new words were part of an extensive feminist analysis which recognised that women were always situated sexually between a rock and a hard place and that part of changing this was to re-invent the language around female sexuality.

The 1970s also saw the beginning of prostitute rights organisations and one mid–70s manifesto began, 'The street walker is the most oppressed *working* woman in . . . society today' (Grimstad & Rennie 1975, p. 20, my emphasis). Sex workers were not divided off by some curtain from the rest of the female working population. Rather, the view was that prostitutes are our sisters, working women who have similar workplace struggles to the rest of us, and that no woman should be jailed for trying to earn a living.

In 1979 political lesbian feminists organised the first Reclaim The Night march in Sydney, which was attended overwhelmingly by local lesbian feminists. The march identified pornography as a major cause of the oppression of women and prostitution as the ultimate expression of the view that women have no value except as sexual commodities. The political arguments that 'porn is the theory, rape is the practice', 'porn is violence against women' and 'porn lies at the heart of the oppression of women', were widely taken up and accepted throughout the lesbian feminist community.

Sydney in the early to mid–1980s was a hard place for lesbian sex radicals. Any public discussion about lesbian sexuality was invariably coated with saccharine clichés about 'wimmin love' and 'sisterhood'. A large number of sexual topics were simply taboo and the debates which had occurred in the previous decade about fantasy, desire and erotica had long since been silenced. If you wanted to explore anything other than the accepted sexual 'norms' of the lesbian community, or to experiment with sexual games which were not in any way 'sisterly', you had two alternatives: keep your mouth shut about what you were doing or leave the lesbian feminist community altogether.

In 1980 a major feminist gathering, the Women and Violence conference, was held at Sydney University. The workshops included one on pornography and another on prostitution. Pornography was defined as visual and celluloid rape; this feminist position on pornography was identical to the political lesbian position. The discussions which had begun in the 1970s on a feminist erotica, and what that might encompass, had now ceased. There was only one dissenting voice at the workshop on prostitution, a lesbian prostitute who talked about her experience as both a prostitute and a lesbian. When she criticised the judgmental nature of the lesbian community and defended her right to choose sex industry employment, the workshop erupted in anger and outrage toward her.

During 1981–82 one of the most curious debates erupted within the Sydney lesbian feminist community. It was not caused, but was fuelled, by the distribution in Australia of the English booklet *Love your enemy? The debate between heterosexual feminism and political lesbianism* (Leeds Revolutionary Feminists 1981). Known later as 'the great penetration debate', a great deal of discussion space in lesbian publications, and time at meetings and in political/social groups, was spent discussing whether all penetration was 'male' because it was by its nature phallocentric.

Political lesbian minds snapped shut when anything was decreed to be 'male', especially if it related to sexuality; any

C.Moore Hardy, Australia Day Jelly Wrestling Competition, Leichhardt Hotel, 1992 © C.Moore Hardy

such label was guaranteed to give the subject in question the lesbian kiss of death. As odd at it now seems, this issue aroused a lot of impassioned debate, with the anti-penetration dykes holding the dominant public, if not private, position. *Love your enemy?* provided the quintessential analysis of penetration: 'penetration is an act of great symbolic significance by which the oppressor enters the body of the oppressed' (Leeds Revolutionary Feminists 1981, p. 6).

It is clear from *Love your enemy?* that its discussion of penetration referred to heterosexual sex. However, in what became typical of sexual clashes among lesbians, once a particular practice was deemed oppressive or 'male', it became equally wrong whether it was indulged in by heterosexuals or lesbians. A strange mental slip-over occurred, possibly because lesbians ended up tirelessly debating these sexual subjects among themselves, rather than with heterosexual women as was originally intended.

At this same time, those women who had never had sex

with men at all were deemed to be somehow 'purer' or 'truer' in their lesbianism than those women who had prior sexual relationships with men. It was a brave woman who admitted to having had an enjoyable past sexual relationship with a man and no one admitted to occasionally still doing so.

The sex radical dykes were continuing to live their lives almost completely separately from the political lesbians. One notable cross-over clash occurred in a non-political setting, which was unusual. In 1983 the first lesbian wet T-shirt competition was held at an inner-city Sydney lesbian bar, the Belmore Park Hotel. Many political lesbians loudly complained at the competition's 'male' emphasis on women's breasts, claiming that it was a sad reproduction of the worst kind of heterosexist reduction of a woman's worth to her breasts. Despite threats of demonstrations the competition went ahead anyway and the hotel's beer garden was packed with women.

The first lesbian sex radical group, Sexually Outrageous Women (SOW) formed in Sydney early in 1984, describing itself as 'a group for all women interested in exploring/experimenting in diverse sexual activities (including SM)'. SOW met monthly at the Gay Centre in Sydney and attracted a regular group of fifteen women to its meetings. In addition, they held special open events addressed to the broader lesbian community, such as the first women-only night at a gay male baths in Oxford Street, which was hugely successful.

Other SOW activities included public readings of sexual fantasies, demonstrations of vibrators and other sex toys for women (with SOW borrowing the toys from sympathetic gay male sex shops); later came an SM demonstration and a night of dungeon play (in a straight brothel where one of the SOW members worked). Advertising for a SOW video night reflected the fact that, even though lesbians were becoming increasingly interested in erotic videos made for and by dykes, there was still no product available. The promo for the video night read, 'hopefully we will have discovered some woman-to-woman erotica by this date'. SOW eventually folded in 1985 (SOW leaflets 1984; O'Sullivan 1991, pp. 22–24).

In 1986 the great penetration debate resurfaced in print in

Melbourne in the long-standing lesbian magazine, *Lesbian News*. It defined lesbianism as 'women-loving-women; it has nothing necessarily to do with sex', an exact restating of the early 1970s position. A new Melbourne group, The Joy of Lesbian Sex collective, began a debate based on the belief that 'there are lesbian sexual techniques', referring to penetration, which 'mimic heterosexual intercourse' and that these should be discarded for other 'non-violent sex' techniques. There had been a change in the lesbian nation since the first penetration debate though, and there were furious rebuttals by happily sexualised lesbians in the letters pages of *Lesbian News*. Later *Lesbian News* grudgingly admitted that lesbianism in some cases included a physical desire to become sexually close (*Lesbian News* 1986–87).

The first American lesbian sex magazine produced by and for dykes, *On Our Backs*, began distribution in Australia in 1986. It was started two years previously in San Francisco, trail-blazing discussions about 'politically incorrect' sex in all its guises and challenging what had been portrayed as authentic lesbian sex. Unashamedly pro-sex toy, pro-sexual fantasy, pro-SM and pro-sex work (with one of its founders being an open lesbian stripper), it had an enormous impact on the lesbian community upon its release in Australia. It sold out quickly at the only two bookshops willing to stock it, with lesbians leaving their names on a list to reserve a copy as soon as the latest issue was received. The list eventually became so long, and the stock so limited, that the magazine never actually hit the shelves.

The first lesbian-produced lesbian porn videos, *Private Pleasures and Shadows*, by San Francisco company Fatale Films, the same people who published *On Our Backs*, became briefly available in Australia through an ACT mail order adult video company, Leisuremail. These videos made it into the company's catalogue through the agitation of a lesbian who was working within the advertising section of the company. However, the videos were poorly promoted and sold badly and when the company was taken over the titles were deleted from their stock list.

January 1988 saw the first edition of Australia's first lesbian-produced lesbian sex magazine, *Wicked Women*. To the lesbians who were desperate for a sexual forum *Wicked Women* was an oasis in the erotic desert of political correctness. The two publishers, editors and lovers Francine (now Jasper) Laybutt (who had been active in SOW) and Lisa Salmon, credited *On Our Backs* with giving them the inspiration for *Wicked Women*. The publishers were young and apolitical, and at the time, as neither identified as a feminist, were unaware of the fiery sex debate into which they had inadvertently stumbled. They were surprised and unprepared for the degree of hostility the magazine engendered. The first edition was a photocopied zine-like publication of 28 pages, hand-collated and stapled, with a print run of only 90 copies, yet it took Sydney by storm. Reflecting on the magazine's beginnings Laybutt said later, 'We wanted to create a magazine which reflected what we were doing and the sort of sex we were having at a time when nothing in the lesbian community validated this at all' (O'Sullivan 1993, p. 120).

The same year at Sleaze Ball, the huge annual Sydney Gay & Lesbian Mardi Gras party, the first lesbian performance was held, a four-woman display of bondage and erotic whipping. For the first time a lesbian sexual underground was forming in Sydney, growing up around the activities organised to raise funds for *Wicked Women*. A year after its debut, *Wicked Women* held its first party, pioneering a style which was to continue until 1993. The magazine's parties, film nights and performances propelled the publication from being just a magazine to an active participant in creating and celebrating the sexual culture it explored in print. Ironically, some the magazine's events are almost better known than the publication itself.

Wicked Women parties took the name Be Wicked; the first, Be Wicked 1, was held in an old warehouse with lesbian porn gracing the walls, spaghetti wrestling, a public sex space and even an *a cappella* singer. When the police raided in the early hours of the morning and the 300 or so dykes and a sprinkling of gay men were herded out, the infamy of *Wicked Women* events was assured. Further dance parties were held, mainly at the Gunnery, a huge abandoned warehouse on Sydney Harbour, which was then an artists' squat. The Gunnery was in a state of total decay, with an erratic power supply (meaning sudden power blackouts at any time during the night), and was prone to flooding in the rain (meaning pools of ankle-deep water in the most unexpected places). However, it was an extraordinary space with an underground, grungy, subcultural atmosphere which suited the parties perfectly.

A typical *Wicked Women* party had its own resident DJ, SM and bondage performances, enlarged and projected sex slides and non-stop video porn all evening. There was always lots of erotic artwork and performances from the confronting to the totally obscure. After being forced to leave the Gunnery these parties, which regularly attracted over 500 party-goers despite very little advertising, continued at another inner-city space dubbed by the organisers The Love Hotel. They were the first lesbian events to give out safe sex information and safe sex packs.

In addition to the parties, *Wicked Women* ventured into the arts and held a number of art exhibitions and film nights known as Wicked Acts. One of *Wicked Women's* most notorious events was Girl Beat, which took place in 1990 in a male-only fuck bar, The Den, on Oxford Street. The venue was hired from the men for one night and nearly 100 women braved its seedy confines to dance, watch dirty videos and cruise, with many having sex or openly voyeuring other women's sexual scenarios.

1990 saw the Ms. Wicked competition instituted, with the winner becoming the first lesbian titleholder in Australia. The contestants were challenged to show the organisers and the audience their interpretation of the word 'wicked'. A series of heats was held, over the years spreading interstate to Brisbane, Canberra and Melbourne. The competition ran from 1990 to 1993 and crowned four titleholders.

The US feminist sex wars of the 1980s (Vance 1989) were mirrored in Australia, but here they were known as the lesbian feminist sex wars. There were some debates in heterosexual

C.Moore Hardy, Lesbian Performance Night at Buckland St Studio, 1992 © *C.Moore Hardy*

circles about SM, role-play, fetishes and sex toys, but there was no Australian feminist equivalent of Andrea Dworkin or Catharine MacKinnon taking these issues to a wider heterosexual feminist audience. The ferocious hostility between women took place almost exclusively within lesbian circles. In 1991 the Sydney Lesbian Festival and Conference was held, with one of the highlights of the week a huge evening concert at the Opera House. On the main stage that night Robyn Archer, a prominent lesbian entertainer, denounced SM dykes and there was cheering and support for her remarks from the lesbian feminist audience.

Despite this, pansexual SM play and pansexual performances became the new area of sexual exploration for many sex radical dykes in the early 1990s. Genderfuck became enthusiastically embraced by lesbian sexual performers and was characterised by strap-on dildoes, false gay male clone-style moustaches and jock straps bulging with socks. 1993 proved to be the year of titleholders with three competitions in Sydney to judge public sexual performance. A second dyke titleholder competition, unconnected with Ms. Wicked, was set up, called Ms. Lesbian. The twelve-hour competition boasted nine categories, including Best Bum in 501s, Best Lingerie/Bra, Best Tattoo, Best Piercings and the Best Most Outrageous. The event turned out to be a one-off but, as with the Ms. Wicked competition, the bar was packed, with hundreds of women being turned away at the door.

In 1993 *Wicked Women* organised a Mr. Wicked as well as a Ms. Wicked competition. This was the first gay male titleholder competition organised by lesbians anywhere in the world and created a storm of sexual controversy from a number of different angles. Many gay men were appalled that lesbians had the nerve to set up a competition to judge their sexual performance, while many sex radical dykes saw the competition as diverting scarce resources and money into supporting male sexual expression when more was needed for their own. For those lesbian feminists who had always opposed the magazine's existence and activities the Mr. Wicked competition confirmed that *Wicked Women* was really 'male' at heart.

Since 1990 leather and SM dykes have become active in Sydney Leather Pride Association, the city's only leather and SM community activist organisation. Regular sexual performances are now held in lesbian bars as part of the standard entertainment and, at every dyke art event and reading night for writers, the work contains, as a matter of course, a high level of sexual content. The exploration of lesbian sexuality now has a high public profile and culturally the lifestyle lesbians hold the dominant social ground.

Despite this, it seems that battles which were fought a decade ago over SM, but in reality were about all kinds of sexual expression, are set for another resurgence. When US academic Janice Raymond visited Australia in 1994 for the International Feminist Book Fair she was strongly promoting her theory that the unfortunate demise of political feminism was tied to 'a tyranny of tolerance'. She vocally opposed 'sex as salvation', which she saw as propaganda from the lifestyle lesbians who were guilty of re-sexualising women (Raymond 1991, pp. 7–21).

Raymond's visit caused much debate within the lesbian communities. Fundamental questions have been raised by the resurgence of political lesbianism. Specifically, what does it mean to insist that tolerance is a tyranny? What is happening when lesbians who proudly admit they have had no personal experience of any kind of transgressive sex set themselves up as experts on other lesbians' sexual and emotional lives? The lesbian sex wars continue, with sexism still being confused with sex itself. Lesbians remain deeply divided over pleasure and desire, in a way which is far more than just academic. Lesbian desire is the most visible face of lesbianism, yet the least understood. For political lesbians, sex continues to be the litmus test of a life well lived or a life just squandered. For lesbian sex radicals, unconditional sexual freedom is a necessary precondition to a good life.

10
Lesbian erotica and impossible images

C.MOORE HARDY

My desire to be an artist and photographer, to create and capture images of people, began a long while ago, with my father giving me a small camera for Christmas one year. In the past ten years I have concentrated on developing a dialogue with and about lesbian images and more recently, erotic images for women.

During my days at the College of Fine Arts (1988–90) my interest in women's images was awakened by the feminist theory practised at that time with its aspiration to create new images of women that would challenge the stereotypical patriarchal images. Influenced by some of the contemporary artists (e.g. Helen Grace, Anne Ferran, Sandy Edwards and Julie Brown Rapp), through the use of my own body I began to express myself and my sexuality. In the exhibition entitled 'Fundamental Attack' (curated by Cath Phillips and held in 1989 during the Sydney Gay & Lesbian Mardi Gras) I installed a work that used continuous slide-projected nude images of my body and screenprinted works resembling the slides. This was an attempt to find a space for myself and create a dialogue about my body/a woman's body and its representation. The images were self portraits of numerous poses and revealing gestures. My objective was to subvert the way the female body is seen, through repetition and ever-changing imagery. I used my own body with the intention of not exploiting other women's bodies (see *Self Portrait*).

This work was never published, my rationale being that all images could be modified and altered when placed into another context, a situation I was attempting to subvert, to avoid being misrepresented. It was important to be able to create images that were read with my feminist intention and not seen through the 'male gaze', catalogued alongside all the other female nudes: exploited, objectified and consumed.

Women artists during the late eighties were creating works that reconstructed the images that had been created by men of women. Men's perception and expectations of women, a woman's image and her objectification and subjection to the male gaze, were under review. *The Female Gaze* by Lorraine Gamman and Margaret Marshment, published in 1988, challenged the notion that women were passive viewers.

During this time my head, heart and philosophy were aware of and conditioned by feminist theory to the extent that I did not wish to exploit another woman's body by photographing it. The Old Masters had painted female nudes for centuries; objectification was the cycle I was trying to break.

The *Australian Oxford Dictionary* defines pornography as 'the explicit description or exhibition of sexual activity . . . intended to stimulate erotic rather than aesthetic feelings'. In contrast, pornography as defined by reactionary feminists Dworkin and MacKinnon is 'the sexually explicit subordination of women, graphically depicted . . .' Neither definition allows much difference between erotica and pornography. Within the Dworkin and MacKinnon definition there exists no room for lesbians and their sexuality, especially those who engage in sadomasochism (SM) or bondage and discipline (B&D). My work attempted to engage in a dialogue representing erotic images for lesbians.

In the late 1980s the lesbian magazine *On Our Backs* arrived from America. Its title was a parody of the feminist magazine *Off Our Backs*, which ran an anti-objectification of women, almost anti-sexuality line. *On Our Backs* was devoted to a different form of representation of women, involving a celebration of sexuality. Yet what I began to see was really inanimate porn, and erotic images that were mere photo documentation, and fairly unimaginative images of women by women. When I saw what was being produced, and realised that it could only be improved upon, I felt encouraged to attempt my own images and began to engage in the debates where the legitimacy of lesbian erotica was discussed. It was important to involve myself in what I could do, or at least attempt to do, rather than be disillusioned with what did exist. The time had come for lesbians to be out and proud, visible and represented sexually (see *SM Performance at Midnight Shift*).

Lesbians were beginning to create images that defined their sexuality and desires. Images of simulated 'lesbian sex' have been man-made for decades, with the intention of titillating the male gaze. This exploitation of heterosexual women to represent lesbians and their sexuality became more obvious as lesbians created the images of their own fantasies.

My 'politically correct' style of the early 1990s was probably seen as a 'vanilla' (non-penetration sex) approach in comparison to the style of two other lesbian photographers, Jasmine Hirst and Linda Dement, who were depicting more explicit images of fisting and SM scenarios.

As photographers within the lesbian culture, lesbians were caught up in the Australian version of the sex wars (discussed by Kimberly O'Sullivan in chapter 9). Sheila Jeffrey's claim that pornography was 'propaganda of woman hatred' meant that any form of representation of explicit lesbian sexuality was taboo. On the other side, women like X-porn star and performance artist Annie Sprinkle were educating women to appreciate their sexuality and experience multiple orgasms. I continued to follow the sex-positive approach in celebrating the female body.

The lack of financial support magnified by zero Australia Council funding, the marginalisation of lesbian artwork, limited emotional support and negative response to aspects of the work continued to discourage my efforts in developing my lesbian erotica series. I decided to battle on and I began to make pictures that would enhance sexual pleasure or expand the imagination. Although I still had concerns about being misrepresented, I felt that by being published in lesbian magazines and exhibiting in these texts, I could only be read as lesbian.

These images would attempt to avoid the 'male gaze' and its exploitation of women, especially when published in underground/subculture magazines with a limited audience. It was the existence of this limited audience that made the dissemination of my images a conceivable option. I believed that, viewed within a specific context, the works would engage in a dialogue that would best represent my ideas. These spaces became very important for me and other lesbians to express ourselves and the images that we were creating. Of course, it is unrealistic to imagine that men did not view these works, as any publication can be bought and sold, making the material available to anyone who wanted it and knew where to obtain it.

About this time (1990) an exhibition from Canada called 'Drawing The Line' opened in Sydney during the Sydney Gay & Lesbian Mardi Gras. This exhibition exposed many fantasy images for a visually-starved lesbian audience. Never before had an entire mainstream gallery displayed works of this calibre. The pivotal aspect of this exhibition was its interactive process, where the (lesbian) viewer could write comments on the walls next to the photographs while they were looking at them. (Male comments were not accepted on the walls and had to be written in a separate book.) Comments ranged from pleasure to disdain, depending on the content of the images. Discussions organised during the exhibition with the artist/photographer Susan Stewart both enlightened and enraged women who attended. This work was a catalyst for many changes in attitude towards expressing lesbian sexuality.

This exhibition signalled the change in my own attitude towards the representation of lesbian images and the need to examine the 'constructed' guilt from feminist philosophy around objectification, representation and voyeurism. If

LESBIAN EROTICA AND IMPOSSIBLE IMAGES

C.Moore Hardy, Lisa and Gabrielle, 1992 © C.Moore Hardy

lesbians are to exist, then their sexuality needs to be represented, nurtured, encouraged, developed and expressed. I understood it was important and necessary to create images that could represent my ideas and desires.

The other way of expressing a lesbian erotica was through written word and performance. The many lesbian performance artists of the time also caught my attention and inspired me. There was a distinct tribe of exotic, unique and rebellious outcasts who performed regularly in girl bars and nightclubs and at opening nights to entertain and shock lesbian audiences. The most fabulous and witty Mistresses of Ceremony duo were Izzy and Angie (see *Izzy and Angie*). Other memorable artists were Anna Munster, Lisa Salmon, Larissa, Groovii Biscuit and Azaria Universe. These 'mistresses of the stage' exhibited, crossdressed and tantalised lesbian and gay audiences irregularly, although sufficiently often to build an adoring fan club. In the early days of the Wicked Women Contests (performances of lesbian erotica competing for the title of Ms Wicked), most photographers had to hand in their cameras at the door. A particularly painful experience for a dedicated documenter like myself, but this measure protected the privacy of those performing lesbian artists and contestants who had careers and responsibilities and did not want their sexual performances to be revealed to the general public. There was and still remains a closet lesbian scene for professionals, public figures and performers unable to express their sexuality due to homophobia and fear of reprisals.

SM performance and bondage scenes were taboo in most sections of the lesbian culture and with the SM subculture being so small, almost everyone knew each other's inclination, or thought they did. My participation as a voyeur annoyed some women, whereas others accepted my position and encouraged me. My intention was to record the events as they were happening and I enjoyed watching this new generation of young sex radical lesbians, who needed support and encouragement as they became the pioneers of the new lesbian sexual revolution. Although there was only a limited outlet for my work, I recorded as much as possible. By documenting live performance work I also engaged in building up the history of a period when lesbian sexuality was being openly celebrated, discussed (albeit in heated debates), performed and encouraged through magazines such as *Wicked Women* (Sydney), *Bad Attitude* (US) and *Quim* (UK). The more 'vanilla' or 'non penetration sex' groups were vehement in their attacks on the explicitly sexual lesbian performance artists, much the same as male heterosexuals condemn female sluts in their society. These vanilla girls were against any form of open expression of sexuality or 'exhibitionism' for fear that the mainstream would find out how lesbians had sex. I presume that this knowledge

C.Moore Hardy, Groovii Biscuit with Anna Kisses at Sex Subculture Party © C.Moore Hardy

would mean that 'lesbian secrets' would be out, and hence the mystique lost.

Lesbian myths and secrets were being exposed in the mainstream anyway, as *Cleo*, *Cosmopolitan* and *HQ* attempted to discuss lesbian issues. Articles for mainstream publications always appeared to be written by gay men who became the authority on lesbian sexuality whereas, on the streets and in the community, lesbians were empowering themselves and their bodies with an explicit and vibrant sensuality, something only previously imaginable in the nightclub scene in Berlin during the twenties. It was out with the checked shirts and overalls for some and into laptops, luxury and lacey lingerie.

Before the demise of the Ms. Wicked competitions in 1994 came the Sex Subculture parties, where lesbians performed alongside queers and homosexuals. The underground decadence of Sydney's inner-city crowd of entrepreneurial sex-performance artists began to take over the party performance scene that I was documenting. Gay men were being

C.Moore Hardy, Miss Lesbian contestants at Exchange Hotel, Darlinghurst, *1993* © *C.Moore Hardy*

exposed to lesbian sex, and were amazed at what they were finding out about lesbians. This was the underground extension of 'coalition politics' that most major gay and lesbian organisations (e.g. PRIDE, Gay & Lesbian Rights Lobby, and Mardi Gras) were encouraging politically (see *Sex Subculture Party*).

Mixed into this underground was the SM scene and the tattooing and piercing elite. Body art and ornamentation became a new body language. Running parallel to this gay and lesbian party subculture was the mainstream media's interest in pseudo-leather fetish and SM. *Vogue* dabbled with glamour models in chic leather, *Australian Women's Forum* analysed it as the new sensation, and *Black & White* sanitised it, making it the latest style thing. Rubber, vinyl and latex became fashion accessories among trend-conscious straight yuppies. However, there was no mention of how leatherfolk engaged in the

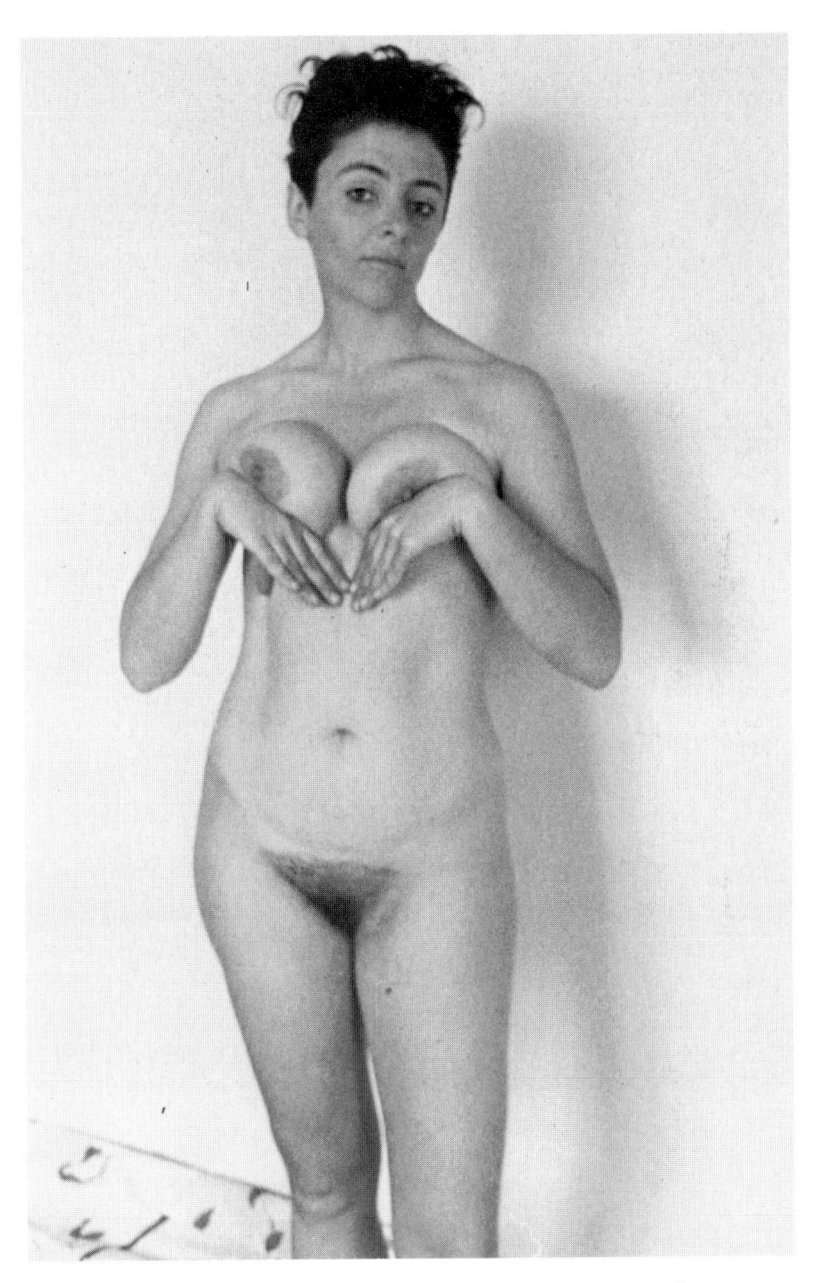

C.Moore Hardy, Self Portrait, 1988 © C.Moore Hardy

C.Moore Hardy, SM Performance at Midnight Shift, *1990*
© *C.Moore Hardy*

C.Moore Hardy, Izzy and Angie © *C.Moore Hardy*

C.Moore Hardy, Sex Subculture Party, *1993* © *C.Moore Hardy*

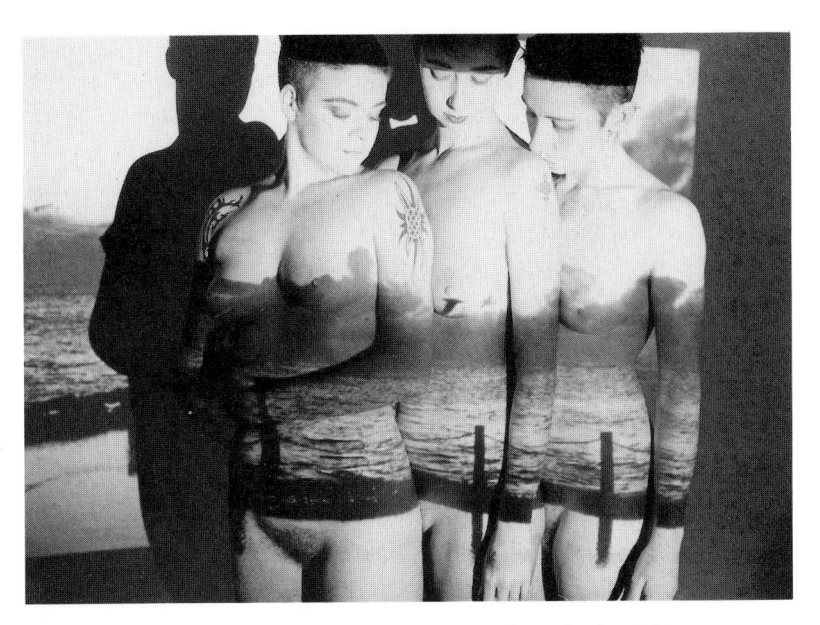

C.Moore Hardy, Lesley, Katrina and Rachael, 1993
© C.Moore Hardy

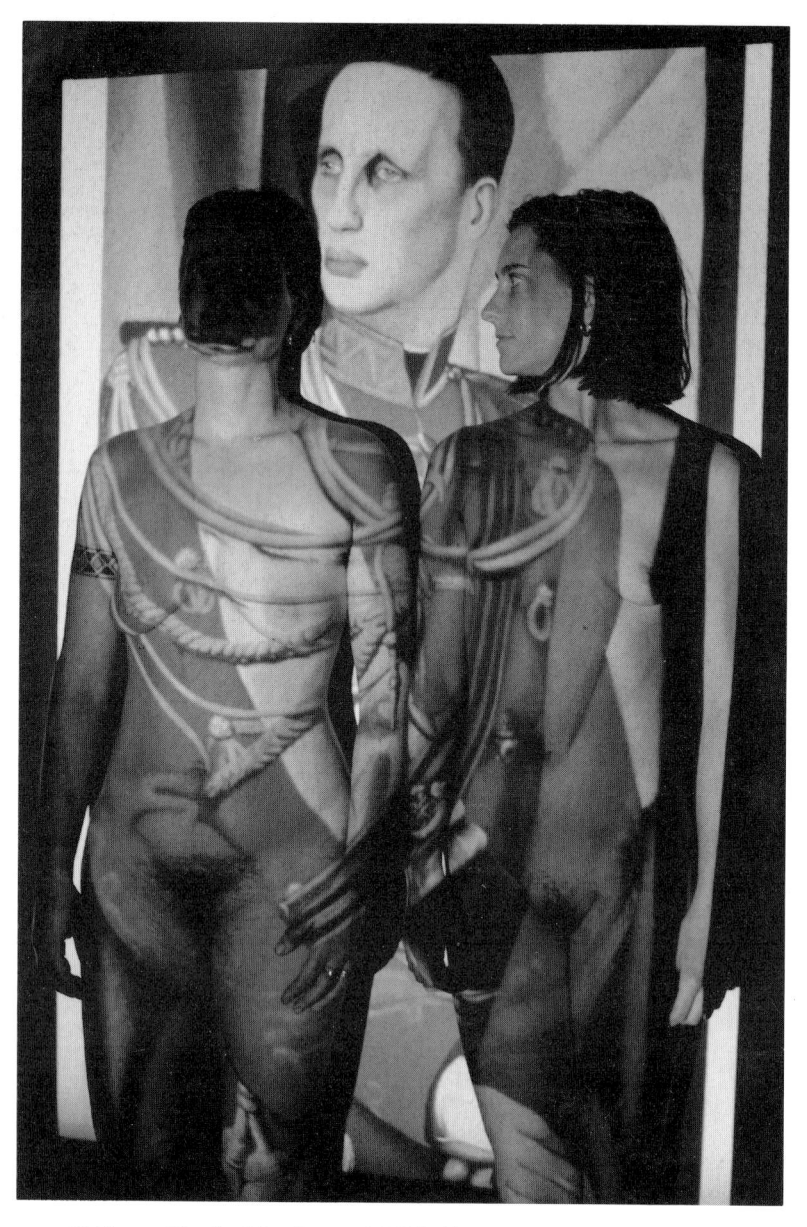

C.Moore Hardy, Martien and Michelle, 1995 © C.Moore Hardy

David McDiarmid, Safe Love, Safe Lust, 1992, *watercolour*.
Reproduced courtesy of AIDS Council of NSW.

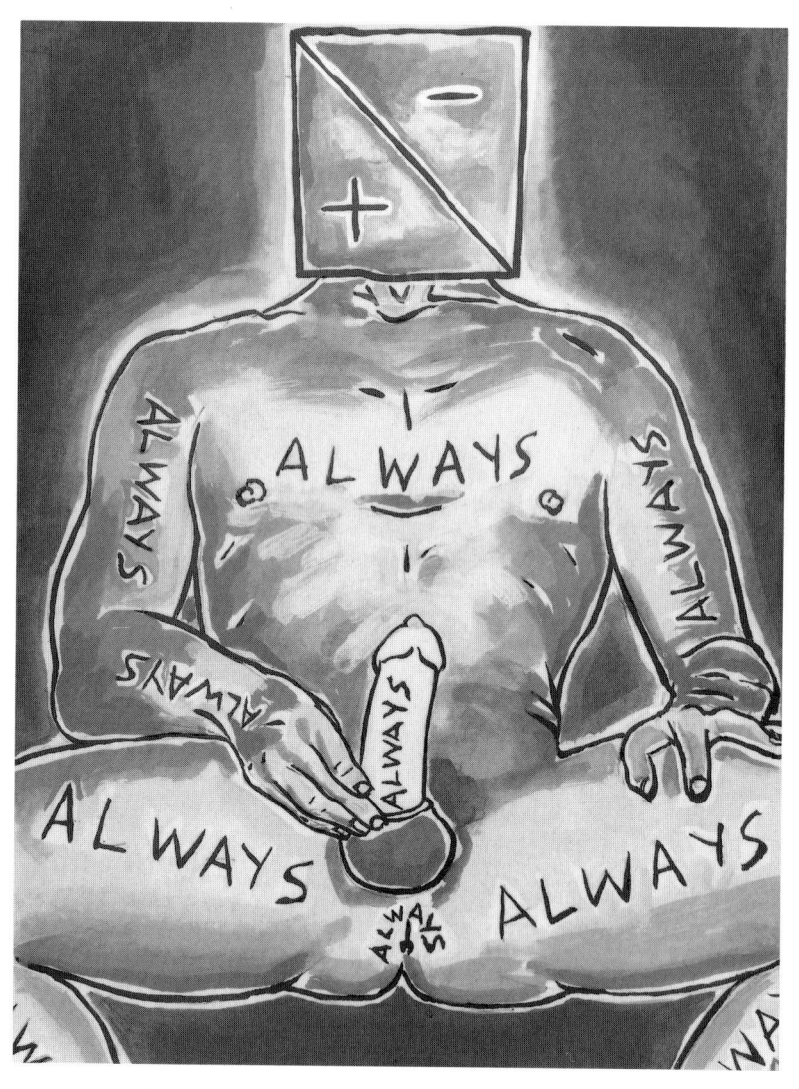

David McDiarmid, Always, 1992, watercolour. Reproduced courtesy of AIDS Council of NSW.

David McDiarmid, That's Miss Poofter to You Asshole, *1994*, computer-generated Canon laser print on craftwood. Reproduced courtesy of the Estate of David McDiarmid.

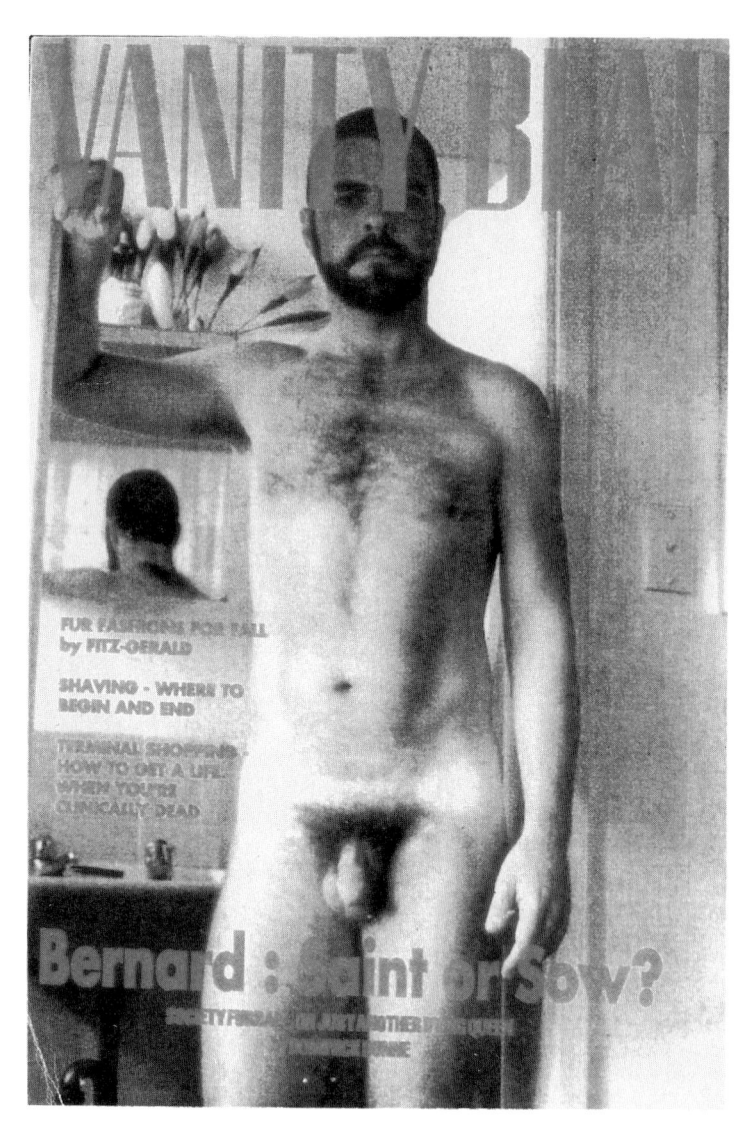

David McDiarmid, Vanity Bear, *1993, Canon laser print. Reproduced courtesy of the Estate of David McDiarmid.*

Obitchery

NAME : Bernard Fitzgerald

AGE : Forty-ish

PROFESSION : Ex-psychiatric nurse, ex-gardener, ex-telephonist

LIFESTYLE : Blank

FAVOURITE COLOUR : Redheads

STAR-SIGN : Ex-Leo

HOBBIES : Telephone

BEDSIDE READING : Final Exit, Mim's Pharmaceutical Dictionary

FAVOURITE FILM : Robinson Crusoe on Mars

FAVOURITE ACTOR : Frank Vickers

FAVOURITE ACTRESS : Frank Vickers

FAVOURITE OPINION : His

FAVOURITE CHARITY : Crippled prostitutes

FAVOURITE ART : Free

FAVOURITE SCENT : Men

FAVOURITE PASTIME : Shaving hairline

FAVOURITE CURE : AZT for bad knees

FAVOURITE OXFORD ST. VENUE : Karen Zoellner

CLAIM TO FAME : His friends

David McDiarmid, Vanity Bear (inside list), *1993, Canon laser print. Reproduced courtesy of the Estate of David McDiarmid.*

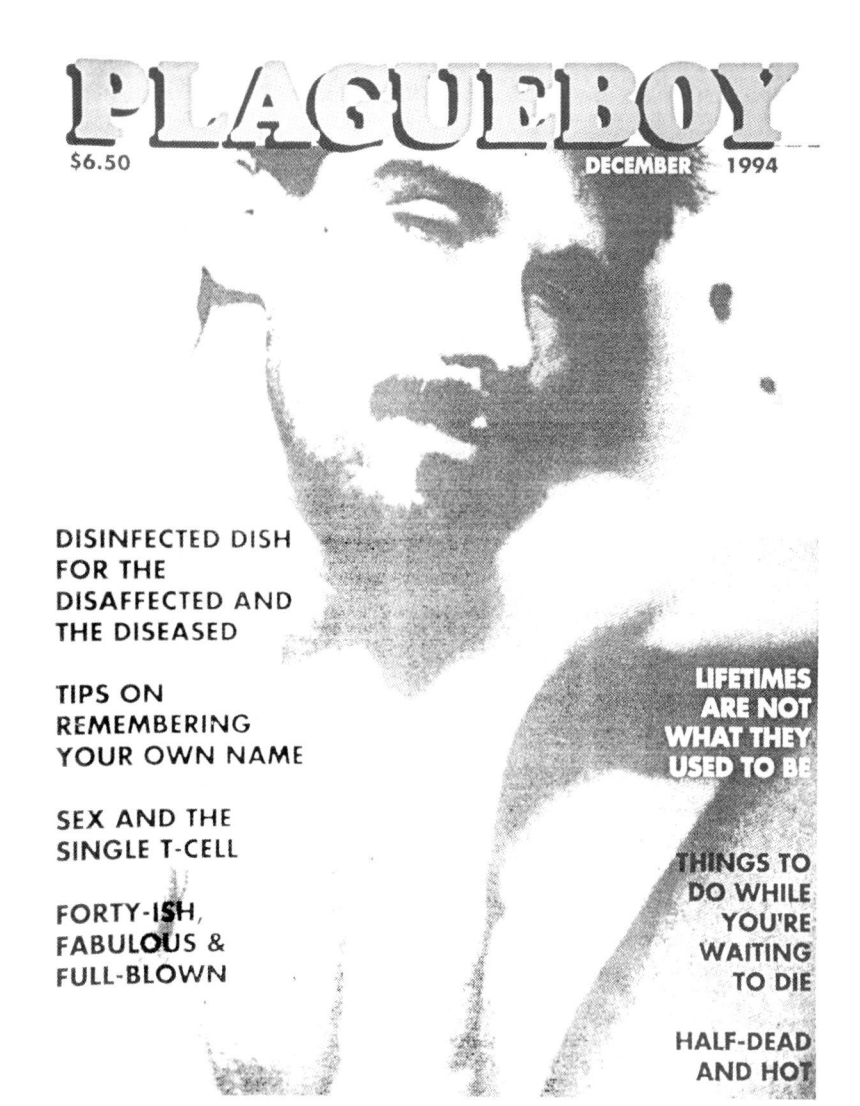

David McDiarmid, PlagueBoy, 1994, Canon laser print.
Reproduced courtesy of the Estate of David McDiarmid.

Marion Moore, Michelle, *Butch Baby Butch Series*
© Marion Moore

Marion Moore, Kimberly and Mel, *Butch Baby Butch Series*
© Marion Moore

Marion Moore, Bo, Butch Baby Butch Series © Marion Moore

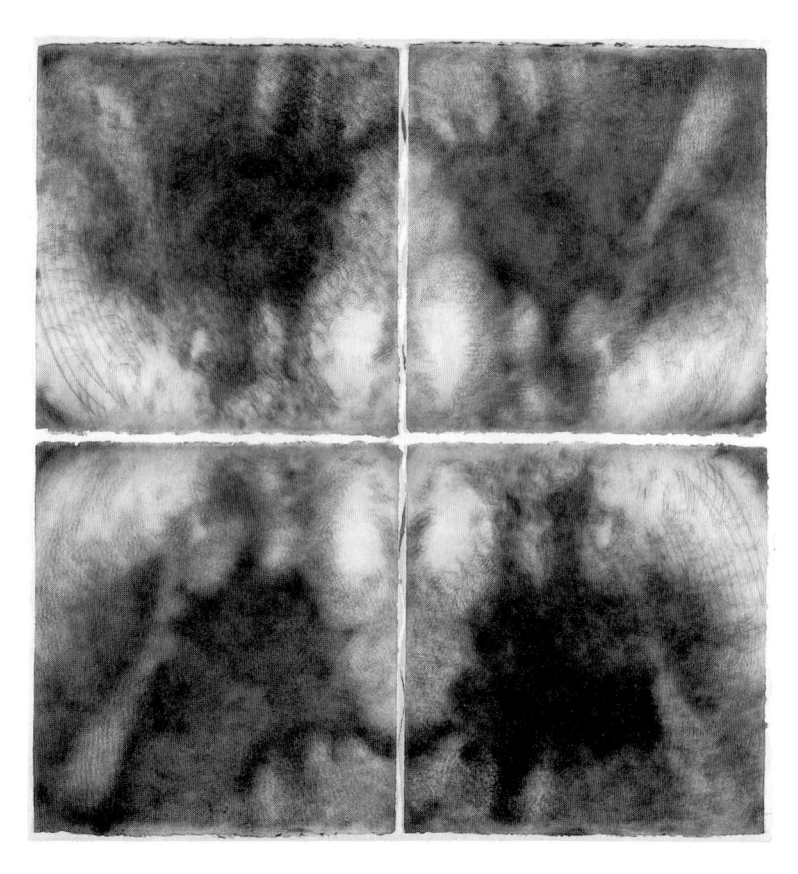

Suzanne Boccalatte, Corporeal Landscape: Head, *mixed media,
120 x 120 cm © Suzanne Boccalatte*

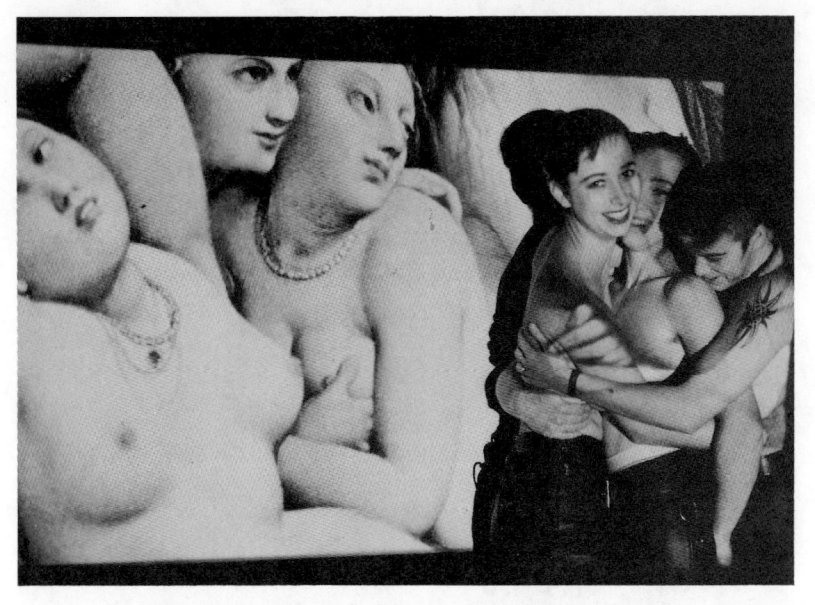

C.Moore Hardy, Katrina, Rachel and Lesley, *1993*
© C.Moore Hardy

politics of leather and latex, no mention of the way rubber is fetishised in its own subculture, and no understanding of the lesbian and gay leather subculture. It was a very easy game to be seen playing at, especially since Robert Mapplethorpe's photos had made leather and rubber so seductive. Apart from Mapplethorpe's work, the images that circulated around the fashion scene presented a superficial and romanticised version of what the leather/SM culture was all about. There was no dialogue about consensual safe sex, or that it was about sexual games, fantasy and pleasure/pain and the imagination of the individuals involved.

I mention this period because the mainstream media had become increasingly interested in gay culture, especially the lipstick lesbians (or the glamour dykes). Once lesbians looked appealing they could again be commodified, packaged and consumed. Because they conformed to the male fantasy image of lesbians, they could still appear to be available to men.

C.Moore Hardy, From the Lesbian Calendar: Giu and Pip, 1993 © C.Moore Hardy

At Sydney College of the Arts (1992–93), where I began seriously working on lesbian erotica, I discovered that creating these images was not as easy as I had imagined. First, the stigma attached to the models being identified as lesbians (from the photographs), as well as engaging in sexual activity, was problematic for most lesbians. It was a small community and not many lesbians were available to pose for me. Secondly, I could not afford to pay the models who were available, so instead I gave them some photographs as an honorarium. From this period I have a small collection of images which I still continue to develop (see *Lesley, Katrina and Rachael* and *Martien and Michelle*).

Over the period 1991 to 1994 I tried to photograph lesbian couples prepared to openly express their sexuality to another audience, beyond their bedroom. Couples were always more harmonious with one another and prepared to play in front of the camera. Had I been profit motivated I would never have had financial problems, as there has always been a market for lesbian erotic photographs. The mainstream porn publications generally portray two women together (who engage the male viewer by glancing back into the lens of the camera); the other scenario is usually two women and a man, suggesting that only the male can truly satisfy the women.

Lesbian erotica generally portrays women as engaging in sexual activity for their own pleasure. There is a subtle but obvious difference, important because of the market the images are aimed at.

It is extremely difficult to survive in lesbian publishing because of the limited advertising revenue, which in turn means that gay publishing still pays very little in comparison to mainstream publications. There is also the notion within the lesbian community that artists will continue working for the love of it, but the financial reality is that very few lesbian artists and photographers survive on selling their artwork. The lesbian community still suffers from lower income discord. Politically correct publishers are reluctant to produce a lesbian erotica book. Sex is still a sensitive subject matter in the 1990s.

My final end-of-year work at Sydney College of the Arts was an installation, which consisted of a darkened room with a bed and a chair surrounded by latex gloves. Above the bed was a spotlit image of a shaved cunt. The work was about lesbian sex, safe sex and lesbian dreams and was titled 'Holy Cunt'. This work received a great response. Creating a space for the inclusion of lesbian erotica and the dialogue around my work had been achieved by persistence and much support from my lecturer, Bradford Buckley.

My work has lesbian content and intent, and attempts to engage in a lesbian dialogue. The strategies I have employed have included using lesbian couples to represent relationships, preserving the integrity of my work by strategic placement in exhibitions and controlling where the images are reproduced, and trying to maintain control over the context in which the work is seen and reproduced.

In 1993 Martien Coucke, my partner, and I collaborated to produce the Lesbian Calendar (1994), which is in the National Library Archive in Canberra. Later in 1994 I was commissioned by the National Portrait Library for a lesbian family portrait. My freelance work for the *Sydney Star Observer* includes photographing lesbians in the community, and I view this process as vital for the preservation and visualising of lesbians for the future.

My passion for lesbian erotica continues, but my other documentary and commissioned work takes precedence. In March 1996 at the State Library of New South Wales I was included in the exhibition 'Images from everyday life'. When the NSW Parliament debates changes to legislation on de facto relationships, my series of twenty lesbian, gay and queer families will be seen in the NSW Parliament foyer as part of the Gay & Lesbian Rights Lobby supporting campaign.

Sponsorship, publication of a book of lesbian erotic images, regular exhibitions and to continue making and creating images that celebrate and document lesbian lives is the agenda for my future.

11
Sex and the single T-cell: the taboo of HIV-positive sexuality in Australian art and culture

TED GOTT[1]

The back rooms and the saunas are power centres for our dead sisters' ghosts. They are laboratories for my studies, as I can learn more there than at University campuses. Every time I orgasm, in a cubicle, I feel I am invaded by at least three entities who share my orgasm. This may or may not be AIDS dementia. Is it sensible to deny these experiences? . . . If this is real, do these entities want to stay in these spaces? Or should they progress to *the great Sauna in the sky where nobody says no.* . . . As I researched the gloom of the *Den* once: sucked a cock to the left, licked an arse to the right, and tickled a few testicles ahead simultaneously, *"shit"* I accidentally knocked out someone's *catheter.*

This hadn't happened to me when I gave everyone oral at the AIDS ward last year (Thomas-Clark 1994).

The bitter-sweet climate in which many Australian gay men have sex with each other every day is captured perfectly here

---

[1] The author would like to thank Jamie Dunbar, Bernard Fitzgerald, Michael Hurley, Derek Hand, Andrew Thomas-Clark (now Fletcher Jetspree), Lou McCallum, Beowulf Thorne, Bill Whittaker, Kathryn Weir, Richard Pedvin, Brenton McGeachie, Sally Gray and the late David McDiarmid for their assistance during the preparation of this article. This article is dedicated to the memories of David McDiarmid (1952-1995) and Andrew Morgan (1962-1995).

by Andrew Thomas-Clark. Diagnosed as HIV-positive at age twenty, Thomas-Clark faced 'outing' and social judgment early. He recalls that during a spell in hospital while an undergraduate art student in Newcastle, 'my lecturer showed my [HIV-related] work to the other students and told them that I felt strongly about the issue because I had AIDS and didn't have long to live!' (Thomas-Clark in Urquhart 1994, p. 23).

In recent years Thomas-Clark has turned this, and other surreal experiences consequent upon his HIV-positive diagnosis, into a digitally-imaged live performance monologue, *The Illustrated Story of a Queer Boy*, which narrates, in his own words, his 'life journeys, from feisty androgyny as a kid, to self-empowerment'.

The startling and frank nature of Andrew Thomas-Clark's performances serves to highlight the fact that, in Australia, few instances of the imaging of HIV-positive *sexuality* have entered the public domain since the AIDS epidemic began. Such imaging remains taboo in a society which views sex negatively at the best of times and insists that HIV-positive people, and especially gay men, should automatically switch off their sexuality after diagnosis, and 'place their dicks on ice'. Only the 'murderously' promiscuous gay 'sexual avenger' and the 'lower-than-low' HIV-positive prostitute reach our media outlets as sexually functioning (while dying) beings; and then only in the context of a flood of terrified and vindictive calls to turn off their erotic faucets for fear of what horrors may leak from them.

Such misunderstandings create a conundrum for the positive representation of HIV-positive gay sex. In the minds of the 'mainstream' populace, gayness is limited solely to the sexual act, reflecting what Vito Russo has termed the 'old stereotype, that homosexuality has to do only with sex while heterosexuality is multifaceted and embraces love and romance' (Russo 1987, p. 132). Following from this, for most people, all representations of gay sex and, more widely, gay affection and friendship are now, *ipso facto*, representations of certain AIDS transmission, so stigmatised has the gay community become as the whipping boy of the AIDS epidemic.

Clearly, gay men in their tens of thousands, regardless of their HIV status, are having sex every day in Australia, and having fabulous safe sex which is not transmitting HIV/AIDS. But how do we get this across? How do we reconsider and reclaim sexuality; how do we express the validity and joy of HIV-positive sexuality, which is as legitimate and can be as safe as any other form of sexual expression?

In this chapter I want to examine the few instances of the imaging of HIV-positive gay sexuality which have entered Australian art in recent years; and look at the problems provoked by one image in particular, the now notorious March 1994 cover of the *National AIDS Bulletin*.

Apart from a few anti-discrimination posters showing darkened faces, the first public and *pro-joy* imaging of HIV-positive gay men occurred in the watercolours commissioned by the AIDS Council of NSW (ACON) from Sydney artist David McDiarmid in 1992, and subsequently turned into a safe sex poster campaign. The radical simplicity and *readability* of these works makes it easy to see why they have been acclaimed worldwide (see *Safe Love, Safe Lust*).

McDiarmid's figures are depicted waving hard-ons, buttfucking, flashing arse-holes, glowing with drug-hazed desire. Anything but demure, they are palpitating, quivering 'hot zones' waiting to be penetrated, fingered, sucked, eaten out, fucked stupid. McDiarmid's posters want to sit on your cock as soon as you look at them. Their tripping acid colours and magnetically arousing images are perfect for the dark and sexually-charged climate of gay men's bars and sex palaces. For the first time in Australia an artist had spoken directly to his peer group of party-going, recreational drug-using, sexually active gay men.

More significantly, for the first time the artist, his subjects *and* a directly identified part of the audience were visibly HIV-positive. The + and − symbols scattered liberally across each work offered a perfectly clear visual message. Luminous text on the posters spelled this out further with aphorisms like 'Some of us have HIV, some of us don't / All of us fuck with condoms—every time!' On the postcard versions of the poster designs which ACON produced and distributed free for men to take away from gay venues, an artist's statement recorded that, 'It is often important to be able to clearly and explicitly depict or represent HIV+ people in [information] resources as there is usually an assumption that safe sex messages are only directed at those who are HIV negative'; and another message from the 'sponsors' recorded that ACON 'commissioned David, an artist who is HIV+, to look at AIDS in a way which is both pro-gay and pro-sex'. This was revolutionary. That this is still so, is very sad.

The iconic status of the McDiarmid images was recognised in 1993, when the designs crossed over into the Sydney Gay & Lesbian Mardi Gras Parade in the form of a float filled with over-life-sized painted 'flats' and peopled by body-painted human actors, all modelled after McDiarmid's figures.[2] While the artist himself felt that 'the nuances of emotion and language achieved [in his original watercolours] had been diluted within the confines and imperatives of the AIDS industry' (McDiarmid 1993, n.p.), so appealing were his posters that today they still adorn most gay sex-on-premises venues, long after their production date. Indeed, in March 1995, giant painted murals modelled on two of the posters, *Yes* and *Always*, were unveiled at The Den, a busy fuck-bar in Sydney, and at KKK or Ken's Karate Klub, a legendary men's sauna just off Sydney's gay strip (see *Always*).

About the same time as McDiarmid's posters first appeared in the streets of Sydney, AIDS activist Andrew Morgan was wanting to create a visual representation of the sexualities of people with HIV/AIDS. McDiarmid's posters convinced Morgan that HIV-positive sexuality could be portrayed as sexy, loving and safe, rather than seeping, contagious and shameful.

In early 1993 Morgan collaborated with Sydney photographer Jamie Dunbar and a group of HIV-positive friends to create a moving and honest series of photographs which

---

[2] For a photographic witness of the cross-over of McDiarmid's posters, see Gerry North, (ed.) *The Night of Your Life 1993 Sydney Gay & Lesbian Mardi Gras*, Sydney, Rural and City Media Services, 1993, n.p.

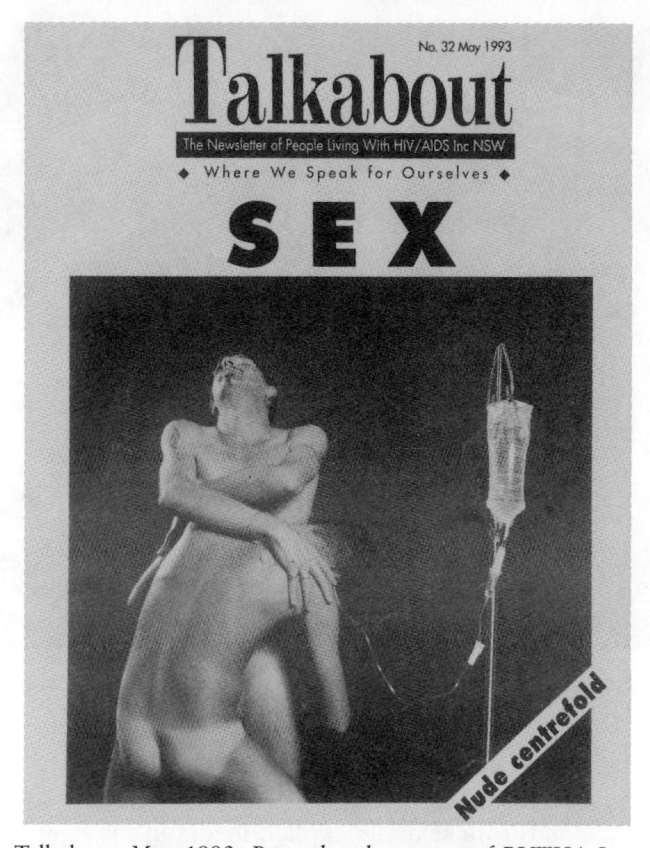

Talkabout, May 1993. Reproduced courtesy of PLWHA Inc. NSW, Jamie Dunbar and the Estate of Andrew Morgan.

directly confront the issue of human sexuality and its place in an HIV-positive world. This 'visual and photographic representation of the sexualities of people with HIV/AIDS', as Morgan himself initially called the project, was first published under the collective title of 'Love, Sex & T-Cell Counts' in the May 1993 issue of *Talkabout*, the newsletter of people living with HIV/AIDS in New South Wales (PLWHA Inc, NSW). The project had in fact been financed by *Talkabout*, with additional funds coming from PLWHA.

An accompanying editorial told *Talkabout*'s readers frankly that 'it is not acceptable for people with HIV/AIDS to continue

PositHIV Sexuality Postcards, *1994. Reproduced courtesy of PLWHA Inc. NSW, AIDS Council of NSW, Jamie Dunbar and the Estate of Andrew Morgan.*

to be excluded from sexually explicit media in the fight against AIDS', and urged them to applaud Morgan's and Dunbar's models, 'proud and loud people fighting for their rights and sexual identities [who] deserve our admiration and respect for their bravery, their honesty, their beauty and their commitment' (*Talkabout* 1993, p. 11).

These are very special photographs, at once cathartic and healing for their subjects, and instructive for all who study them. They received an overwhelmingly supportive response from the readership of *Talkabout*, and from HIV-positive constituencies in and around Sydney. Many HIV-positive colleagues requested a further development of the project, and thus was born the PositHIV Sexuality Campaign.

In Andrew Morgan's opinion, 'PositHIV Sexuality is about people with HIV infection reclaiming their territory in the

SEX AND THE SINGLE T-CELL

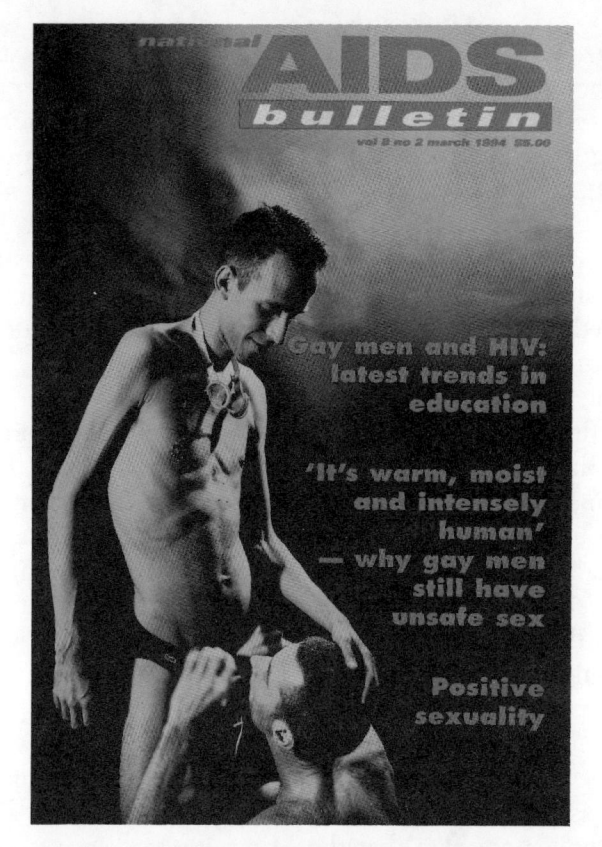

National AIDS Bulletin, *March 1994. Reproduced courtesy of AFAO.*

sexual arena . . . for too long people living with HIV/AIDS have been receiving messages that tell us we shouldn't be allowed to be sexual beings after receiving a positive diagnosis. This misconception has to change' (Morgan in Hoskins 1994, p. 5).

In conjunction with the HIV Strategy and Support Unit and the Community Development Unit of the AIDS Council of New South Wales (ACON), a select number of the Morgan and Dunbar photographs were turned into a print campaign, consisting of two posters and four postcards. Funds for this campaign, a meagre $8000, were raised independently by

ACON, with no state or Commonwealth monies involved (*National AIDS Bulletin* 1994a). This point is an important one, given the subsequent threat to withdraw Commonwealth funding from the Australian Federation of AIDS Organisations (AFAO), which I will come to shortly.

Launched at the time of the 1994 Sydney Gay & Lesbian Mardi Gras, the Dunbar/Morgan photographs and posters met with community acclaim. Until, that is, one of the images appeared on the front cover of the March 1994 issue of the *National AIDS Bulletin*.

What the cover did was provoke a letter from the Minister for Health to the President of AFAO, the publishers, protesting that 'I find the cover to this month's *National AIDS Bulletin*, depicting an oral sex encounter between two men, to be gratuitous, offensive and damaging to public acceptance of the National HIV/AIDS Strategy and its safe sex message'. The letter went on to complain about the cover's 'suggestive copy apparently advocating anything but safe sex', along with the fact that it constituted a leaking into the public space of imagery that should have been 'properly targeted' to only the gay community. It concluded that 'you should be aware that I will be looking very carefully at Commonwealth funding of AFAO as a result of this incident'.[3]

I should note here that the Minister's reference to 'suggestive copy apparently advocating anything but safe sex' related not to the *cover* of the journal, but to the PositHIV Sexuality poster on the *inside back page*, which bore the text: 'Hold him there. Let him up for air then get back to it. Put it in your mouth, lick, suck, slow and easy, fast and hard.'

Reactions such as this signal the subtle underlying homophobia which continues to oppress forthright and reasoned discussion around HIV/AIDS and sexuality. The message of the Minister for Health's letter is clear on two points: the explicit imaging of gay sex in the public realm is not admissible; and

---

3   Letter from Senator Graham Richardson, Minister for Health, Commonwealth of Australia, to Tony Keenan, President of AFAO; partially quoted in 'Anger at sex cover of AIDS magazine', *The Australian*, Wednesday 23 March 1994.

cock-sucking is definitely not safe and is always AIDS-transmissive. Both points must be vigorously challenged. As Michael Bartos has stressed, in fact the cover's 'depiction is of the adoration of Speedos (a safe act), the potential enactment of oral sex (considered safe, with some qualification, in Australian safe sex guidelines), and sex implied to be between two positive men, where there is no prospect of an uninfected individual becoming HIV infected' (Bartos 1996).

Indeed, if homophobia and AIDS-phobia are to be truly combated, images both of HIV sexuality and gay sexuality must be *properly* targeted—at the whole country; otherwise the 'dirty secret' tag remains. Every time the 'general public' is protected from what may offend it, its own bigotry is allowed to continue unchecked.

The consequence of the Minister's threat to withdraw funding from AFAO for its image transgression has created a new climate of reticence in Australia, in an already sufficiently paranoid vortex of AIDS educators and image-makers. In the November-December 1994 issue of the *National AIDS Bulletin*, an act of censorship occurred which was directly related to the 'cover-boys' controversy, and which was also provoked by the unmentionable issue of HIV-positive sexuality.

In the journal's own words, placed in one corner of an otherwise blank double-page spread, '"Butt Plugs", a piece of AIDS fiction by Sydney writer Stephen Dunne, was deemed by the Australian Federation of AIDS Organisations to be too controversial for publication . . . Earlier this year, the funding for the *National AIDS Bulletin*, the majority of which is provided by the Commonwealth Department of Human Services and Health, was threatened when it published an erotic picture of two HIV-positive men on its cover. AFAO judged at the eleventh hour that using Dunne's story at this time could be provocative, and not appropriate for the audience of the *National AIDS Bulletin*' (*National AIDS Bulletin* 1994b). This suppression of information happened despite AFAO's own disclaimer, placed regularly amongst the journal's imprint details, that 'views expressed in the *National AIDS Bulletin* are those of the authors and do not necessarily reflect the views of AFAO'.

To their credit, the journal's editors brought prominence to this censorial action by leaving the offending pages so dramatically blank, and offering to mail out the story to anyone interested. A further touch of irony is to be found in the fact that the suppression of 'Butt Plugs' occurred ten pages after Michael Hurley's telling 'Select Bibliography of HIV/AIDS Censorship', in the same issue. The reason for this censorship seems clear—a wish not to rekindle the ire of the Minister for Health and reinvoke the earlier threat to withdraw funding from AFAO (and therefore the *Bulletin* itself).

Stephen Dunne's story addresses with biting humour the complex issues of viral load, safe/unsafe HIV-positive sex, and AIDS envy (the phenomenon of a person, surrounded by the infected, pretending to also be HIV-positive so as to feel 'one of the gang'). In the climax of the tale Peter, a gay PLWHA rediscovering his libido, makes a grab for his carer Daniel:

> Fingers tighten[ed] on Daniel's tits while exquisite pain shot through him. [. . .] Daniel gladly acquiesced until he saw Peter reach for a very ancient jar of Vaseline. Daniel sat up as Peter's finger slid in.
> 'Um, hang on. That's um . . . not safe, um . . .'
> Peter didn't care, index finger prodding a prostate.
> 'Not safe? C'mon, you can do better than that. Fuck, you don't actually believe in reinfection do you? Listen honey, let's swap viral loads.'
> Daniel gulped hard. Shit.
> 'Um, listen . . .'
> 'What?'
> Two fingers now, alternating strokes, getting faster.
> 'I lied.'
> 'What darling?'
> Three, easy.
> 'I lied. I'm negative' (Dunne 1995a, p. 37).

One has to ask, if a piece of fiction such as Dunne's darkly amusing narrative concerning HIV-positive sexuality cannot be published in the *National AIDS Bulletin*, where on earth can it find a home? Who is the *National AIDS Bulletin* aimed at, if not people living with HIV (who are having the very sex in question) and in large part the medical and health-care professional world, all of whom should surely by now (and I write this in full recognition of the irony that it is *not* so), a decade and more into this epidemic, be both well aware of and able to deal with their clients' sexualities?

In any case, this act of self-censorship only served, as always, to draw greater attention to the piece under suppression. 'Butt Plugs' has, for example, subsequently been printed in full both in the Australian gay glossy *Campaign*, and in the London equivalent, *Rouge* (Dunne 1995a; 1995b). Despite this, it is hard not to draw parallels with the paranoia currently rampant in the United States, where arts bodies are engaged in an orgy of over-zealous self-regulation in the wake of Senator Jesse Helms's sexuality-related attacks on the National Endowment for the Arts. It is a pity that such timidity seems now to have crept into Australia—an intercontinental form of Acquired Information Denial Syndrome?

The simple fact, however, is that, despite ministerial fulminations and despite censorship from the AIDS bureaucracy, HIV-positive sexuality is here, is both queer and non-queer, and will not go away. What we need is not more 'targeting' or censorship, but a gutsy, head-on approach.

Hence the popularity of David McDiarmid's ACON posters, which mirror the manner in which gay men in particular, whose communities have been hardest hit by HIV/AIDS, are dealing with the issue of HIV-positive sex every day. And only David McDiarmid has continued to image our tactical response to what could have been an Armageddon for *homo*-sexuality.

This is evident from the series of works McDiarmid embarked upon in 1993–94, which at the time of his death in May 1995 had only just begun to emerge into the public space. The taboo of HIV-positive sexuality became the central focus of this last phase of McDiarmid's art.

In 1992 David became enamoured of the numerous 'gayzines' which had sprung up in response to the AIDS-phobia and homophobia of mainstream American media culture. He

Queer with Class: The First Book of Homocult, 1992 (detail), photocopy.

avidly collected 'gayzines' such as the San Francisco-based *Homoture* and the Los Angeles-based *Infected Faggots' Perspective*.[4] He was especially taken with the subversive British queer group Homocult, whose confrontational graphics eschewed any attempt at nicety in the face of the homophobic legacy of Thatcherite England.

The style and tone of these 'gayzines' (or 'queerzines') inspired McDiarmid's own vitriolic publication, his book *Toxic Queen*, which employed both shocking humour, and contrasting images of eroticism and infection, to explore the psychological realms of HIV-positive sexuality. A subsequent series of Rainbow Aphorism laser prints took McDiarmid's black humour to an almost blasphemous brink, lending a queer

---

4   For an introduction to 'gayzines', see Stephen Dunne, 'Inter/erupt ! Queer Zine Scene ?', *Media International Australia*, no. 78, November 1995, pp. 53-68.

David McDiarmid, Toxic Queen, 1992 (detail), colour photocopy on paper. Reproduced courtesy of the Estate of David McDiarmid.

new meaning to the terms 'sick joke' and 'dying laughing' (see *That's Miss Poofter to You Asshole*).

It was in a final sequence of simulated magazine-cover prints, however, that McDiarmid proffered his most confronting meditations on the taboo of his own HIV-positive sexuality. The first of these was designed in November 1993 as the invitation to an alternative Christmas party thrown by his best friend Bernard (see *Vanity Bear*). The cover of the invitation bore the colour image of a naked, bearded and bodily hairy Bernard. Over Bernard's birthday glory McDiarmid stencilled in piercing red text the 'cover' title *Vanity Bear*. Inside the card, recipients were invited to Bernard's Summer Solstice Celebration party. Across from this, an 'Obitchery' poked fun at the artist's and model's shared HIV status, informing us, for example, that Bernard's lifestyle is Blank; his favourite bedtime

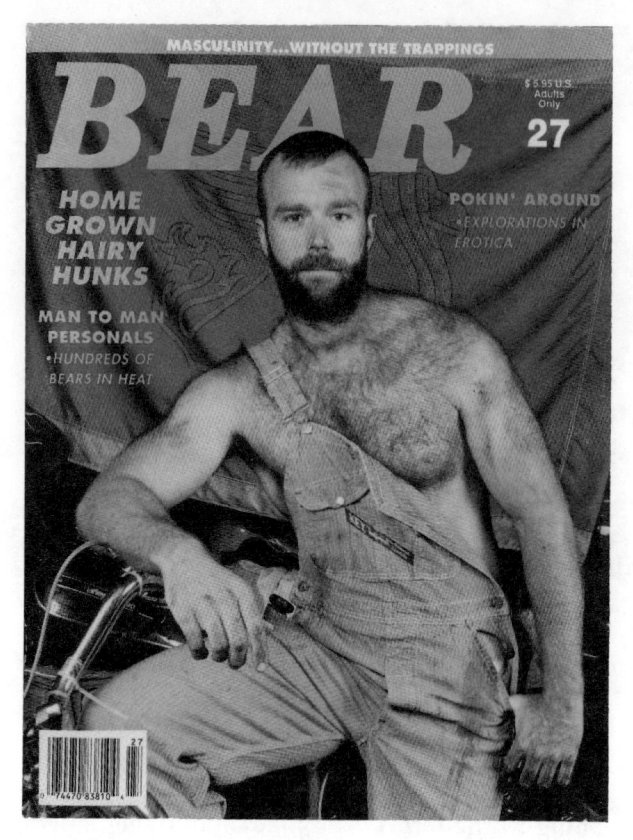

Bear Magazine, *no. 27. Reproduced courtesy of Brush Creek Media, San Francisco.*

reading is *Final Exit*, or MIM's *Pharmaceutical Dictionary*; his favourite scent is men; and his favourite cure is AZT for bad knees. (see *Vanity Bear [inside list]*).

The joke embedded in the invitation's cover works on many levels. There is of course the wickedly ironic hubris of an HIV-positive reading of the drop-dead elegance of *Vanity Fair* magazine being subverted by its 'homo' derivative *Vanity Bear*. It also functions as a send-up of the voluminous genre of gay men's 'stroke' magazines, such as *Torso, Honcho, Handjobs*, etc.

But the core of the joke relies both upon the observer's knowledge that in gay circles 'bear' is a code-word for a 'furry'

Diseased Pariah News, *no. 9. Reproduced courtesy of* Diseased Pariah News.

man with plenty of facial, chest and bum hair; and, especially, on the viewer's one-handed familiarity with *Bear* magazine, a San Francisco-based 'softish' porn publication devoted to photographic depictions of 'Buck-Naked Bare-Assed Hairy Men!!!' whose by-line describes itself as the journal of 'Naked Hairy Homo Smut!'

HIV-positive Bernard is simultaneously reified and deified as the new breed of cover-boy of the AIDS era, part porn-star, part dying queen, part fashion victim. The point is brought across beautifully in the teaser titles McDiarmid has stencilled over Bernard's beefcake cover: 'Fur Fashions for Fall', 'Terminal Shopping—How To Get a Life When You're Clinically Dead', and 'Bernard: Saint or Sow? Society Furball, or, Just Another Dying Queen?'

This new 'edge' to McDiarmid's work was inspired by the artist's discovery of the Californian, definitely post-new-age journal *DPN* or *Diseased Pariah News*. In the journal's own words, '*Diseased Pariah News* is a self-indulgent publication of, by, and for people with HIV disease (and their friends and loved ones). We are a forum for infected people to share their thoughts, feelings, art, writing, and brownie recipes in an atmosphere free of teddy bears, magic rocks, and seronegative guilt.'

The journal's wicked humour is captured best in the *DPN* 'Meat Market' advertisements, such as this one, which appeared under the headline 'Bend Over': 'I'm 31, tallish, hungish, good-looking in a somewhat avant-garde way. My new AIDS diagnosis hasn't affected my honker. Cute buggerable post-twinkies should write DPN Basket #2 quick, before I die or something' (*DPN* 1990, p. 29).

DPN also championed the 'Page 3 Boy', whose salient features are presented in mock-defiance of the traditional (and always perceived to be seronegative) beefcake imagery of gay soft-porn publishing. This irreverent respect for the sexual rights of all was explained in the fourth issue of *DPN*:

> 'But why emulate other skin magazines?' you may ask. Well, your Prurient Editors have thought about this for a while, and decided one of our goals is to eroticise the person with HIV. That's the reason why you see so much smut in this magazine. We're all still sexual creatures, no matter how much our ever-so-concerned sero-negative caregivers would like us to live in saintly abstinence, so there's no reason why we shouldn't find ourselves and others like us attractive (*DPN* 1991).

DPN will doubtless offend well-meaning heterosexuals who love to smilingly approach gays as lovable victims (what we can perhaps term the 'ET complex'). But it is hysterically funny and real to countless gay men who daily negotiate the zones of HIV sexuality.

Continuing in this *DPN*-inspired vein, McDiarmid followed his first foray into the twisted world of the mock AIDS 'fanzine' with a further series of laser prints, such as his premier issue of *Tired & Bitchy*, whose tattooed rough-trade cover-boy offered 'Attitude and Fashion Tips for the Infected'. These continued to rework the language of traditional gay soft porn magazines—borrowing the same appeal of seduction, but marrying it to a new language of sedition (see *PlagueBoy*). The monumental *PlagueBoy* features on its cover a sultry-eyed, moustached queen inviting the reader to devour articles such as 'Disinfected Dish for the Disaffected and the Diseased', 'Forty, Fabulous and Full-Blown', and the irresistible 'Half-Dead and Hot'. Blown up to colossal scale, *PlagueBoy* formed part of the interior decoration for a sex-radical soirée staged as an alternative to the March 1995 Sydney Gay & Lesbian Mardi Gras dance party.

That McDiarmid's humour hits the right note within its 'target community' is shown most simply by my favourite AIDS-era obituary notice: 'FAREWELL to a man with a HEART as BIG as his DICK!', which appeared in the gay newspaper *Sydney Star Observer* early in 1995.[5] This may seem like just more gallows humour to some; but I don't read it that way. I read it as a message full of love and, not so curiously after all, joy for having shared so much with the deceased.

Both McDiarmid's hornily-HIV cover-boys, and Jeff's 'big-dicked' farewell to his friend, offer us perfect reflections of the pragmatism of Australia's gay communities in recognising that just as AIDS seems to be here to stay for the conceivable future, so has the vibrancy and joy of human sexuality been here all along on the ride, to help us deal with this shadow.

Gay men in the nineties have realised and by and large dealt with the fact that both the heady plateaus of sexual desire and the health-compromising minefields of HIV/AIDS now

---

5   Obituary for Stuart Buggy 1954-1994, from Jeff; *Sydney Star Observer*, Thursday 12 January 1995, p. 12.

have to be accommodated, without further fuss, within the realm of everyday life. When will the rest of 'society' follow our lead and just

GET OVER IT?

12
Stirred heart and soul: the visual representation of lesbian sexuality

ELIZABETH ASHBURN

If you live in Sydney it is possible year-round to attend sophisticated and professional art exhibitions dedicated to the exploration of lesbian sexualities. These exhibitions peak during the Sydney Gay & Lesbian Mardi Gras Festival, a one-month program of visual and performing arts. In 1996 the Festival program included seven joint exhibitions of gay and lesbian work and eleven exhibitions dedicated solely to lesbian art, in which possibly as many as 140 lesbian artists from around New South Wales and from interstate exhibited work. This flowering of the visual arts reflects the diversity within lesbian communities which as yet manifests no single dominant approach or style.

When any artist who is a member of a minority group, and who is conscious of being so, enters into art, they do so obliquely. Lesbian artists are equally as concerned about problems of form as straight artists but 'also they cannot help but be stirred heart and soul when their subject is . . . "that which dares not speak its name". . . that which they find everywhere though it is never written about' (Wittig 1992, p. 62). Lesbian art is that art which is produced by an artist stirred heart and soul by her subject—the exploration of experiences arising from her lesbian sexuality or from issues relating to her sexuality. There are some visual artists who although they are lesbians do not always make their sexuality the subject of every art work, and some never choose to explore their sexuality through their art at all. But within Western culture the art practice of all lesbians has been constrained and marginalised.

The battle of the lesbian creator is waged on two fronts: 'on the formal level with the questions being debated at the moment in literary [or art] history, and on the conceptual level against the that-goes-without-saying of the straight mind' (Wittig 1992, p. 65). The homophobic strategies which exist within society have previously functioned to make lesbians invisible as individuals or as groups. Even today, the world which is constructed by major institutions such as the media remains overwhelmingly straight. Lesbians are absent from dominant representations in the same way that Aboriginal and other ethnic groups have been erased. When lesbians do appear they cannot be anything other than lesbian and are represented *only* by their sexuality. Their sexual preference *is* their identity and they must wait for this lesbian sexuality to be confirmed by the kiss or embrace of another woman.

In the United States and Britain, the long-term agenda of the conservative right has helped to maintain deep reservoirs of ignorance and sexual bigotry, so that the hegemonic control over the State exercised by the right in these countries has renewed and deepened its hold over erotic behaviour (Rubin 1982, p. 193). Lesbian artists have had to fight against discrimination, censorship and loss of funding. The situation for lesbian artists has been different in Australia, where the political climate has given them real possibilities for exploring issues surrounding their lesbian sexuality in the arts.

Australia, in common with the United States and Britain, was a site of extensive and successful morality campaigns in the late nineteenth and early twentieth centuries against prostitution, obscenity, contraception, abortion and masturbation, which established 'state policies, social practices, and deeply entrenched ideologies which still affect the shape of our sexual experience and our ability to think about it' (Rubin, p. 192). But since the early 1970s in Australia, the right has not controlled the State as it has in the United States and Britain. The continuous government of the Labor Party at federal level for the thirteen years to 1996 slowly generated policy positions, such as multiculturalism, which encourage tolerance toward racial and sexual diversity. The development by the Labor government of anti-discrimination legislation made it unlawful for citizens to discriminate against lesbians in many aspects of civil life, although this apparent acceptance of lesbian sexuality is still a thin veneer over deeply-held homophobia and misogyny. These beliefs, which occasionally still break through, could rapidly re-surface under a conservative regime.

Flowing from this relative lack of discrimination, a climate was generated in the visual arts that enabled lesbians to create and exhibit images of a sexual nature which would probably be censored or not shown publicly in other countries. In Sydney, in areas such as Newtown and Paddington where there is a concentration of gays and lesbians, their powerful 'pink vote' and visible presence has allowed diverse and vigorous open expression of homosexual sexualities. Elsewhere in this book, Kimberly O'Sullivan and C.Moore Hardy discuss the development of the sex-radical underground and its performance art in Sydney. The infrastructure needed to support gay and lesbian arts, such as sympathetic venues and funding for lesbian art, has been slowly increasing, particularly in the larger cities. The policies of government arts agencies, educational institutions and the art industry have included initiatives which allow for the production and exhibition of specifically lesbian and gay art. Some visual arts administrators have proposed policies for straight galleries and public museums which are sensitive to the representation of lesbian and gay sexuality. The Sydney Gay & Lesbian Mardi Gras organisation offers grants, scholarships and artists' residencies to encourage specifically gay and lesbian works and exhibitions.

Such an open lesbian visual art culture was not possible before the shift in government sensibility to a policy of anti-discrimination. An increasing acceptance of exhibitions which explore aspects of lesbian sexuality has been shown by Sydney mainstream galleries, such as the Roslyn Oxley Gallery and the Barry Stern Gallery. Specifically lesbian work has also been shown at significant art events such as the Sydney Biennale. However, the situation for lesbian artists in predominantly heterosexual areas can remain restrictive. There have been incidents where local government councils outside these centres have behaved in discriminatory ways. When the lesbian artist Cath Phillips exhibited in the country centre of Mildura she was prosecuted for making art which was described as 'offensive' to public morals. Recently, councils have banned images of topless women in an 'Images of Family' exhibition when the subjects were identified as lesbians,[1] and have censored safe sex posters for lesbians. In the climate of tolerance developed under anti-discrimination policies, incidents such as the removal of the safe sex poster, Dam Dykes, was criticised in both the gay and straight press.[2]

The opportunity to exhibit artworks centred around lesbian sexuality has encouraged sections of the lesbian community to become active in the visual arts, and lesbian artists to become involved in developing lesbian content. Thus, artworks motivated by such a passion for their subject can flow directly from within lesbian groups or emerge in the art practice of individual artists. These twin sources have produced strong and celebratory works which have attempted to develop powerful images of lesbian sexuality. Marion Moore is an artist who has worked collaboratively with other artists, and in consultation with lesbian groups, to produce strong and positive images of butch lesbians and of lesbian mothers. Suzanne Boccalatte, who works as a traditional visual artist, formulates her projects around new modes of representing the body. This body is not immediately recognisable but slowly becomes an expression of a lesbian erotic, both seductive and unsettling.

---

[1] Having previously allowed the exhibition of photographs of totally naked Aboriginal women the councillors were able to demonstrate that their attitudes were both homophobic and racist: 'Bernie Shehan in *Dyke* collage likened to "girlie" pinup' in *Sydney Star Observer,* 17 November 1994.

[2] As well as the local gay press, *The Brisbane Courier Mail* May 1994 reported this incident.

Both of these artists have developed specific art processes which are intrinsic to their work and each endeavours to produce positive statements about lesbian sexuality.

Marion Moore has been an artist working with the community on several projects which have used powerful visual images of individual lesbians to attempt to change attitudes within society towards lesbians as a group. She describes herself as 'a documentor of the lesbian community' (Moore 1995, p. 32); however, her involvement with the community extends beyond mere documentation. Lesbians wherever possible want to take control of their own representation. These collaborative projects have been designed in consultation with, and on behalf of, sectors of the lesbian community and provide an alternative model for the production of artwork. However, for such projects to be successful, all parties concerned need a high level of communication skills. Even though a collective basis of involvement in art production can be a way to allow all parties input into the final work it takes creative decision-making to produce a strong image. Artists like Moore consult with their subjects throughout the development of each image about the way their sexuality is to be depicted. Many of these subjects, and some lesbian artists themselves, have concerns about particular audiences viewing specific images, however, and refuse to be included in certain exhibition venues or publications.

Community-based lesbian artists see such collaborative projects 'as a way of representing ourselves as lesbians . . . ; images of us, by us and for us' (Elisa Hall in Ashburn 1996, p. 43). Catherine Fargher, who has worked as a community artist and writer since 1985, says that 'often lesbian groups are under-resourced or over-stretched, or we are putting energy into the social and political struggles of other groups. I feel it is really important to put energy into creating our own cultural products, to take responsibility for our own visibility and demand our right to be heard and seen' (Catherine Fargher in Ashburn 1996 p. 43).

Marion Moore has collaborated with Elisa Hall and Catherine Fargher on a major community-based project as part of

Marion Moore, Some Kids Have Two Mums, 1 and 2, *Lovely Mothers Poster Series, Word of Mouth III* © Marion Moore

Marion Moore, She Loves Me, 1 and 2, *Lovely Mothers Poster Series, Word of Mouth III* © Marion Moore

Word of Mouth, a lesbian art collective. Word of Mouth began in 1991 with a community-based mixed-media exhibition and performances at the Performance Space. Devised after a series of public forums, Word of Mouth aimed to provide an outlet for both practising artists and those previously un-art-skilled.[3] In 1993 The Lovely Mothers' Poster series was designed to highlight lesbian mothers and children and lesbian-based families. Created as part of Word of Mouth III, this project was funded by the Community Cultural Development Board of the Australia Council for the Arts. After the success of these posters, The Lovely Mothers' Billboards project was further developed by Catherine Fargher and Deborah Kelly as part of Word of Mouth IV to develop the images from these posters into billboards in highly visible sites at railway stations around Sydney.

These artists intended using strong and positive visual images to raise the awareness of the general public to lesbian-based families and to increase visibility, acceptance and support of both parents and children. In the straight world, lesbian mothers are sometimes portrayed as unsuitable parents because of their sexuality and have even lost custody of their children. By encouraging the inclusion of lesbian-based families under the broader spectrum of the constitution of *family*, these artists hoped to decrease the violence, negativity and homophobia surrounding lesbians.[4]

In the thematic exhibition 'Butch Baby Butch; Contemporary butch profiles' Marion Moore chose to present photographs of individual lesbians as a means of presenting the face of contemporary butch sexuality (see *Michelle; Kimberly and Mel*). This exhibition consisted of black and white photographs of sixteen butch lesbians, with a handwritten statement from each subject concerning her experiences as a butch superimposed on the background behind her portrait. Each photograph described a specific individual who identified

---

3   This information was provided by the *Word of Mouth* collective.
4   The information for *The Lovely Mothers' Poster* series and *The Lovely Mothers' Billboards* project was provided by Elisa Hall and Catherine Fargher.

Marion Moore, Helen, *Butch Baby Butch Series*
© *Marion Moore*

herself as butch and commented on her own history and attitudes as a butch. Although their appearance and comments were recognisably butch, collectively their diversity challenged the existence of a single butch stereotype. Their comments made it clear that they were aware of the stereotype and the power such stereotypes generate, but they frequently used ironic comments to send it up, such as Cris who is a SNAB, 'a sensitive New Age Butch', or Denny who has a gourmet butch role (Moore 1995, pp. 20, 22). The catalogue essays by Shân Short and Kimberly O'Sullivan discussed the way the place of the butch and femme in the lesbian community had been contested, and the perception of the early lesbian feminists of the seventies that butch was a role-play derived from the world of heterosexuality. This exhibition was an attempt to recognise the diversity of butch lesbians, to vindicate their lifestyle as a valid choice for today and to encourage their support by both straight and lesbian viewers.

Suzanne Boccalatte's aim to create artworks which articulate the corporeal in a new way is far less lesbian-specific. These works do not produce an immediately recognisable lesbian image in the way that the work of Marion Moore intends, but they are nevertheless shaped by a strong lesbian erotic. Boccalatte has had extensive training in painting and printmaking within TAFE and the Sydney College of the Arts, Sydney University, and is one of the many lesbian artists whose practice is strongly informed by formal art studies. Art colleges and universities require students to relate their own art production to the histories and theories of art. Consequently, their programs provide studies in contemporary art theory, women's studies, and in some cases the growing field of lesbian, gay and queer theory. The work of these lesbian artists is increasingly technically skilled and theoretically sophisticated, often utilising the writings of Australian lesbian academics and scholars such as Elizabeth Grosz.

When Boccalatte examined the work of other women artists, such as Louise Bourgeois, Kiki Smith and Helen Chadwick, she recognised that although each artist used the body in her own unique way, there was a strong notion of fragmentation. Boccalatte's early art practice had been to use Polaroid close-ups of bodies—of her own, of her friends, and of specific animals. Close-ups are a means of fragmenting the whole body and this development of 'body bits' was used to inform her own work. The writer A. Sinnott has suggested that the bits-and-pieces of the body and what we do with them 'could be defined as a metaphor for the psychological, social, political and physical assaults on the individual, a site for the investigation of our most urgent concerns including sexual identity, reproductive rights, homophobia, social inequalities, disease and death' (Sinnott 1993, p. 8). Although Boccalatte uses the processes of fragmentation in her work, and thus repeats this assault, she moves beyond mere fragmentation by creating a new form from the pieces by reintegrating them into an image which is unifying and positive.

To fragment the body is to use a strategy close to pornography. In her early work, Boccalatte was developing fragments which provided an intimacy of detail similar to the way that pornography 'operates on the formal fragmentation and the close-up of the body' (Boccalatte 1995, p. 5). She wanted these fragments to become 'sumptuous and desirable' and yet avoid the pornographic with its concern with issues of voyeurism, heterosexuality and spectatorship. Within the context of straight representation, images of lesbian sexuality operate mainly as erotic stimulation for heterosexuals. Such images are not involved with the representation of lesbian sexuality but are often part of a straight cautionary tale which leaves the lesbian abandoned (or dead). In pornography, the fragmented body remains abstracted and unrecognisable. Boccalatte moves beyond pornography by re-assembling these body bits into new articulations which give a new and often surprising wholeness to these fragments.

In building a fresh vocabulary for the body, Boccalatte has concentrated on richness of colour and density of composition to achieve the fragility of a body surface with the flesh removed. She quotes Elizabeth Grosz describing the surface of the body, where 'the skin moreover provides the articulation of orifices, erotogenic rims, cuts on the body's surface, loci of the exchange between the inside and outside, points of conversion of the outside into the body and of the inside out of the body' (Grosz 1994, p. 36). Boccalatte combines various techniques from painting and printmaking in the same work to subject her images of body bits to a further blurring of identity. These hybrids formed by using multiple techniques Boccalatte calls printed paintings. The art process begins with an initial process of fragmentation. By making Polaroid prints of a body, she encourages the image of the body as a whole to break down. She then scans the Polaroids into a computer and continues the further disintegration of the body by cropping, distorting and re-arranging images. These fragments are printed out as a template and covered by a perspex plate which is gouged, cut and punctured. Thin layers of oil paint placed on the perspex are further pushed, manipulated and wiped and the plate is printed using an etching press. These images now bear traces of many techniques, and it is as difficult to determine the processes which formed them as it is to identify what the original image represented.

The most important, and the final, stage in making these works is the joining together of the printed paintings into new configurations where the artist brings wholeness to the fragments. Making square multiples of these images, she joins them into a grid within a larger square. The fragments, mirrored and reversed now, look like a Rorschach test producing 'new aesthetic bodies' within their own space and contexts (Boccalatte 1995, p. 5). The assemblage of the body parts within the grid framework asserts an idea of completion but, because this formation allows the easy addition of more images, closure retains the possibility of further extension. These works remain ambiguous and abstract until they are seemingly offered as a matrix forming the whole which again repeats the refusal of closure and identity. It is this dynamic of the representation of a female body which is erotic and repeated, yet resists classification, that reveals the strength of Boccalatte's images as metaphors for aspects of lesbian sexuality (see *Corporeal Landscape: Head*).

This re-creation of the image by the artist is intended initially to seduce and then to unsettle the viewer. In works such as *Corporeal Landscape: Head* she describes the seduction as being achieved through 'rich, luminescent colours—reminiscent of classical painting techniques in close-up, *an intimate look at the sensuality of the dark and the hidden*' (Boccalatte 1995, p. 5, my emphasis). The chiaroscuro, the glowing colour, and the 'soft smoothness and sensual surface' the artist has created through her multiple techniques extends her evocation of the erotic female body. This is never a single female body because it is continually mirrored and multiplied until every space is filled, creating a totally female universe.

The viewer is unsettled by these isolated and juxtaposed images. By fragmenting close-ups of familiar aspects of the body, strange cavities and protuberances are formed which appear to bear little relationship to the names of the works. Simple subtitles of *Back, Front* or *Head* suggest possible familiarity for the viewer, but the rejoining of the pieces encourages confusion and ambiguity by their refusal to indicate which part of the body is imaged or indeed if there is a body at all. In these works the viewers are left again to search for their own resolution.

Interestingly, in their latest works Moore and Boccalatte both explore the dimension of the masculine/feminine. In *Ox*, Boccalatte uses the image of cows' udders as a metaphor for desire. This desire can be read as containing both male and female characteristics, as udders have the hermaphroditic qualities of being simultaneously voluptuous and erect. She sees this piece as influenced by Louise Bourgeois in its pursuit of a gender-bending metamorphosis (Nochlin 1994, p. 54) and as a continuation of her intent to blur strict categories. In her exhibition 'Centrefold', Marion Moore also aims 'to dissect, explore and challenge preconceived ideas of the masculine and feminine within the theatre of sexual interplay'.[5] She has developed this exhibition around Bo, a body builder who appeared in 'Butch Baby Butch; Contemporary butch profiles' (see *Bo*). Bo's physical development gives her a non-specific gender identity, an ambiguity which Moore exploits by placing Bo in the context of the gender-stereotyped centrefold. By using the nude centrefold she intends to stress the constructed rather than the biological nature of gender.

Australian lesbian art has rapidly developed a cultural base that has both breadth in the numbers of individual artists and depth from the growing body of artworks and exhibitions. Many artists such as Moore, Boccalatte and C.Moore Hardy are now able to build on previous work to extend their art practice into a stronger and more systematic investigation of

---

5   Marion Moore quoted in the *1996 Sydney Gay and Lesbian Mardi Gras Guide* p. 41.

issues of sexuality. As Wittig (1992) points out, the work of lesbian artists can change 'the angle of categorisation as far as the sociological reality of their group goes, at least in affirming its existence' (Wittig 1992, p. 64). Lesbian artists make lesbian presence increasingly visible. Powerful lesbian art has the potential to transform the visual reality of our time. This growing maturity and vitality within lesbian visual art culture encourages the lesbian viewer to look to lesbian artists for new representations of lesbian sexuality and suggests to the wider art community that lesbian art requires serious consideration in its production of significant works of art.

13
I was a teenage romance writer

JENNY PAUSACKER

In a world of continually changing icons, romance writers are a rare constant, appearing regularly in TV programs, magazine articles and newspaper features where they elicit equal amounts of gentle satire and rueful admiration for their earning power. We all know what romance writers are supposed to be like. Either defenders of the faith or cynical exploiters—or possibly both at once. Women of a certain age with carefully coiffed blonde hair and elaborate make-up, swathed in chiffon draperies and preferably clutching small silky dogs, a style that pays homage to Barbara Cartland, the icon of icons—over 600 romance novels and still counting.

In other words, romance writers and the romances that they write are conflated to an unusual degree. As far as I know, writers of horror novels aren't expected to look like Boris Karloff, any more than thriller writers are expected to be muscled and athletic or detective story writers to have homicidal tendencies. Indeed, I've written novels and short stories in all three of those genres without feeling any pressure to adjust my self-image. But when I became, more or less by accident, a writer of romances, I instantly found myself part of a strange sexual subculture, the locus of all sorts of unpredictable confidences, moralities, questions and expectations.

Maybe the expectations are higher because romance has been such an enduring genre, represented among the first English language novels by writers like Fanny Burney and Jane Austen and mutating steadily ever since—although for a while, in the seventies, it seemed that Women's Liberation was going to challenge the hegemony of romance writers. Germaine Greer (1970) led the way with pronouncements like, 'The titillating mush of Cartland and her ilk is supplying an imaginative need but their hypocrisy limits the gratification to that which can be gained from innuendo: by-pass the innuendo and you shortcircuit the whole process', while other feminists criticised the way romance confined women to the personal and domestic. But imprints such as Mills and Boon responded by incorporating relatively explicit descriptions of sexual activity and relatively high-flying career women into the formula. Before long feminist theorists were writing about the pleasures, as well as the dangers, of romance and romance writers went back to being icons again.

How to explain the ongoing fascination with this particular sexual subculture? Does the world of the romance writer evoke a mythically simpler time when men were men, women were women and romance writers created rituals for negotiating the impasse? Is the genre subvertable or not? Is it monolithic, part of a pre-packaged global culture, or does it take on different forms and meanings in different places? Have romance writers survived simply by being as adaptable as the cockroach or is romance still filling 'an imaginative need' not met anywhere else? I'd like to place some of these questions in a specifically Australian context by telling the story of the time when I was a teenage romance writer.

As a kid, I always used to pounce on series novels, from the Bobbsey Twins and the Famous Five to Ivan Southall's Simon Black books, because it was comforting to know that, if I liked one of them, there was a whole shelf full of similar titles ready and waiting. At the same time I've always been irritated by the popularity of American teenage romance series, because it bugged me to think of Australian readers fetishising proms and cheerleaders and colleges and drugstores and homecoming queens.

So when Belinda Byrne rang to say that Greenhouse wanted to establish an *Australian* teenage romance series, I was already predisposed towards the idea. At the time I was writing children's and young adult fiction for my own satisfaction, and educational kits to pay the rent, although I was starting to feel irked by the continual shift between fiction and non-fiction. I was also stony broke and suffering from Chronic Fatigue Syndrome and Greenhouse was offering a flat fee on receipt of manuscript (later changed to half the fee on receipt of manuscript and the other half on publication—but that still didn't take as long as waiting for advances and royalties to come through). I had practical reasons and theoretical reasons for accepting Belinda's offer—and I had one more reason as well.

I wanted to see whether I could do it.

Some years before, I'd tried writing for Mills and Boon, in collaboration with a friend of mine. We'd both been dedicated feminist activists in the seventies and we were moderately annoyed that no one had ever asked us to sell out, so we decided to arrange it for ourselves. We read through a huge stack of Mills and Boon romances, constructed a plot around a heroine who cooked and a hero who was a cross between a saint and a rapist, struggled for months with the drawn-out, introspective Mills and Boon housestyle and finally posted off our manuscript.

To our dismay, Mills and Boon wrote back to say that we'd obviously done our research but that our novel was a bit old-fashioned. I raced into Coles, read the back blurbs of a dozen current Mills and Boons and discovered that the typical mid-eighties heroine was busy trying to choose between love and career—and discovering in the final chapter that she could have it all. Ironically, if my friend and I had decided that we were going to bring feminism into Mills and Boon, we might've achieved our ambition after all.

As it happened, writing teenage romances turned out to be a very different sort of experience. Where Mills and Boon novels basically revolve around two characters, him and her, the teenage romance genre allows for a whole range of friends and schoolmates and parents and siblings, who share the stage with the main protagonists. What's more, with teenage romances the readers are well aware that even if the heroine and hero are together on the final page, they're highly likely to break up two weeks after the novel ends. Consequently, teenage romances don't have the self-enclosure and the 'all or nothing' intensity of adult romances.

The process of publishing an Australian teenage romance series was also very different from the popular stereotype of multinational publishing firms with extensive marketing campaigns, intensive research and unlimited finances. Understandably, most people assumed that the Dolly fiction series was an offshoot of *Dolly*, a mainstream magazine aimed at young women readers, but in fact the link was more tangential. Sally Milner, the publisher at Greenhouse, dreamed up the series for the same reason as I was interested in writing for it—because she wanted to provide an alternative to British and American teenage romances. At that time Greenhouse was owned by Australian Consolidated Press (ACP), who publish *Dolly*, and the connection between magazine and series was made because it was felt that the power of the *Dolly* name would help to establish the series in the marketplace. However, although the staff at *Dolly* vetted the synopses, they played no part in commissioning or editing the books.

Dolly Fiction was launched in September 1987. In 1989 ACP closed Greenhouse and sold most of the titles on its list to other publishing firms—with the exception of the Dolly Fiction series, which it retained as a separate entity. For the next few years the series led a kind of gypsy existence, owned by a magazine publishing conglomerate that was not set up to distribute books and run by Belinda Byrne working from home as a freelance editor. Always under-resourced, its future continually in doubt, it nonetheless continued on until, at Belinda's suggestion, James Fraser at Pan licensed the series from ACP in 1991. After a trial run, Pan decided to drop the Dolly connection and change the name of the series to Paradise Point. Twenty-four Paradise Point titles were published before the series was discontinued in December 1993.

The initial print runs for the first Dolly Fiction titles were a wildly optimistic 25 000 but by the time Pan took over the series, print runs had been revised to 10 000 and finally stabilised at 8000. Two titles were published every month and by the time the series ended, there were 118 Dolly Fiction titles in all. Readers were, on average, between eleven and fifteen, although Belinda Byrne received letters from girls as young as nine and as old as 24. Invariably, these readers would explain that they loved Dolly Fiction because the books offered characters and situations that they could relate to, sometimes even mentioning particular fictional scenarios that had helped them in their own lives.

Looking back over the series, Belinda Byrne comments:

> I was always conscious of treading a fine line. The books were never meant to be worthy or instructive and yet we were writing for an impressionable and, in some ways, vulnerable audience. In defiance of their genre, Dolly Fictions were resolutely politically correct and they moved further and further in that direction as the series went on and I clarified what I was trying to do with it. The earlier Dolly Fictions were probably closer to their UK and US counterparts; later books encompassed more complex issues and a bolder approach towards depicting 'real' teenage lives. Once the link with *Dolly* magazine was severed, we were a lot freer, because *Dolly* imposed fairly strict guidelines about what could and could not be mentioned. (No alcohol, no cigarettes, no drugs, no sex . . .)

Writing for Dolly Fiction turned out to be a very relaxed and collaborative experience. Although the writers for the series never formally met together, we heard a lot about each other's work via Belinda, which meant that basically we were writing for each other, for Belinda and for the young women who sent in letters. I enjoyed this sense of a group project

Dolly Fiction and Hot Pursuit teenage romances © James Spence

right from the beginning and I soon found out that there were other pleasures in writing teenage fiction.

Between 1988 and 1992 I wrote fifteen novels in the Dolly Fiction series and four novels in Penguin's Hot Pursuit series, devised by Merrilee Moss and myself. A lot of my ideas were the result of playing games with genre. In order to prepare myself for writing my first Dolly, I borrowed a stack of Sweet Dreams from the local library and started coming to grips with the American prototype. I followed the model—more or less—in my first book but from then on I entertained myself by seeing how far I could stretch the boundaries of the formula without moving out of the romance genre altogether.

Thus, at various times, I tested out a fat heroine and a Greek-Australian heroine, a socialist hero and a Koori hero, a male narrator and a gay subplot, as well as writing about drugs, gossip, lesbian mothers and depression. The overseers at *Dolly* magazine passed all my experiments without a flicker, until they came to the synopsis of the novel with the fat heroine. They wrote back to Belinda Byrne, saying, 'We're not sure about this one—but she's written twelve books for the series already, so we're prepared to give it a go.' Which was a relief, because I'd been braced to argue my case. I wrote the synopsis for *Bigger and Better* after judging a *Dolly* competition where readers sent in their own suggestions for a Dolly Fiction plot. Having scanned dozens of synopses along the lines of, 'Betty really fancied John but John didn't even notice her, then Betty lost weight and John asked her out', I felt that there was a definite need for a corrective—and to my further relief, *Dolly* passed the completed text without changing a line.

The sticking point for *Dolly* magazine was the idea that a young woman could be fat and sexy. The sticking point, as far as I was concerned, was the issue of happy endings. Despite Belinda Byrne's constant urgings, I only once managed to write a novel where the hero and heroine *weren't* together at the end. At one point I was questioned stringently about this by a class of very romance-literate girls, who were anxious to know whether the happy endings in their favourite light reading were the result of a publishing directive. They were satisfied when I told them, 'It's not because I'm ordered to supply happy endings—it's because I like happy endings.' But the experience left me with a few questions of my own.

I've never thought of myself as a romantic. I don't sigh over happy couples in the street and I feel positively unnerved whenever I see anyone investing the whole of their emotional life in one other person. So what was I doing, working in a genre that—face it—focused on the manic moments of falling in love? Okay, I could tell myself I wanted to show young women that you could fall in love without falling for all the associated claptrap . . . but in that case, why wasn't I grateful to be working for an editor who actively encouraged me to leave my heroines unattached and feeling fine about it at the end of the novel?

To cut a long story short, I don't know. My parents had a classic fifties romance that came to a sticky end and I've sometimes wondered whether I'm trying to rewrite their story in order to make it come out right. But I'm not sure of the value of this kind of psychobiography: it certainly can't account for all the thousands of romance writers and millions of romance readers. At other times I suspect I'm simply acknowledging a cultural imperative—the pleasure of the expected ending, whether it's the solution at the end of a detective story, the triumph of the white hats at the end of a Western, or the kiss at the end of a romance. (Although this doesn't explain to me why I've found myself writing romances, rather than detective stories or Westerns.)

After I'd been writing Dolly Fictions for a year or so, I was intrigued to realise that I was being asked to speak on the subject of romance writing far more often than I was asked to speak about my 'serious' fiction. At a panel during the 1992 Melbourne Writers Festival, after Ken Methold had offered a devastating and hilarious parody of the Barbara Cartland syndrome, I pushed back my shaggy hair, hitched down my baggy windcheater and got a laugh simply by saying, 'I'm a romance writer.' It was all very interesting and entertaining but over time I started to get rather tetchy about the way people seemed simultaneously to be fascinated by romance and to feel a need to distance themselves from the genre. I'd expected teachers and librarians to be pleased that there were some Australian teen romances to set against the American imports—but they weren't. I'd expected reviewers to notice the little-Aussie-knocker approach of homegrown romance writers—but they didn't. The books were now there but the climate, the discourse, the forbidden nature of romance writing hadn't changed.

So what did I learn from my travels through the subculture of romance writing? First of all, I found that romance, for all its high mainstream profile, offers the lure of the forbidden. The principal agent of this particular taboo is the laugh. You can get a laugh in adult circles simply by saying 'Mills and Boon' and you can get the same laugh in children's literature circles with the words 'Sweet Valley High'. After listening to this laugh for a while, I finally recognised it. It's the laugh we used to laugh in primary school whenever we heard the word 'bosom', as in 'bosom of the ocean', or 'poo', as in 'Pooh Bear'. It's the laugh that you laugh when somebody breaks a minor taboo and, just as my primary school class was fascinated by the forbidden topic of sex, so people these days are fascinated by romance. They flock to the panels on romance writing and they know all the Mills and Boon circulation figures—although, at the same time, they are always careful to explain that they themselves don't, of course, actually read romances.

Hence, over time, I've started to get the distinct impression that writing about love, especially love between a man and a woman, is one of the unacknowledged taboos of our time. Something to do with the impact of sixties sexual liberation and the counterculture on fifties definitions of romance? Yes, probably. Something to do with the remnants of the British class system where 'only servant girls read romance'? Yes, I suspect so. Something to do with feminism? Yes, for sure—but what, exactly?

For this particular feminist, the taboos surrounding romance have had two sharply contrasting effects. The eternal deviant in me is delighted to find itself breaking the rules again and recognises that part of the attraction of romance writing is the fact that romance, unlike science fiction and detective stories and horror films, has not suddenly become intellectually respectable. The activist in me, on the other hand, is stirred by the thought that the romance genre is denigrated primarily because it's seen as being women's business. I'm a pre-modernist feminist, after all. My mob didn't believe in toying with mainstream discourses; we actually believed in taking them over and changing them.

So, at least on a part-time basis, I've come to regard myself as a militant romance writer. I was disappointed when Pam Gilbert and Sandra Taylor (1991) analysed the way that the first eighteen Dolly Fiction titles represented codes of femininity, parents' occupations and girls' and boys' hobbies and career choices, without offering a similarly detailed analysis of the way the writers constructed the central romantic relationships. As a second wave feminist, I learned that 'the personal is political' and I spent a lot of time, in and out of consciousness-raising groups, discussing gay and straight relationships—how they were and how, with a more politicised awareness, they could be. The romance genre strikes me as a logical place to tackle these kinds of issues and I would describe my own endeavour, in a phrase borrowed from feminist theorist Sheila Jeffreys, as an attempt to 'eroticise equality'.

Given both my academic and my feminist backgrounds, I made it my business to catch up on the various studies of the romance genre that came out of women's studies and courses on popular culture and children's literature. While some writers talked about the pleasurable subversions of romance, others assumed an inherent contradiction between romance and feminism. But neither side of the debate left me feeling any more enlightened about what I was doing. Matched against my own experience, the belief that romance was inherently anti-feminist seemed too simple, the belief in pleasurable subversions too convoluted.

The most useful article that I came across during this time was 'A place for us: adolescent girls reading romance fiction' (1987), probably because its author, May Lam, was also trying to make sense of her own experiences. As an English teacher and school librarian, Lam had been involved in preparing a non-sexist book list and made a special effort to promote books with 'positive role models and an emphasis on challenging and rewarding careers'. However, she found that '[w]hile girls at my school often cheerfully read and reported that they had enjoyed many of the titles I recommended them, at least as many girls (and often the same ones!) would ask for romance stories'. At this point, Lam decided to investigate. Working with a group of 42 keen romance readers, she discovered that their attitude to romance fiction was not uncritical ('I hate the American schools with the American football teams and the prettiest girl gets the lead guy in the football team') and that although romances could create feelings of inadequacy ('It makes you feel sort of sad because it makes you feel "I wish I was as pretty as her and had her life and all of that"'), they could also encourage a sense of realism ('I've learnt that love isn't always a lot of fun, it's probably made me be more mature with guys I'm going with. I take love more seriously now than before I started reading romances'). Most of all, these young women liked romance novels because they were about 'feelings'—not necessarily romantic feelings but feelings of all kinds, placing emotional responses at the centre of the narrative. Their honest appraisal had its effect on Lam. Having begun by promoting 'challenging and rewarding careers', she ends by saying that 'we need to address ways of showing how love and work do not have to be mutually exclusive'.

To Lam's 42 young women, romances represented an accessible way to start assessing love and sexuality. In a similar fashion, romance writing has represented the accessible face of literature to women writers ever since Jane Austen and the Brontës. As a self-confessed romance writer, I had a lot of people sidling up to me at seminars or launches or parties and I was startled to find out just how many closet romance novelists there are in this country. Over the past seven years I must've talked to more than 40 women who were working on a romance or had several chapters and a synopsis tucked away in a bottom drawer. And none of them fitted the stereotype, ranging as they did from lesbian feminists and country booksellers to modern girls and university lecturers—indeed, at least one of the other contributors to this collection has had a go at a Mills and Boon.

The Dolly Fiction series offered a starting point from which writers like Goldie Alexander and Merrilee Moss have gone on to write precisely the kinds of novels that critics like Sharyn Pearce (1991) regard as antithetical to the teen romance. Indeed, I'd argue that the series itself in no way fits Pearce's description of series romances as 'fairy stories which ignore dilemmas like divorce, the dole or single parenting'. After writing *Bigger and Better* (Dolly Fiction Number 58), where the heroine doesn't lose weight and gets the guy, I was rapt to come across Gerri Lapin's *Slim Pickings* (Dolly Fiction Number 84), where the heroine puts on weight and gets the guy—a characteristically iconoclastic contribution to a teen culture that spends a lot of time promoting anorexia.

Mind you, there's more to romance writing than values or ideology. While I readily agree with George Orwell that 'all art is propaganda', my most enduring interest in writing series romances has been a literary one. I dislike the generally accepted divide between high culture and popular culture and yet at the same time I know that my own novels all fall neatly into one or other category. Hence my use of pseudonyms. I started writing as Jaye Francis and Mary Forrest by accident—*I* remember Belinda Byrne telling me that I had to use a pen-name, *she* states firmly that she said no such thing. Still, even after I'd stopped to think about it, I decided to keep the pseudonyms going because, much as I resent the high/popular culture split, I (reluctantly) accept that I can't change the entire situation single-handed.

Nevertheless, I continue to hope that, by working on both sides of the divide, I may gradually overcome the split in my own sensibility. Maybe some day Jaye Francis, the fluent yarnspinner, and Jenny Pausacker, the meticulous reviser, will be able to get together. Maybe some day I'll see a change in the mindset where, in Ursula LeGuin's words, 'The Canoneers of Literature still refuse to admit that genrification is a political tactic and that the type of fiction they distinguish as serious, mainstream, literary, etc., is itself a genre without inherent superiority to any other.' Maybe some day it will become intellectually respectable to say that most people, women and men alike, spend a significant portion of their lives thinking about how to love and be loved, and to value writing that deals with this directly and reflectively.

In the meantime there's a lot of entertainment to be got from working the divide.

References

Introduction

Anderson, Benedict, 1983 *Imagined Communities: Reflections on the Origin and Spread of Nationalism*, London: Verso

Eisenstein, Hester, 1991 *Gender Shock: Practicing Feminism on Two Continents*, Sydney: Allen & Unwin

McGregor, Fiona, 1996 'I am not a lesbian', *Australian Queer*, Special issue of *Meanjin* vol. 55, no. 1, pp. 31–40

Rubin, Gayle 1984 'Thinking sex: notes for a radical theory of the politics of sexuality', in Carole Vance (ed.) *Pleasure and Danger*, New York: Routledge, pp. 267–319

Whitman, Walt 1945 *The Portable Walt Whitman*, selected by Mark Van Doren, US: Viking

Yeatman, Anna, 1990 *Bureaucrats, Technocrats, Femocrats: Essays on the Contemporary Australian State*, Sydney: Allen & Unwin

Yeats, W.B., 1945 *Selected Poetry*, edited by A. Norman Jeffares, London: Macmillan

Watson, Sophie (ed.), 1990 *Playing the State: Australian Feminist Intervention*, Sydney: Allen & Unwin

REFERENCES

1 Nothing personal

Baudrillard, J. 1990, *Seduction*, New York: St Martin's Press
Fraser, N. 1989, *Unruly Practices: Power, Discourse and Gender in Contemporary Social Theory*, Cambridge: Polity
Hartley, J. 1992, *The Politics of Pictures*, London: Routledge
Landes, J.B. 1988, *Women and the Public Sphere in the Age of the French Revolution*, New York: Cornell University Press
Meyrowitz, J. 1986, *No Sense Of Place*, New York: Oxford University Press
Morris, M. 1990, 'Banality in cultural studies', in P. Mellencamp (ed.) *Logics of Television*, Bloomington: Indiana University Press

2 Screen sex

Ballard, J.G. 1984, *Re/Search*, nos 8–9, p. 157
Barthes, R. 1974, *S/Z, An Essay*, New York: Hill and Wang
—— 1976, *Sade/Fourier/Loyola*, trans. Richard Miller, New York: Hill and Wang
Cowie, E. 1984, 'Fantasia', *m/f*, no. 9, pp. 71–105
Creed, B. 1993, *The Monstrous-Feminine: Film, Feminism, Psychoanalysis*, London: Routledge
Dibbell, J. 1994, 'Rape in cyberspace', *Good Weekend, The Age Magazine*, pp. 26–32
Freud, S. 1905, 'Three essays on sexuality', *The Standard Edition of the Complete Psychological Works of Sigmund Freud, 1953–1966*, 34 vols, trans. James Strachey, London: Hogarth vol. 7, pp. 123–230
—— 1900, 'The interpretation of dreams', *Standard Edition*, vols 4 & 5
—— 1918, 'From the history of an infantile neurosis', *Standard Edition*, vol. 17, pp. 1–22
Haraway, D. 1985, 'A manifesto for cyborgs: science, technology and socialist feminism in the 1980s', *Socialist Review*, vol. 15, no. 2, pp. 65–107
Harmon, A. 1994, 'Sex a la "seedy Rom"', *The Age*, March 1, p. 32
Lacan, J. 1977, *Ecrits,* London: Tavistock

Laplanche, J. & Pontalis, J-B. 1985, *The Language of Psychoanalysis*, London: The Hogarth Press
Lyotard, J-F. 1988–9, *Discourse*, no. 11, pp. 74–87
Morales, J. 1995, 'Cybersnare', *Advocate*, pp. 24–25
Mulvey, L. 1989, *Visual and Other Pleasures*, London: Macmillan
Pryor, S. & P. Scott, 1993, 'Virtual reality: beyond Cartesian space', in Philip Hayward & Tana Wollen, *Future Visions: New Technologies of the Screen*, London: BFI Publishing
Rheingold, H. 1991, *Virtual Reality*, London: Mandarin
——1994, *The Virtual Community*, London: Minerva
Springer, C. 1991, 'The Pleasure of the interface', *Screen*, no. 32, p. 3

3 The economy of pleasure and the laws of desire

ABT (Australian Broadcasting Tribunal) 1992, 'Exploration of attitudes towards film, TV and video classification: a marketing research report' conducted by Frank Small & Associates
ABA (Australian Broadcasting Authority) 1993, 'Community standards for Pay TV interim report' based on the first of two studies carried out by Keyes Young
——1994, 'Community standards for Pay TV, report on national survey' based on two studies carried out by Keyes Young
Commonwealth of Australia, Classification (Publications, Films and Computer Games) Act 1995
Eros Foundation Survey 1995
Good Weekend Magazine, Sydney Morning Herald 28 October 1995
New South Wales Indecent Articles and Publications Act 1975

4 Grief and the lesbian queer/n

Butler, Judith 1990, *Gender Trouble: Feminism and the Subversion of Identity*, New York: Routledge
Califia, Pat 1983, 'Gay men, lesbians and sex: doing it together', *The Advocate*, July 7, Los Angeles
de Lauretis, Teresa 1991, *Differences*, vol. 3, no. 2, Providence: Brown University

Hart, Lynda 1994, *Fatal Women, Lesbian Sexuality and the Mark of Aggression*, Princeton: Princeton University Press

Raymond, Leigh 1992, 'Who're you calling queer!' and 'New queers on the block', *Capital Q*, nos. 13 and 14, Sydney

Sedgwick, Eve Kosofsky 1993, *Tendencies*, Durham: Duke University Press

Signorile, Michelangelo 1992, *Queer in America: Sex, the Media and the Closets of Power*, London: Abacus

Smyth, Cherry 1992, *Lesbians Talk Queer Notions*, London: Scarlet Press

White, Edmund 1994 [1977], 'The joys of gay life' in *The Burning Library: Writings on Art, Politics and Sexuality 1969–1993*, London: Picador

5 Bisexual mediations

Bartos, Michael, Jon McLeod & Phil Nott 1994, *Meanings of Sex Between Men*, Canberra: Department of Human Services and Health

Baxter, John 1996, 'Bisexual chic', *Weekend Australian*, 20 January, p. 30

Bernhard, Sandra 1993a, *Confessions of A Pretty Lady*, London: HarperCollins

——1993b, *Love, Love and Love*, London: HarperCollins

Connell, R.W. & G.W. Dowsett 1992, *Rethinking Sex: Social Theory and Sexuality Research*, Melbourne: Melbourne University Press

Davis, Klemmer & G. Dowsett 1991, *Bisexually Active Men and Beats: Theoretical and Educational Implications*, The Bisexually Active Men's Outreach Project, AIDS Council of NSW & Macquarie University AIDS Research Unit

Deleuze, Gilles 1977, *Proust and Signs*, London: Allen Lane

Deleuze, G. & F. Guattari 1984, *Anti-Oedipus: Capitalism and Schizophrenia*, London: Athlone Press

Dessaix, Robert 1993, *Australian Gay and Lesbian Writing: An Anthology*, Melbourne: Oxford University Press

Dowsett, G.W. 1991, *Men Who Have Sex With Men: National HIV/AIDS Education*, Canberra: Department of Human Services and Health

Garber, Marjorie 1995, *Vice Versa: Bisexuality and the Eroticism of Everyday Life*, New York: Simon & Schuster

Grosz, Elizabeth 1994, *Volatile Bodies*, Sydney: Allen & Unwin

——1995, *Space Time and Perversion*, Sydney: Allen & Unwin

Guattari, Felix 1995, *Chaosophy*, New York: Semiotext(e)

Hutchins, L. and L. Kaahumanu 1991, *Bi Any Other Name: Bisexual People Speak Out*, Boston: Alyson Publications

Jackson, A. & J. Lindsay 1991, *Evaluation of 1991 National Gay/Bisexual Campaign*, Canberra: Department of Human Services and Health

Kippax, Susan Crawford, Rodden & Benton 1994, *Report on Project Male Call: National Telephone Survey of Men Who Have Sex With Men*, Canberra: Department of Human Services and Heath

Munster, Anna 1993, 'Hateness of straightness', in K. Bashford, J. Laybutt, A. Munster & K. O'Sullivan, *Kink*, Sydney: Wicked Women Publications

New Weekly, 12 June 1995

Off Pink Collective 1988, *Bisexual Lives*, Off Pink Publishing

Sedgwick, Eve Kosovsky 1993, *Tendencies*, Durham: Duke University Press

Wark, McKenzie 1993, 'Let's Perform', *Meanjin*, vol. 52, no. 4, Summer

——1994a, *Virtual Geography: Living With Global Media Events*, Bloomington: Indiana University Press

——1994b, 'In-your-face observations of the irony lady', *Weekend Australian*, 30 April

Weise, Elizabeth Reba 1992, *Closer To Home: Bisexuality and Feminism*, Seattle: Seal Press

Wittig, Monique 1992, *The Straight Mind and other Essays*, Boston: Beacon Press

Wolff, Charlotte 1979, *Bisexuality: A Study*, London: Quartet Books

REFERENCES

6 Sexual conduct, sexual culture, sexual community

Altman, Dennis 1979, *Coming Out in the Seventies*, Sydney: Wild & Woolley

Callen, Michael 1983, *How to Have Sex in an Epidemic*, New York: News from the Front Publications

Crimp, Douglas (ed.) 1988, *AIDS: Cultural Analysis, Cultural Activism*, Cambridge Massachusetts: MIT Press

D'Emilio, John 1983, *Sexual Politics, Sexual Communities: The Making of the Homosexual Minority in the United States, 1940–70*, Chicago: University of Chicago Press

Donovan, Basil, Brett Tindall & David A. Cooper 1986, 'Brachioprotic eroticism and transmission of retrovirus associated with Acquired Immune Deficiency Syndrome (AIDS)', *Genitourinary Medicine*, vol. 62, no. 6, pp. 390–2

Dowsett, Gary W. 1996, *Practicing Desire: Homosexual Sex in the Era of AIDS*, Stanford: Stanford University Press

Duberman, Martin Bauml, Martha Vicinus & George Chauncey Jr (eds) 1989, *Hidden from History: Reclaiming the Gay and Lesbian Past*, New York: New American Library

Fogarty, Walter J. 1992, '"Certain habits": the development of a concept of the male homosexual in New South Wales law, 1788–1900', in *Gay Perspectives: Essays in Australian Gay Culture*, eds Robert Aldrich & Garry Wotherspoon, Sydney: University of Sydney, Department of Economic History Occasional Publications Series, pp. 59–76

Foucault, Michel 1976, *The History of Sexuality, Volume I: An Introduction*, trans. Robert Hurley, Harmondsworth: Penguin

Goldberg, Jonathan 1992, *Sodometries: Renaissance Texts, Modern Sexualities*, Stanford: Stanford University Press

Gott, Ted (comp.) 1994, *Don't Leave Me This Way: Art in the Age of AIDS*, Canberra: National Gallery of Australia

Greenberg, David F. 1988, *The Construction of Homosexuality*, Chicago: University of Chicago Press

Hughes, Robert 1987, *The Fatal Shore*, London: Collins Harvill

Koestenbaum, Wayne 1993, *The Queen's Throat: Opera, Homosexuality and the Mystery of Desire*, New York: Poseidon Press

Lifson, Alan R., Paul M. O'Malley, Nancy A. Hessol, Susan P.

187

Buchbinder, Lyn Cannon & George W. Rutherford 1990, 'HIV seroconversion in two homosexual men after receptive oral intercourse with ejaculation: implications for counseling concerning safe sexual practices', *American Journal of Public Health*, vol. 80, no. 12. pp. 1509–11

Mann, Jonathan, Daniel J.M. Tarantola & Thomas W. Netter (eds) 1992, *AIDS and the World*, Cambridge Massachusetts: Harvard University Press

National Centre in HIV Epidemiology and Clinical Research 1995, *Australian HIV Surveillance Report*, vol. 11, no. 2 (April)

(not only) Blue 1995, no. 1 (February)

Saslow, James M. 1986, *Ganymede in the Renaissance: Homosexuality in Art and Society*, New Haven: Yale University Press

Sedgwick, Eve Kosofsky 1990, *Epistemology of the Closet*, Berkeley: University of California Press

Shilts, Randy 1988, *And the Band Played On: Politics, People and the AIDS Epidemic*, Harmondsworth: Penguin

Watney, Simon 1987, *Policing Desire: Pornography, AIDS and the Media*, London: Methuen

Weekend Australian, 15–16 July 1995

Weeks, Jeffrey 1990, *Coming Out: Homosexual Politics in Britain from the Nineteenth Century to the Present*, rev. ed., London: Quartet Books

——1985, *Sexuality and its Discontents: Meanings, Myths and Modern Sexualities*, London: Routledge & Kegan Paul

Woods, Gregory 1987, *Articulate Flesh: Male Homoeroticism and Modern Poetry*, New Haven: Yale University Press

Wotherspoon, Garry 1991, *City of the Plain: History of a Gay Subculture*, Sydney: Hale & Iremonger

8 Degrees of separation

Atkinson, Ti-Grace 1974, *Amazon Odyssey*, New York: Link Books

Cheney, Joyce (ed.) 1985, *Lesbian Land*, Minneapolis: Word Weavers

Copper, Baba 1981, 'Land-based separatism, a personal account' in Sarah Hoagland & Julia Penelope (eds) 1988, *For Lesbians Only: A Separatist Anthology*, London: Onlywomen Press, pp. 320–2

REFERENCES

Frye, Marilyn 1983, 'Some reflections on separatism and power' in *The Politics of Reality: Essays in Feminist Theory*, Freedom, California: The Crossing Press, pp. 95–109

Gilman, Charlotte Perkins 1915/1979, *Herland*, London: Women's Press

Hess, Langford & Ross 1980, 'Comparative separatism' in Sarah Hoagland & Julia Penelope (eds) 1988, *For Lesbians Only: A Separatist Anthology*, London: Onlywomen Press, pp. 125–32

Hoagland, Sarah Lucia 1989, *Lesbian Ethics: Towards New Value*, Palo Alto, California: Institute of Lesbian Studies

Jackson, Margaret 1984, 'Sexology and the universalization of male sexuality' in L. Coveney et al., *The Sexuality Papers: Male Sexuality and the Social Control of Women*, London: Hutchinson, pp. 69–84

Morgan, Robin 1978, *Going Too Far: The Personal Chronicle of a Feminist*, New York: Vintage

Penelope, Julia 1986, 'The mystery of lesbians: 1' in *Gossip: A Journal of Lesbian Feminist Ethics*, no. 1, pp. 9–45; also reprinted in Sarah Hoagland & Julia Penelope (eds) 1988, *For Lesbians Only: A Separatist Anthology*, London: Onlywomen Press, pp. 506–47

Steinem, Gloria 1980, 'The way we were—and will be' in Levine & Lyons (eds) *The Decade of Women*, New York: Paragon, pp. 7–25

Sunday Telegraph, 19 July 1987, pp. 16–17

Sydney Women's Liberation Newsletter 1974, p. 5

Treblicot, Joyce 1986, 'In partial response to those who worry that separatism may be a political cop-out: an expanded definition of activism' in *Gossip: A Journal of Lesbian Feminist Ethics*, no. 3, pp. 82–4

Wagner, Sally Roesch 1982, 'Pornography and the sexual revolution: the backlash of sadomasochism' in Robin Ruth Linden et al. (eds) *Against Sadomasochism: A Radical Feminist Analysis*, San Francisco: Frog In The Well, pp. 23–44

9 Dangerous desire

Grimstad, K. & S. Rennie (eds) 1975, 'The politics of women's sexuality' and 'The Oldest Profession', *The New Women's Survival Sourcebook*, New York: Knopf

Leeds Revolutionary Feminists 1981, *Love Your Enemy? The Debate Between Heterosexual Feminism and Political Lesbianism*, London: Onlywomen Press

Lesbian News, 1986–87, nos 18–21, Melbourne

O'Sullivan, Kimberly 1991, 'SOW', *Wicked Women*, vol. 2, no. 3, p. 22–24

——1993, 'Five years of infamy', in Bashford, Laybutt, Munster & O'Sullivan, *Kink*, Sydney: Wicked Women Publications, pp. 119–24

Radicalesbians 1971, 'The woman identified woman', in Anne Koedt & Shulamith Firestone (eds) *Notes from the Third Year*, New York: Notes from the Second Year Inc

Raymond, Janice G. 1991, 'Putting the politics back into lesbianism', *Journal of Australian Lesbian Feminist Studies*, vol. 1, no. 2, pp. 7–21

SOW leaflets, 1984, Sydney

Vance, Carole S. (ed.) 1989, *Pleasure and Danger: Exploring Female Sexuality*, Pandora Press, London

10 Lesbian erotica and impossible images

Gamman, Lorraine & Margaret Marshment 1988, *The Female Gaze: Women as Viewers of Popular Culture*, London: Women's Press

11 Sex and the single T-cell

Bartos, Michael 1996, 'The queer excess of public health policy', *Australia Queer (Meanjin)*, no. 1, pp. 122–31

DPN 1990, 'Statement by editors Beowolf Thorne and Tom Shearer', *Diseased Pariah News* no. 1, p. 1

DPN 1991, 'The totally amazing DPN 3-D centrefold', *Diseased Pariah News*, no. 4, insert between pp. 16–17

REFERENCES

Dunne, Stephen 1995a, 'Butt plugs', *Rouge*, no. 19, pp. 35-7
——1995b, 'Butt plugs', *Campaign*, February 1995
Hoskins, Mark 1994, 'Enjoy this', *Talkabout*, no. 41, pp. 4-5
McDiarmid, David 1993, 'A short history of facial hair', speech for the forum 'HIV: Towards a Paradigm' at the Positive Living Centre, Melbourne, 19 April 1993 for the National Centre for HIV Social Research, University of Queensland; reprinted as speaker's abstract in notes accompanying the conference 'Harmed Circles: Cultural Responses to the AIDS Crisis', National Gallery of Australia, Canberra, 11-12 November 1994. Also reprinted in this volume
National AIDS Bulletin 1994a, 'Positively sexual', vol. 8, no. 2, p. 29
——1994b, 'Butt plugs: too hot to handle?', vol. 8, no. 10-11, p. 37
Russo, Vito 1987, *The Celluloid Closet: Homosexuality in the Movies*, revised ed., New York: Harper & Row
Talkabout 1993, 'Editorial: let's talkabout sex', *Talkabout: The Newsletter of People Living With HIV/AIDS Inc NSW*, no. 32, p. 11
Thomas-Clark, Andrew 1994, 'Spooky HIV sweetness', *Talkabout: The Newsletter of People Living With HIV/AIDS Inc NSW*, no. 48, p. 21
Urquhart, David 1994, 'Positive art: interview with Andrew Thomas-Clark', *Talkabout: The Newsletter of People Living With HIV/AIDS Inc NSW*, no. 40, pp. 23-24

12 Stirred heart and soul

Ashburn, E. 1996, *Lesbian Art: An Encounter with Power*, Sydney: Craftsman House
Boccalatte, S. 1995, Whole Fragments: An Honours Research Paper, Sydney College of the Arts, The University of Sydney
Grosz, E. 1994, *Volatile Bodies: Toward a Corporeal Feminism*, Sydney: Allen & Unwin
Moore, M. 1995, *Butch Baby Butch: Contemporary Butch Profiles*, Catalogue

Nochlin, L. 1994, *The Body as Pieces: The Fragment as a Metaphor of Modernity*, London: Thames and Hudson

Rubin, G. 1982, 'The leather menace: comments on politics and S/M' in *Coming to Power*, edited by members of Samois, Boston: Alyson Publications

Sinnott, A. 1993, *The Body Social*, London: Routledge

Wittig, M. 1992, *The Straight Mind and Other Essays*, New York: Harvester Wheatsheaf

13 I was a teenage romance writer

Francis, Jaye 1990, *Bigger and Better*, Sydney: Australian Consolidated Publishing

Gilbert, Pam, and Sandra Taylor 1991, *Fashioning the Feminine: Girls, Popular Culture and Schooling*, Sydney: Allen & Unwin

Greer, Germaine 1970 *The Female Eunuch*, London: McGibbon and Kee

Lam, May 1987, 'A place for us: adolescent girls reading romance fiction', *Equal Opportunity Newsletter*, vol. 6, no. 1

Lapin, Gerri 1992, *Slim Pickings*, Sydney: Pan

Pearce, Sharyn 1991, 'Growing up gender-wise: what we give to girls', *Magpies*, no. 5, November

Index

Acquired Immune Deficiency Syndrome (AIDS) 81–3, 93, 94, 95–6, 140
adult (sex) shops 33–5
advertising 79–80
AIDS Council of NSW (ACON) 94, 95, 141, 142, 145–6
Alexander, Goldie 180
Altman, Dennis 65
And the Band Played On 93
Angie 131
Anything That Moves 73
Archer, Robyn 124
Australian Federation of AIDS Organisations (AFAO) 146, 147–8
Australian Women's Forum 10, 134
Azaria Universe 132

Bad Attitude 132
Ballard, J. G. 16, 21

Barrett, Virginia 70
Barrymore, Drew 74
Barthes, Roland 25
Bartos, Michael 147
Basic Instinct 74
Baudrillard, Jean 2–4, 10, 11
Bernhard, Sandra 74, 75
bisexual 65–74
  chic 74–5
  'problem' 64–5
  vectors 69, 75–7
Black & White 134
Boccalatte, Suzanne 160, 165–6, 167, 168
bondage and disipline (B&D) 128
Bourgeois, Louise 165, 168
Burchill, Julie 12
Byrne, Belinda 172, 173, 174, 176, 181

cabaret 35–6
Campaign 149

Chadwick, Helen 165
Cleo 10, 12, 133
Coucke, Martien 138
Cronenberg, David 16, 17
cyberspace 17–21, 24, 28–30
culture, Australian 80

de Lauretis, Teresa 58, 71
D'Emilio, John 89
Dement, Linda 129
Dessaix, Robert 72
Dolly 173, 176
Dolly Fiction 173–5, 177, 179, 180, 181
Dunbar, Jamie 142, 144
Dunne, Stephen 148
Dworkin, Andrea 124, 128

Esquire 7, 8, 12
Everett, Kenny 96

fantasies 25–7
   cyber 28–30
Fargher, Catherine 161, 163
female
   eroticism 28–9, 118
   sexual fantasies 116
   sexuality 97, 117
The Female Gaze 128
feminism 13, 15, 97
   lesbian 114–16
   and pornography 117–18, 128, 129
   and romance writing 178–81
   separatist beginnings 98–101
   and sexuality 4–6, 116–118

feminist
   sex wars 123–4
   theory 117, 171
Forrest, Mary 181
Francis, Jaye 181
Freud, Sigmund 21–2, 23, 25, 26, 27
Friday, Nancy 7
Frighten the Horses 73
frigid 97, 117
Frye, Marilyn 99, 105
Future Sex 10

Gamman, Lorraine 128
Garber, Marjorie 75
Gay & Lesbian Rights Lobby 138
Gay Liberation Movement 80, 81, 88, 91
Gay Men's Health Crisis 93
gender 14–15, 24
Gilbert, Pam 178
Greer, Germaine 171
Groovie Biscuit 132
Grosz, Liz 66, 70–1, 165, 166
Guattari, Felix 70, 71

Hall, Elisa 161
Haraway, Donna 24
Hardy, C.Moore 159, 168
Harmon, Amy 19
Hartley, John 6
Hirst, Jasmine 129
homosexuality 78–90, 91–6
Homoture 150
Human immunodeficiency virus (HIV) 81–3, 94, 95–6, 139–56

The Importance of Being Earnest 70
Infected Faggots' Perspective 150
International Feminist Book Fair 125
Internet 17–21, 24, 28–9, 38, 39
The Interpretation of Dreams 25
Izzy 131

Jeffrey, Sheila 129, 179

Kelly, Deborah 163
Ken's Karate Klub 142

Lam, Mary 179–80
Larissa 132
law reforms 80
Laybutt, Francine 122
Leichhardt Women's Health Centre 116
LeGuin, Ursula 181
lesbian
  chic 12
  communities 97–113, 160
  erotica 127, 128, 129, 131, 132, 136–8
  feminism 116–17
  and pornography 121, 128, 129–30
  sexuality 13–14, 119–20, 122–6, 127–129, 132–4, 157–69
  and social attitudes 160–1
  theory 98–9
Lesbian News 121

lesbianism
  defined 120
  political 114–26, 129
Love your enemy? The debate between heterosexual feminism and political lesbianism 118–19
Lyotard, Jean-Francois 29

McDiarmid, David 91–6, 141, 142, 149, 151, 154–5
McGregor, Fiona 12
MacKinnon, Catharine 124, 128
magazines
  and lesbians 10, 12, 121–2
  and feminism 4–5, 10
  and masculinity 8–9, 10
  on sexuality 7–8, 9
Mapplethorpe, Robert 135
Mardi Gras *see* Sydney Gay & Lesbian Mardi Gras
Marshment, Margaret 128
masculinity 7–10
media 4–5, 10, 12–13, 100
  and lesbian sexuality 158
  sexual 38–40
Melbourne Powerhouse Women's Theatre Group 105
Men's Fitness 8
Men's Health 8
Methold, Ken 177
Meyrowitz, Joshua 13
Milner, Sally 173
monosexuality 67–70
Moore, Marion 160, 161, 163, 165, 168
Morgan, Andrew 144

Morris, Meaghan 4
Moss, Merrilee 175, 180
Mulvey, Laura 23
Munster, Anna 67, 132

National AIDS Bulletin 141, 146, 147, 148–9
New South Wales
 Women's land 101–13
No Sence of Place 13
(not only) Blue 78, 79
nymphomaniac 97, 117

Off Our Backs 128
On Our Backs 10, 121, 122, 128–9
O'Sullivan, Kimberly 159, 164

Pausacker, Jenny 181
Pearce, Sharyn 180
Penelope, Julia 98, 99, 105
Phillips, Cath 127, 160
PlagueBoy 155
Poersch, Enno 93
The Politics of Pictures 6
polyvalence 72–4
Popham, Paul 93
pornography 22, 27, 166
 computer 17–19
 and feminism 117–18, 128, 129
 in film 22, 26
 lesbian 121, 128, 129–30
 and literature 84
 and photography 84
prostitutes' rights 117

prostitution 32–3, 42, 43, 45, 46–7, 49

queer, academic theorisings 58–61
Queer Nation 60, 61, 62
Quim 132

Raymond, Janice 125–6
Reclaim the Night 117
regulation of sex industry 40
 Australian Capital Territory 42–4
 federal government 41–2
 New South Wales 44–5
 Northern Territory 48–9
 Queensland 46–7
 South Australia 48
 Tasmania 47
 Victoria 49
 Western Australia 45–6
Rethinking Sex 65
Rheingold, Howard 29
Roberts, Ian 78–80, 90
romance writing taboos 178
Rouge 149
Russo, Vito 140

sadomasochism (SM) 128, 132
safe sex 82, 93–4, 95, 123, 141
Salmon, Lisa 122, 132
Sedgwick, Eve Kosovsky 70
Senate Select Committee on Standards Relevant to the Supply of Services Utilising Technologies 19, 38

INDEX

sex
  and feminism 4–6
  industry 31–49
  virtual 19–21, 22
sex subculture parties 133, 134
sex-radical underground 118–26, 127–38, 159
sexual
  fantasies 16–30, 116
  harassment 18
  media 38–40
  subculture 133, 134, 171
Sexually Outrageous Women (SOW) 120
Shilt, Randy 93
Short, Shân 164
Sinnott, A. 165
Smith, Kiki 165
Springer, Claudia 21
Sprinkle, Annie 129
Stewart, Susan 130
Sydney Gay & Lesbian Mardi Gras 13, 64, 68, 74, 78, 80, 83, 94, 122, 127, 130, 142, 146, 155, 157, 159
Sydney Leather Pride Association 125
Sydney Lesbian Festival and Conference 124
Sydney Star Observer 82, 138, 155

Talkabout 143, 144
Taxi Club 51

Taylor, Sandra 178
technology, new
  identification 23–5
  narrative 25
  primal fantasies and virtual pleasures 25–7
  sex 38–9
  voyeurism 21–3
Thomas-Clark, Andrew 140
Tierney, John 19, 38
Toxic Queen 96, 150

Vanity Bear 151–2
Vanity Fair 12, 152
Videodrome 16–17
videos 36–8, 41, 43–4, 121
Volatile Bodies 66, 70
voyeurism 21–3, 132

X-rated videos (non-violent erotica) 36–8, 41, 43–4

Warhol, Andy 7
Wicca 106, 107, 108–10, 112
Wicked Women 10, 122–3, 125, 132
Wittig, Monique 67, 169
Wolff, Charlotte 73
Women and Violence conference 118
Women's Liberation Movement 92, 97
Word of Mouth 163

197